Schnorrers

Wandering Jews in Germany 1850-1914

Roni Aaron Bornstein

Schnorrers
Wandering Jews in Germany 1850-1914

Roni Aaron Bornstein

DEKEL PUBLISHING HOUSE

Schnorrers - Wandering Jews in Germany 1850-1914
Roni Aaron Bornstein
Copyright © 2013

Dekel Academic Press
www.dekelpublishing.com

North American rights by
Samuel Wachtman's Sons, Inc.
ISBN 978-1-888820-53-9

All rights reserved. No portion of this book, except for brief review, may be reproduced, stored in a retrieval system, or transmitted in any form or by any means – electronic, mechanical, photocopying, recording, or otherwise – without written permission of the publisher. For information regarding international rights please contact Dekel Academic Press, Israel; for North American rights please contact Samuel Wachtman's Sons, Inc., U.S.A.

English translation: Benjamin Rosendahl
Language editing: Liron Rubin
Cover design: Yuda Deri

Interior design and typesetting by:

For information contact:

Dekel Publishing House	**Samuel Wachtman's Sons, Inc.**
P.O. Box 45094	2460 Garden Road, Suite C
Tel Aviv 61450, Israel	Monterey, CA 93940, U.S.A.
Tel: +972 3506-3235	Tel: 831 649-0669
Fax: +972 3506-7332	Fax: 831 649-8007
Email: info@dekelpublishing.com	Email: samuelwachtman@gmail.com

This book is dedicated to my beloved family.
My wife Lilach, and to our three sons,
Gideon, Alon and Jonathan

TABLE OF CONTENTS

	Thanks	8
	Introduction	9
Chapter 1:	Door-to-Door Beggars	17
Chapter 2:	The Beginning of the Unified Struggle against Beggars	37
Chapter 3:	Change in Perception	49
Chapter 4:	Characteristics of *Wanderarme*	72
Chapter 5:	A Demographic Survey of *Wanderarme* Occupation	88
Chapter 6:	German Jews and the Fight against *Wanderarme* and Beggars	121
Chapter 7:	Centralized Solutions to the Jewish *Wanderarme* Problem: Mechanism, Deployment, and Spheres of Influence	142
Chapter 8:	Regional Activity	170
Chapter 9:	The Establishment of Jewish Worker Colonies	189
Chapter 10:	Hostels for Homeless Jews	223
Chapter 11:	The Weimar Republic and the End of the Jewish Beggar	243
	Bibliography	251

Thanks

I would like to thank Jürgen Schäffler, historian and director of the Lemgo Museum, whose help accompanied the whole process of writing this book. At a meeting with him in Tel Aviv, he convinced me to have this work, originally published in Hebrew only, translated into English. I am, of course, more than thankful to him for that suggestion.

In addition, I would like to express my gratitude to Mr. Benjamin Rosendahl, the translator and to Ms. Liron Rubin, the English editor, whose excellent work enabled me to present this book to an international audience.

INTRODUCTION

This book deals with the large number of German Jews who, during the 19th century, lived at the bottom of the social ladder. These included poverty-stricken individuals, beggars, paupers and "wandering Jews" (*Wanderarmen*, meaning "wandering poor") who moved from community to community in search of income, and who were often entirely dependent on the support of the local Jewish population and Jewish organizations. Such figures were not a new phenomenon in the 19th century and had, in fact, existed before then. Beginning in the 1850s, however, this phenomenon underwent fundamental changes. This study attempts to describe and analyze these changes. We will focus on the *Wanderarmen*, Jews who depended on charity (from individual local Jews or by way of the community's social network) while wandering through Germany.

Most of the historical studies on German Jews, especially those written by contemporaries, tend to focus on the established and successful members of society. The lives and activities of successful businessmen and capitalists, salesmen and industrialists, intellectuals and writers, social leaders and statesmen have been documented extensively. There is, however, relatively little updated research on the Jewish lower classes in Germany. What little research can be found on poverty in Germany in general, and the Jewish underclass in particular, is either unsystematic or oblivious to the standards of academic rigor. These studies often describe the activities of charities (organizational and private) but are silent about the indigent Jews themselves, their behavior, their numbers, and their daily difficulties.

Although a great deal of documentation was lost when the Nazis decimated the well-organized Jewish communities of Germany, many relevant documents are still available in community archives. These archives, among other sources, tell the story of poor Jews, be they poor natives of Germany or destitute immigrants from other countries. This study, then, attempts to illuminate the relationship between two sectors within German-Jewish society: the established classes and those at the very bottom of the social ladder. Considering the fact that modern and German historiographies have recently shed a great deal of light on the underclasses of different societies, it is ironic that so little has been written about the lower Jewish classes of Germany.

The *Wanderarmen*, by passing through Jewish communities all over Germany and seeking charity, forced their problems on Jews of far more established political and economic status. The communities saw to the needs of the *Wanderarmen* while at the same time fiercely battling manifestations of Jewish beggary with the aim of putting an immediate stop to the practice. In the beginning, Jewish beggars appealed directly to other Jews by knocking on doors and begging for aid, small as it might be. Later, as this practice intensified and became a real burden, the communities united in order to prepare for a real struggle; strictly regulated charities were funded for *Wanderarmen* for the purpose of eradicating beggary.

At the end of the 19th century, industrialization in Germany gained momentum, the highlight of which was called *Hochindustrialisierung* (full industrialization), characterized by a marked mobility of both merchandize and people (Jews and non-Jews alike). Years of impressive economic success and growth, however, were followed by years of severe economic recession, triggering unemployment and the very social problems that were typical of developing industrial societies. The demand for labor, another characteristic of the German economy during the last quarter of the 19th century, rose so quickly that it opened doors for non-German migrants who entered the country looking for ways to earn a living; among these were many Jews who, seeking employment or any other source of income, wound up destitute and had no choice but to approach the local Jewish community for shelter, material support, food, and, sometimes, encouragement, or a piece of advice for the journey. This chapter in German history, one in which the presence of beggars (Yiddish: *Schnorrer* or *Gauner*, or beggars and small-time crooks, respectively) became increasingly common, has yet to be recognized in historical research.

The *Wanderarmen* phenomenon became a serious problem during the 1870s, demanding a quick solution. Accordingly, the *Deutsch-Israelitischer Gemeindebund* (German-Jewish Community Federation, or DIGB) was founded in Berlin on June 29, 1869, after which the problem was discussed regularly on the pages of the DIGB's publications, Jewish newspapers of the period, and in local and regional community debates. Later, in the 1880s, the DIGB implemented a number of measures designed to battle the *Wanderarmen*, begging, and other poverty-related activities. These measures included a fund for the support of transients, non-German migrants, almshouses, loans for those in times of need, laborers' housing projects, employment agencies, and training centers. Responsible for fundraising within the Jewish communities in Germany, on behalf of the *Wanderarmen*, these institutions provided detailed accounts of the *Wanderarmen's* movement, accounts which form an important source of information for this study.

At the end of the 19th century, regional organizations were founded in order to centralize local efforts to deal with beggars and *Wanderarmen*. Later, on the eve of WWI (in 1910), a federal organization was founded in Berlin with the purpose of centralizing these regional organizations.

This study covers the period between the 1850s and WWI, years during which the Jewish minority in Germany experienced many significant changes. The core issue of this study has its origins in the 1870s, when the presence of *Wanderarmen* became a threatening nuisance and a problem demanding an immediate solution. By the end of WWI, the specific problem of *Wanderarmen* (but not the general problem of Jewish poverty) had been greatly alleviated.

Wanderarmen were still a minority at the beginning of the 19th century, obliged, in the words of the renowned Jewish philosopher Moses Mendelssohn, to pay a "poll tax" worth the price of "a Polish cow." Mendelssohn himself was forced to pay this humiliating tax when he was arrested at the entrance to Berlin; incidentally, this occurred at the very peak of his renown as a philosopher.

By the eve of the First World War, the Jews of Germany had already been granted equal rights: They took part in the Reichstag

Introduction 13

elections, paid their taxes, and were about to join the army in order to fight Germany's enemies. Prior to that, only a few members of Germany's Jewish minority – namely, the "Court Jews" – had attained certain privileges and a status of sorts. During the 20th century, however, Jews became a large and influential group, many members of which were among Germany's most affluent and influential: parliamentary representatives, professors at elite universities, artists, intellectuals, and economists. In short, Jews made an indelible contribution to modern German history.

The Jewish minority in Germany was comprised of two influential poles. On the one hand, there were the settled local Jews who tried to strengthen their legal, social and economic status vis-à-vis the German authorities in particular and Gentiles in general. On the other hand, there were the *Wanderarmen*, made up largely of immigrants from the countries bordering Germany on the East, but also of destitute German Jews seeking employment and temporary residents who hoped to move on to the countries of the Mediterranean.

The topic of this book, the lower classes of German Jews (including beggars and charity-seekers) was not an isolated, marginal phenomenon in the annals of German-Jewish history. The beggars were not beggars in the folkloristic sense, nor were they "anti-social" figures who refused to integrate into normative life. Rather, they were people who strove to escape economic destitution even if the cost was losing their self-respect and begging from their Jewish brethren in Germany. Many of these impoverished Jews were dealt with as "foreign poor," a group common in Germany before the *Wanderarmen*.

It is only natural that a topic of this nature leads to difficulties in the matter of sources. The protagonists of this story – poverty-stricken people, beggars and, in general, the lower classes of German Jews – were not likely to write down the stories of their lives, as their time was spent on the burdensome routine of scrounging a few coins, daily bread, and enough money to continue until a community would absorb them. Their self-imposed vagabond lifestyle makes it impossible to locate them within the Jewish communities, as they were only temporary guests there. Accompanied by hardship and suffering, their lives were not considered worthy of documentation.

The historian trying to research these people and their stories must find existing material, e.g., community archives and reports of the organizations responsible for dealing with the poor and the weak. Although most of the existing documentation comes from these charitable organizations, it is necessary to question their motivation and to consider the point of view of the *Wanderarmen* themselves.

As a result of the immense difficulties involved in finding sources dealing directly with the group under analysis, I did not *a priori* limit the sources I would consult. In addition, I did not limit the debate to specific geographic boundaries, as any attempt to deal with vagabondism requires one to take into account the overall picture, rather than just a specific region. In order to understand these events within the context of and in relation to German history, I simultaneously researched and analyzed similar phenomena in German society. We are not dealing here with a Jewish phenomenon occurring within a vacuum, but, rather, with Jewish developments occurring within the overall German setting, the circumstances and conditions of which need to be recognized. The dearth of secondary sources on this topic requires the historian to consult both Jewish and non-Jewish primary sources.

Most of the consulted sources are located in thirteen archives in Germany and Israel; and most of the documentation can be found at the Central Archive of Jewish History in Jerusalem, Israel. The archive contains remnants of material from German-Jewish communities that were transferred to Israel in the 1960s in accordance with an early post-war agreement between the Israeli and Federal German governments. Although the documents I consulted while preparing this study are not homogenous, most deal with known and recognizable events in different parts of Germany. The regional archives of Bavaria in particular and of Southern Germany in general are the most complete, and contain extensive material not only on the activities of *Armenkommissionen* (poverty commissions) of different Jewish communities, regional organizations and community welfare organizations, but also on the communities' policy vis-à-vis foreign Jews. Working with the archival material was relatively complicated, for the information was often fragmented. Of the accumulated material, I dealt only with those topics and places whose extant documentation was sufficient enough to allow me to describe the workings of the communities. Wanting to approach the topic from all angles, I approached official German institutions whose files could help shed light on the topic of Jewish poverty and vagabonds: the archives of the Interior Ministry of the Reich, ministries of other countries, the police and the municipalities. These documents touch upon many topics, but I focused primarily on those dealing directly with Jews. It should be noted that although I examined a vast amount of files on welfare and anti-poverty measures in Germany, I did not find any evidence of German welfare institutions that dealt with Jewish indigents; it is possible, however, that these institutions neglected to record the Jewish backgrounds of their clients. In order to quantify the phenomenon, I consulted censuses (which were conducted regularly, especially in Bavaria and in Prussia) of the German Bureau of Statistics and of other organizations. Additional data were taken from the Jewish newspapers and publications of the period, reports of activities, and yearly balance statements of relevant Jewish organizations. These documents helped me to prepare the study, as did DIGB publications and Jewish newspapers, published in Hebrew, from Eastern Europe.

The topic under discussion raises a number of methodological problems with which the researcher must deal. Although the group of *Wanderarmen* and beggars can be defined and characterized, we are dealing with a relatively long period, spanning many years, during which Germany experienced drastic changes. These changes, evident in all aspects of life, including German-Jewish society and its sub-class of Jewish beggars and vagabonds, did not stem solely from the relationship between Germans and Jews, but also from internal developments within the Jewish community and, most pertinent to the following study, between Jewish vagabonds and settled German Jews. The study of these relationships can contribute to an understanding of the development of the German-Jewish minority during the years leading up to the establishment of the Weimar Republic.

CHAPTER 1:

DOOR-TO-DOOR BEGGARS

Demographic changes and population growth were central characteristics of the Jewish population in Germany since the beginning of the 10th century. Several factors triggered this increase, among them better living standards, higher life expectancy, and a trend of societal improvements, especially in the economy. These changes were recognized by the Jews of Germany, who were granted equal rights in 1812. There is no doubt that Jewish migration within Germany contributed to the development of German Jewry. Migration took place throughout the 19th century, particularly and most intensively during the second half. Although migration strengthened the Jewish communities and contributed to the workforce, it was often a burden for the members of the communities in which the migrants arrived, for the veteran members were required to allocate resources to and support the migrants.

The subject of Jewish migration to Germany and within Germany, during the period covered here, will clarify the central topic of this book: the *Wanderarmen* (wandering Jewish paupers). These two topics are intertwined: Without the massive migration occurring in Germany at the time, the *Wanderarmen* issue would not have become a crucial problem demanding a solution from the Jewish communities. On the other hand, it can be assumed that these circumstances increased the Jewish population of Germany and, hence, turned it into a defined and dominant entity at the beginning of the 20th century.

Several scholars have attempted to analyze 19th-century Jewish migration to Germany, but the dimensions and influence of the Jewish minority's rise within Germany is still unclear. It is particularly difficult to suggest a precise figure for the period leading up to the 1880s, as it was only after 1880 that population censuses were conducted in Germany, censuses which categorized citizens according to religious affiliation. These censuses constitute a primary source for this study,[1] but the available statistics on Jewish

---

[1] Israelitisches Jahrbuch für das Deutsche Reich: First published in 1873. In its volumes, different data on population numbers in different parts of the German Reich were listed. Individual cities also published additional data independently by local bureaus of statistics. Confessional statistics, i.e. data that divided the census by religious affiliation, were first published in 1880. These confessional statistics enable us to more precisely quantify Jewish migration. For a statistical publication in which a division according to religious affiliation is provided, see: Vierteljahreshefte zur Statistik des deutschen Reiches, Statistisches Jahrbuch für den deutschen Staat, Statistisches Jahrbuch für das Deutsche Reich, Kalender und statistisches Jahrbuch für das Königsreich Sachsen, Statistik des Deutschen Reiches.

migration reveal but a partial picture. The research on these issues is still far from complete.[2]

Nevertheless, it is obvious that the vagabondism of Jews in Germany until the 1860s differs from that which took period during the period following it. During the first of these periods, vagabondism was limited by local government decrees: A Jew desiring to move from one province to another needed a permit from the sovereign authority he attempted to reach –in other words, from the local government. Furthermore, a Jew had to secure the consent of the Jewish community in order to live in its midst. His only choice, then, was to stay in a place for the shortest time possible, and then leave the boundaries of the community and continue on his way. In the event that a Jew did stay in a Jewish community that had refused him, he usually stayed with a Jewish family that had agreed to host him and offer him overnight accommodation. Alternatively, he could stay in a "charitable trust" known as "the hostel for poor passersby." Although institutions of this kind existed in different forms in most 19th century Jewish communities, they were unable to address the problem when the population of the *Wanderarmen* increased significantly. Accordingly, charitable activities increased, as did the establishment of independent entities founded with the aim of coping with *Wanderarmen*.

As long as the number of people requesting charity was small (in proportion to the size of the community), it was possible to turn to the regular community support system for the poor and to help

---

[2] A comprehensive study on Jewish demography in Germany is being conducted by the demographer Usiel Schmelz. Some of the study's conclusions have already been published. On the difficulties of a migration study see: Usiel Schmelz, "Die demographische Entwicklung der Juden in Deutschland von der Mitte des 19. Jahrhunderts bis 1933." In: *Zeitschrift für Bevolkerungswissenschaft*, 1982, p. 46-47.

the *Wanderarmen* in their absorption process. According to Jewish sources from the period, Jewish communities had no problem supporting *Wanderarmen* until the mid-19th century, the main reason being the relatively small number of vagabonds in proportion to the permanently settled. Sources from Jewish community archives also indicate that the number of occurrences of begging Jews and of *Schnorrer* (Jews who reached Jewish communities and asked for charity) was very low then. Most of the beggars were satisfied with the direct support they received from individual local Jews and, hence, did not approach community institutions. Even though there was occasional friction between the beggars and the community they approached, mostly as a result of the strain on community support organizations, these problems were uncommon. Rarer still were expulsions of individual beggars from the community: There is not even one recorded case in the community archives of groups organizing to expel foreign Jews from their territory.

This picture changed drastically at the end of the 1860s, and especially at the beginning of the 1870s. A clear indication of the changing attitude towards the *Wanderarmen* was the establishment of the German-Jewish Community Federation, or DIGB, in 1869, an organization founded to unify, centralize, and organize the communities' response to the rising wave of Jewish migration. The decision to find a unified solution to the *Wanderarmen* problem marked a turning point of wide-reaching consequences in the relationship between veteran members of the Jewish communities and transient migrants, as indicated by the expansion of the organizational structures for the absorption and support of the *Wanderarmen*. This undermined the hitherto direct relations between the vagabond charity seekers and the established charity givers.

Jewish immigrants to Germany (*Einwanderer*) and migrants within Germany (*Binnenwanderer*) were mostly influenced by the mobility of overall German society. German society was, in fact, less mobile before 1868, but the "Trade Regulation Act" (German: *Gewerbeordnung*) of that year triggered unprecedented free movement within Germany.³ Before that, movement had been limited by a number of restrictions and regulations imposed on people wanting to move from place to place. As opposed to the situation in other countries, migrants were highly noticeable, especially to the police authorities.

In Germany's established, settled society (which was the norm until the 1860s), the appearance of strangers in communities drew much attention. As a result, the supervision of the migrants (Jewish and Gentile) was meticulous. German archives, in fact, include several files on governmental action against the unwanted arrival of Jewish strangers. Despite the fact that Jews entering cities or towns with Jewish communities were normally looking for support from local Jews, they were often barred from entering the settlement at all, even if the Jews living there were able to support them. A testimony from 1814 on the arrival of Jewish beggars in a district of Saxony-Anhalt illustrates a basic disagreement between the Jewish and the German authorities. Regarding the overnight hosting of Jewish paupers in a hostel, the German authorities refused to allow Jews to stay there overnight, notwithstanding the fact that the hostel normally hosted the poor, i.e., poor local Jews.⁴

---

3   In that year, most provinces within Germany provided economic freedom, which also led to freedom of movement within all parts of Germany. See: Arnold Friedrich, *Die Freizügigkeit und der Unterstützungswohnsitz*, Berlin, 1872. Ernst Rudolf Huber, *Dokumente zur deutschen Verfassungsgeschichte*, Bd II, Stuttgart, 1964, Nr. 192. Angelika Kopecnz, *Fahrende und Vagabunden*, Berlin, 1980, p. 134.
4   *Niedersächsisches Staatsarchiv Hannover* (N.S.H.), Hann.80 Bf. 64: "Im Amte Diepholz soll keine Herberge für Betteljuden geduldet werden. Verpflegung der armen einheimischen Juden 1814".

Wanderarmen were forbidden from moving about freely without a written permit, and local governments actively limited their movement. In April of 1849, for example, the battalion of the city of Ludwigshafen notified the Royal Corps of the district of Pfalz (Palatinate) about the capture of a family of Jewish *Gauner*, consisting of a husband, a wife, and three children. During the first half of the 19th century, the term *Gauner* referred to Jews who were not economically independent and who, therefore, were in need of charity from individuals or institutions. *Gauner*, in addition, were characterized as moving from place to place; their main activities were associated with the underworld, and their organization was associated with gangs.[5] The report points out that the husband held a passport issued in Strasbourg, where the rest of the arrested family members were from as well. The Ludwigshafen battalion announced the following: "This Jew wandered all over Germany and wanted to come to Pfalz to stay there during the fair."[6] Another example of governmental supervision regarding foreign Jews can be found in the records of the city of Frankenthal. In 1849, local police updated the Royal Ministry of the Interior of Pfalz about expelling a female Jewish *Gauner* after it turned out that she had falsely identified herself as Sarah Reinhard:

We were informed yesterday about the fact that the data regarding this woman were counterfeited. In the meantime, we were also informed, through the district court, that the name of the woman is Sarah Reinen, and that she is the widow of Yoseph Levi from France, who had arrived in the town for the purpose of *Landstreicherei* [loitering]. The woman was arrested and interrogated, but released in the

---

5 On *Gauner* and the differences between them and *Bettler* as well as *Schnorrer*, see hereinafter p. 12-20.

6 Speyer Landesarchiv, H3/610, "Bezirk der Pfalz, 1848-1849", *Allgemeine Zeitung des Judentums* (AZJ), December 12th, 1899.

end. As suspicion arose that she is a member of the Jewish community, she was expelled from the boundaries and transferred to the local commissioner. Description: Approximately 59 years of age; 152 cm tall; thin, high forehead; gray-blue eyes; long nose; big mouth; long facial features; light skin color; does not have any other salient features. Signed: Office of the local commissioner, Frankenthal.[7]

Even before the constitution of 1869 went into effect, granting Jews equal rights within the North German Confederation (*Norddeutscher Bund*) and complete freedom of movement in almost all of Germany, *Wanderarmen* had the right to move, albeit in a limited manner and under the suspicious eyes of the local authorities. The motives behind granting Jews freedom of movement can be found in a simple manner of raison d'état: The migrants were economically significant, for many were traders of various kinds. Local mayors or provincial governors, interested in boosting their sovereignties' trade and economy, also allowed the Jews to move about.

The Jewish communities of Germany, however, did not always welcome the vagabond Jews: For example, the local government of the town of Speyer – a town in the Palatinate whose Jewish community traced its roots to the Middle Ages – published, in 1849, a proclamation warning its local Gentile population of the arrival of Jewish *Gauner*:

News has arrived of Jewish *Gauner* from Prussia arriving with carts and dealing in linen cloth. This merchandise is not properly woven, and is probably fake. This news has arrived to us from authorized sources and from police reports, dating January 1843, and March 1844. These *Gauner* make a large profit. Be warned about them and the way they conduct their business. In particular, be warned about the merchant Eduard Kaufmann of the city of Aschaffenburg: He is

---

7   *Speyer Landesarchiv,* "Bezirk der Pfalz", August 7th, 1849.

accompanied by his mother Rosita (née Gittinger) of the city of Burg, by his two sisters, and by his brother-in-law Frank Yitzhak of the city of Burg. These Jews operate in the vicinity of the cities of Kissingen and Marburg. Local authorities are instructed to pay attention to these *Gauner* and to act against them by putting them on trial without delay, should they enter their territories. Signed: The Royal Regime of Lower Franconia, Aschaffenburg.[8]

This file contains many documents warning of additional Jewish *Gauner* wandering around the region. The documents not only point out that allowing these people to find a foothold in the region is prohibited, but also specify their names and businesses. Judging from the referenced origins of these *Gauner*, it can be assumed that the vast majority were not foreign Jews but previously settled German Jews. The document also mentions Police Amendment No. 7359 from 1828, which prohibited *Gauner* from wandering the area and defined vagabondism as a violation of public safety.

A different document mentions a Jewish *Gauner* who sold gold rings and who was arrested for eight days. Another case, dating 1856, tells of the capture of a Jewish *Gauner* who revealed, during his interrogation, that he belonged to a group of gold merchants. This same Jew blew the whistle on 26 members of the gang who were subsequently caught and accused, as was he, of illegal trading in gold. Several small villages in the region also reported Jewish vagabondism.

Gauner, Schnorrer and Beggars at the Beginning of the 19th Century

The sight of foreign Jews passing through towns was a common one for many Germans during the beginning of the 19th century.

---

8   *Speyer Landesarchiv*, "Bezirk der Pfalz", October 10th, 1849.

For the large part, these vagrants were Jewish paupers begging for food, clothing, shelter, and money. Although this class of charity seekers and beggars became a clearly defined group as early as the beginning of the 19th century, it was during the following years that it underwent a number of changes. This study will analyze these changes through the lens of the changing status of Jews and living standards in Germany.

Wandering Jews were defined as "foreign Jews," i.e., Jews who were not permanent members of their communities. The continuous presence of foreign Jews in Jewish communities created a whole set of characterizing idioms. The usage of these idioms over the years was neither consistent nor precise, for the groups referred to, as well as its sub-groups, underwent various changes.

Jewish gangs were a known phenomenon at the end of the 18th and beginning of the 19th century. They were united and acted according to clearly defined and agreed-upon patterns of behavior. *Gauner* had developed their own tradition, a tradition that included a language specific to their group (a "sociolect") and a hierarchy in which the group members submitted to the authority of the group leader. There is disagreement about the origins of the word *Gauner*: According to one interpretation, it is connected to the word *Gau*, deriving from Saxonian dialect and meaning "naked or smart person." A different interpretation claims that the word is a distortion of the Hebrew word *Ganav* (thief). The *Gauner* also referred to themselves as *Hochmer*, a word derived from the Hebrew *Hacham* (wise).[9]

---

9 On the origins of the term Gauner see: A.F. Thiele, Die jüdischen Gauner in Deutschland, ihre Taktik, Eigenthümlichkeiten und ihre Sprache, nebst ausführlichen Nachrichten über die in Deutschland und an dessen Grenzen sich aufhaltenden berüchtigsten jüdischen Gauner, Berlin 1842, S. 2, and Helmut Reinicke, "Hebräer und Gauner," in: Christof Sachse, Florian Tennstedt (Hrsg.), Jahrbuch der Sozialarbeit, 1981, S. 132.

These traditions had been adhered to since the Middle Ages. Numerous witness accounts from the 16th and 17th centuries tell of Jews captured by the police and indicted in court for crimes and misdemeanors committed mainly in cities. The issue became a problem for the Jewish communities once the beggars and gang members arrived there, causing the settled members not a little discomfort. It was not uncommon for these gangs to appear "uninvited," in which case the community leader had to seek consultation as to how to react.

These Jewish gangs were a new criminal phenomenon. The police, facing the unprecedented scope of their activities, had to find an appropriate response for the new kind of crime. The people responsible for national security and police work found it difficult to respond, for they were facing organized, mobile groups that operated according to established norms and under an organized hierarchy. Furthermore, the gang members' foreign origins and "secret language" (mostly variants of Yiddish or Hebrew) amplified their mystery and the feeling of helplessness produced by trying to counter them. In the eyes of the policemen, these groups were "the latest thing" in the world of crime, a "mafia" (to use modern terms) whose hidden elements doggedly eluded the authorities. This also explains why the authorities often grossly exaggerated the gangs' numbers and scale.

Criminal gangs, and gangs in general, were not, of course, a specific Jewish phenomenon. On the contrary, Jews joined non-Jewish gangs throughout the years. It would, therefore, be more appropriate to say that these organizations established an infrastructure for equality between Jews and Gentiles.

After the Thirty Years' War (1618-1648), as gangs became common in Germany, the authorities organized themselves in an attempt to end the manifestations of this new phenomenon. Nevertheless, the gangs spread to additional regions within Germany, especially during the 18th century, when the seeds of "pure Jewish" gangs were planted.

The Jewish gangs became a *fait accompli* as a result of the authorities' inability to deal with their great mobility. Germany's separate regions were quite isolated during the 18th and 19th centuries; accordingly, local authorities found it difficult to cooperate with one another on a wide scale, thereby hindering any serious attempt to confront a widespread problem. In order to fight the above-mentioned crime gangs and their far-reaching networks, it was necessary for the local authorities (those responsible for providing police services) to also act freely in territories outside their sovereignty. The Jewish gangs exploited this situation in several ways, each contributing to the difficulty involved in dissolving the gangs and catching their members.[10]

For one, the Jewish gangs weakened the territorial framework by spanning Germany's many regions and crossing provincial borders. Interestingly, Jewish gangs were tolerated in the geographic no-man's land between Germany and other countries, and even between German provinces (with the exception of the big cities).

The gangs largely operated in Northern and Western Germany in the regions of Saxony, Hamburg, Lübeck, and Hannover.[11] According to one theory, the Jewish gangs originated in Poland and,

---

10 Rudolf Glanz, "*Geschichte des niederen jüdischen Volkes in Deutschland. Eine Studie über historisches Gaunertum, Bettelwesen und Vagantentum.* New York, 1968, pp. 82-102.
11 In Kassel, 396 Jews were members of one gang in 1758. See: J.J. Bierenbaür. *Beschreibung derer berüchtigten jüdischen Diebs-Mörder und Räuberbanden.* Kassel, 1758.

between 1810 and 1815, moved their operations to the Rhine River region, to central Germany, and especially to the Brabant region, where police supervision was lax.

The presence of Jewish *Gauner* was particularly acute in the so-called "Low Countries," most likely as a result of the fact that the Jews of those poverty-stricken regions were particularly poor. Poverty was a major contributing factor for people to join gangs. The temptation must have been great in the "Low Countries," for regional documents depict an economic situation in which inhabitants often faced the threat of starvation. In 17th century Amsterdam, for example, there was a Jewish proletarian class, as a result of which Amsterdam became, in addition to Hamburg and Altona, a gathering place for Jewish *Gauner* and Jewish gangs.

In the middle of the 19th century, the number of Jewish *Gauner* was estimated at 10,000. They acted as a criminal gang, stealing property valued at several million *Thaler* a year, an enormous sum at the time. A.P. Thiele, a researcher of *Gauner* gangs, points out that gang members referred to each other as *Hevren* (Yiddish: comrades) or as *Havruseh* (Yiddish: circle of friends). These names would later enter the vocabulary of German gangs as well.

The gangs had permanent meeting points all over Germany. Gang members addressed one another with nicknames referring to profession, physical appearance or geographic background: "Chaim with the Jole," "Itzik the Miller," "Yolches Halberstadt," "Hirgen Neubruck," and so on. In addition, gang members referred to the Hebrew, rather than the German, names of their comrades: "Shimon ben Baruch," "Shimon Moshe," or "Moshe Baruch." *Gauner* were accompanied by wives whose task was to support their husbands in times of hardship and to protect them from possible danger: When a

Gauner was caught and convicted, for example, it was up to his wife to formulate pardon request letters.[12]

Between 1824 and 1847, an investigation against a large group of Jewish gangs, led by one Don Yoseph, took place in Hamburg. The indictment named 238 members of one gang. One source, aiming to prove that some of these gangs had been active for a long time, mentions examples of Jewish gangs that had operated in the Rhine River and Brabant regions for over a century. The author of this source mentions that the Brabant gang was led by Yaacob Moises, son of Ahron Moises, a famous *Gauner* who had led the gangs of Holland. The document also mentions gang leaders Moshe Ocker, Ahron Levi of Hamburg, Jakob Hampel, Abraham Lalengase, Moshe Mainzer, Leon Levi, Shimoen Susskind and Shimon Gas. In the 1830s, members of a gang from Koberg who had been active all over Germany were put on trial.[13]

The Jewish *Gauner* were part of a larger phenomenon called "crime economics," through which those who were unable to find sources of income joined gangs that guaranteed sustenance through criminal activities. According to the law of the 18th century, a homeless, vagabonding or roaming person was considered a criminal, a category that also applied to permanently wandering Jews.[14]

The large number of Jewish gang members translated into an influence on the criminal scene in Germany. Contemporary

---

12   Thiele, *Die jüdischen Gauner in Deutschland*, p. 17.
13   Friedrich Chr. Benedict Ave-Lallement, Das deutsche Gaunertum in seiner sozialpolitischen, literarischen und linguistischen Ausbildung zu seinem heutigen Bestande 1852-1862, Reprint der bearbeiteten und gekürzten Ausgabe von 1914, Wiesbaden.
14   Angelika Kopecny, *Fahrende und Vagabunden*, p. 172.

German crime slang still includes idioms whose origins are from the Hebrew: *Ganoven*, for example, is from the Hebrew *ganav*.[15] It should be noted, too, that the *Gauner* gangs' constant movement generated a considerable amount of attention from local German authorities and local Jewish communities. These gangs became a known phenomenon, and the term *Gauner* was used during an entire period. Later, the term lost its original meaning and was used for all *Wanderarmen*, i.e., all vagabonding Jews, even in cases where they were not *Gauner* (members of a criminal gang).

The Jewish Beggars

The Jewish beggars (German: *Betteljuden*) constituted a class of their own, growing with each year and, as was the case with the *Gauner*, constantly moving in groups, often of 50 people or more. The sight of groups of beggars walking in public was not a rare one in the late 18th and early 19th centuries. Beggars often wandered the main roads connecting communities, sometimes stopping to enter one.

This phenomenon became more and more of a threat to the established Jewish communities. In order to deal with the *Betteljuden* problem, special institutions were established in the 18th century. One such institution was the "hostel for beggars" where vagabonds were permitted to spend one night. If, however,

---

15 See: Friedrich Kluge, Rotweltsch, Quellen und Wortschatz der Gaunersprache und der verwandten Geheimsprachen. Straßburg, 1901 and: L. Günther, Das Rotwelsch des deutschen Gauners. Straßburg, 1905 and: L. Günther, Die deutsche Gaunersprache und verwandte Geheim– und Berufssprachen. Leipzig, 1919.

a beggar arrived on Friday night, he was, as a result of the Shabbat laws, permitted to spend two nights there. The hostels operated according to a set procedure: The beggar received a note from the community's *Gabbai* (the caretaker of the synagogue) on which the vagabond's name and the place he would spend the night were written. In the event that the community did not maintain a special hostel for beggars or vagabonds, they were sent to private houses, in prior coordination with the owners. An extant document outlines the procedure:

If the stranger arrives, including the Jewish *Schnorrer*, with a note mentioning the hostel where he is sent to, he shall stay at the place from Friday until Sunday evening or Monday early morning.[16]

This system, called "the Beillen System" (from *Billet*, or note),[17] worked according to tradition and precedent, according to which *Wanderarmen* were often housed in old-age homes, with the community issuing monthly notes listing the addresses the beggars were sent to.

Even though the community shouldered the problem of *Wanderarmen*, and despite the fact that the beggars received the hospitality of its members, the paupers were still treated as strangers: Jewish cemeteries, for example, had a special section for beggars; in 1830, the Hamburg community added such a section to the Jewish cemetery there. Even graver was the prohibition on Jewish beggars to marry under the patronage of the Jewish community. Hamburg's detailed religious ruling on this issue determined that every individual who paid taxes on an income of less than 100 Marks would not be allowed to enter into matrimony with a "foreign

---

16 R, Glanz,Geschichte der niederen, p. 317.
17 Other variants of the word were *Bilet, Plet* and *Plete*.

poor" (*Arme aus der Fremde*) unless he received permission from the community leadership committee in Altona.[18]

This strange prohibition likely stemmed from the community leaders' fear that the paupers would form bonds with groups living on the margins of society, thereby exacerbating crime and prostitution, something that would have corrupted the community in general and local poor Jews in particular. A stringent attitude towards *Wanderarmen* and *Betteljuden* was characteristic of 18th century Jewish communities. Members of Jewish communities were forbidden from initiating group activities benefiting foreign paupers or from raising funds on their behalf. A trend combining prohibitions on the beggars and supervision of their activities developed in the communities, a prominent example of which was the prohibition of activities that would benefit the *Wanderarmen*. The religious authorities of Hamburg and other communities ratified such a prohibition in 1726: "It is forbidden to publicly raise donations for the poor."[19]

As far as the local German authorities were concerned, the beggars and "foreign poor" were a permanent headache. They fought in vain against these elements, for the Jewish beggars, unlike their Gentile counterparts, had managed to strengthen their hold on the Jewish communities. Accordingly, one finds numerous accounts in German archives of the authorities' attempts to deal with Jewish beggars and *Wanderarmen*.

---

18 The original wording is "Wer unter 100 M versteuert darf keine heiraten, sondern nur mit Erlaubnis des Gemeindevorstands in Altona selbst." In: Max Grunewald, *Hamburgs deutsche Juden bis zur Auflösung der Dreigemeinden 1811*, Hamburg 1904, p. 24.

19 The original wording is "Es sollen keine öffentlichen Sammlungen für Arme veranstaltet werden." In: Max Grunewald, *Hamburgs deutsche Juden bis zur Auflösung der Dreigemeinden 1811*, Hamburg 1904, p. 43-45.

Chapter 1: Door-to-Door Beggars

The terms *Schnorrer* and *Bettler* referred to Jews who received charity from other Jews. Both terms originally referred to a direct relationship, without middleman, between those who sought charity and those who gave it; and both terms, usually referring to Jews who went from door to door seeking charity, were already in use by the end of the 18th century (They did, however, gain more currency at the beginning of the 19th century). Here, too, the usage was not homogenous. Often, the terms were used in reference not only to door-to-door beggars and those who stood on street corners with open hands, but also to Jews who, unable to support themselves, were dependent on community institutions.

Although Gentile beggars were also called *Bettler*, the Jewish beggars were referred to by a nickname coined just for them: When Germans wanted to define a beggar as a Jew, they did not just call him *Bettler*; instead, they referred to him as a *Betteljude* (a begging Jew), which became a term in and of itself. Unlike *Bettler*, the word *Schnorrer* was a uniquely Jewish term. According to one theory, *Schnorrer* refers to the reciprocal relationship between the giver and the receiver, a theory based on the etymological route of the German *Schnurre*, meaning joke, funny story, or tale.

Schnorrer, or storytellers, were known figures in the Jewish communities of Germany, and their way of life was connected to the etymological origins of the word: *Schnorrer* wandered from place to place, knocking on the doors of members of Jewish communities, asking to be let in, fed, and, sometimes, put up for the night. In exchange, the *Schnorrer* would tell stories of their ways, their hardships, and the communities they had encountered. This tradition existed until WWI, with the *Schnorrer* being treated with respect at the dinner tables of many Jewish hosts. According to one witness account, the *Schnorrers* of the beginning of the 19th

century "were not ashamed and self-conscious beggars knocking on doors with shaking hands. Instead, they were treated as friends of the Jewish hosts, who also fulfilled the Jewish commandments that way. *Schnorrers* were known for their humor and the good spirits with which they flavored their witty stories." The writer Jakob Löwenberg (1856-1929) writes the following about Polish beggars who had come to his town in his youth:

We were embarrassed vis-à-vis our Christian friends that those dirty, filthy beggars dressed in torn rags were Jews. On the Shabbat, my father would invite them to the Shabbat meal and study Talmud with them. And then, it turned out that these Polish Jews were actually full of virtue and intellect.[20]

Although Jewish and Gentile beggars were a fairly common sight in 19th century Germany, the Germans emphasized the Jews among them. Was begging more common among Jews, or were Jewish beggars more conspicuous? The available historical research does not provide clear answers to these questions. One study concludes that the presence of Jewish beggars was indeed larger, noting that as early as the beginning of the 19th century, more Jewish beggars were seen in German settlements than non-Jewish ones, a phenomenon that would continue to grow in the years to come.

German authorities regarded Jewish beggars as a homogenous group and, accordingly, did not differentiate between *Gauner*, who were often involved in criminal activities, and "normal" beggars who simply knocked on doors searching for lodging and sustenance. Both groups were judged by the same standards, and both were

---

20 Wilhelm Neumann, "Reform des jüdischen Wanderunterstützungswesens Berlin," 1910, p. 2-4. Quoted in: Ernst L. Löwenberg, *Aus zwei Quellen*. Quoted in: "Jakob Löwenberg: Excerpts from his Diaries and Letters," in: *Leo Beack Institute Year Book*, 1970, p. 206.

suspected of engaging in illegal activities. The authorities, the police and the municipalities viewed them as a true hazard. As a result, a great deal of attention was paid to reports of Jewish beggars and *Gauner* entering German towns. Often, the police was called upon to expel them immediately.

One of the functions of *Wanderarmen* was to pass on news. They acted as "walking newspapers" of sorts, delivering quickly and precisely all manner of news from one Jewish community to another: affairs of the Jewish world and of Jewish communities, economic matters, non-Jewish politics, etc. The authorities, not in possession of such a service, could only comfort themselves with the knowledge that these "walking newspapers," by spreading news on the internal affairs of Jewish communities and institutions, served their interests, too. The police also exploited the news (coming from the *Schnorrer*), the bearers of which were the equivalents of police "informants" or anonymous sources.

The abovementioned examples prove that a continuous presence of foreign Jews in the Jewish communities of Germany had been established long before freedom of movement became German law. The phenomenon, manifestations of which were beggars, *Gauner* and *Wanderarmen*, had many names, later developing into a comprehensive terminological system. The terms deviated from what they had indicated as early as the beginning of the 19th century, and thus became independent of their original usage. For example, travelling merchants were often referred to as *Schnorrer* or *Gauner*, even though they were, in fact, seeking neither charity nor help. The terms *Gauner* and *Schnorrer* later became synonymous with vagabonds, thereby losing their original meanings. It is interesting to note that these terms, despite the negative connotation attached to them (a *Schnorrer* signified a beggar knocking on doors, a *Gauner* a criminal), were not only used as derogatory terms for Jews; they were also adopted by local Jews themselves, mainly to describe the relationship between the charity-giving local Jews and the charity-receiving *Wanderarmen*. The use of these terms, however, was accompanied by a negative tone, criticizing anyone in need of economic support. Even at the close of the 19th century, when the population of beggars, *Schnorrer*, and *Gauner* (in their original meaning) had dwindled significantly, the Jewish communities continued to use these terms, mainly as a way of emphasizing a moral stance which regarded vagabondism as unrespectable.

This terminology, which developed during a period when vagabondism had been limited in scope, continued to be used after Jews were granted equal rights and freedom of movement, i.e. after 1869 in North Germany and after 1871 in the unified German Empire.

CHAPTER 2:

THE BEGINNING OF THE UNIFIED STRUGGLE AGAINST BEGGARS

The continuous immigration of Jews to Germany, and the demands this made on the "established" Jewish communities there, led to an escalation in tensions between the two groups: the *Wanderarmen* and the established German Jews. The increasingly common opinion among German Jews was that the *Wanderarme* were turning into a nuisance, exploiting the communities' financial resources and hurting the fragile relationship between local Jews and their non-Jewish neighbors.

On the one hand, German Jews were expected to help charity seekers. The justifications for this were manifold: helping one's fellow man, especially an adherent of the same faith; and the knowledge that the Jewish communities were the only addresses to which the *Wanderarmen* could turn for charity and shelter, to name but a few. On the other hand, the Jewish communities' resources were often limited, especially during periods of declining membership. In order to deal with the dilemma of needing to allocate more resources, the communities often created new positions (to be filled by welfare seekers), e.g., rabbi, *mohel* (circumciser), and *gabbai* (manager of a synagogue). With time, however, these positions were filled as well, and due to the continuing trend of dwindling membership (mainly in the cities of the periphery and small communities), neither welfare funds nor new jobs became available. Other communities, while willing to help, lacked the financial resources to do so; and still others simply lacked the appropriate infrastructure through which to absorb the stream of shelter seekers, due to either insufficient organization or to insufficient funds.

And so, as the number of charity seekers grew, individual Jews began to gradually abandon their responsibility towards the beggars, preferring instead to renounce the tradition of direct help in favor of coordinated community effort. The Jewish community archives, as well as other sources of the period, attest to this transition, one in which German Jews moved from direct support of the *Wanderarmen* to a unified struggle against them. One of the declared aims was to lift restrictions on the mobility of the *Wanderarmen*, thus alleviating the burden on individual community members (as it encouraged *Wanderarmen* to leave communities they had come to sooner rather than later).

Chapter 2: The Beginning of the Unified Struggle against Beggars

It is interesting to examine the timing of this turning point, and the time it took for it to be completed, i.e., when the communities organized under one umbrella organization in order to turn against their wandering brethren. This turning point did not occur at once, for there were regional differences regarding the necessity of an umbrella organization, depending on the urgency of the problem and the dimension of the threat.

A good example of the abovementioned transition can be found in the archive of the Jewish community in the Bavarian town of Gunzenhausen. The relevant file documents the accepted way in which the community supported *Wanderarmen*: While the community's institutions bore full responsibility for the arrivals, they nevertheless cooperated with other Jewish institutions and those of the municipality, the latter of which tried to supervise the movement of foreigners in their sovereignty. This type of cooperation was relatively common in Bavaria. In the 1840s, all *Wanderarmen* arriving in Gunzenhausen were asked to leave their passports at the local police station for surveillance purposes, a procedure applied to both Jewish and non-Jewish vagabonds. One report from Gunzenhausen describes the work of the "Jewish committee against Jewish beggars," most of whom came from Poland:

> Every Jewish beggar coming to this town, even if for a short period, has to leave his passport at the police station. There, the passport will be kept, and later returned, when he [the beggar] leaves. Should something happen, and the beggar's behavior be inappropriate, the Jewish community will be held responsible for him...The community instructs its members not to let Jewish beggars from Poland stay with them, even if for a short time, unless the police is informed about this and the passports of these people are left with the police. The community hereby declares itself committed

to reporting any such person to the local authorities within 30 days.[21]

From this document, it becomes clear that families in Gunzenhausen provided the Jewish beggars with protection, shelter, sleeping arrangements, and food. Out of a sense of obligation to the municipal authorities, the communal Jewish organizations instructed their members to supervise the beggars' presence. According to documentation from the city of Württemberg, this situation continued to exist in South Germany; in fact, there is no evidence of any change until 1871, when Jewish communities imposed a number of supervisory regulations on the beggars. Only a few records of these regulations have been preserved. An exception is the Jewish community of Esslingen, whose documentation depicts a precise picture of the process. In 1871, the community leadership published new instructions about supervising beggars, making it clear that the cooperation between the community and local police would continue to exist. The new instructions, however, did point to a new direction: While in 1843 (when the old instructions were published), the beggars had to leave their passports with the police and were, apparently, allowed to pass from person to person within the Jewish community in order to seek shelter, work, or financial support, the instructions of 1871 stipulated that Jewish paupers were to receive charity in a centralized manner from the local police office. The document describes the system as follows:

> Every local and non-local pauper will receive a grant from the police station assigned to deal with him (women shall receive a grant as

---

[21] *Central Archive of the Jewish People Jerusalem* (C.A.J.P), Gemeinde Gunzenhausen, "Unterstützung durchreisender polnischer Juden, Verschiedene Anträge und Gericht – 1842", July 17th, 1843.

well) [sic]. Every person with the capacity to work, man or woman until the age of 25, shall receive nine Kreutzer. Children shall receive three Kreutzer each. The sick, disabled and deformed shall receive support as well, as shall Jewish paupers from Württemberg – they shall receive 15 Kreutzer each. These people are required to carry with them a note with an [official] stamp from the police. With this note, they will approach the treasury of the Jewish community and receive the money. The police have received instruction not to allow Jewish beggars to bother the [permanent] Jewish residents. Every person who has received the support is required to sign to that effect; if unable to do so [i.e. if he is illiterate], he shall sign with a symbol. The members of the Jewish community reserve the right to inspect the lists and to change the amount payable.[22]

The main change that took place here was the move towards a centralized method through which communities dealt with beggars in general and *Wanderarmen* in particular, allowing the community and its leadership to determine the amount of charity to be given and thereby reducing the scope of begging by deterring beggars from approaching Jewish homes. In some cases, Jewish communities went so far as to collaborate with local police in order to fight Jewish paupers. In the community of Esslingen, for example, the community wrote to the police and informed them of its intention to eliminate the problem of *Wanderarmen* from Galicia and "[begging] Jews of Hungary and their like." In addition, the community asked for aid in achieving this goal, suggesting the following to police authorities: "Every beggar shall receive a grant from a police officer. This will remove the pressure on us. We would like to inquire whether the police are ready for this, and what the involved costs would be.

---

22 *C.A.J.P*, Wr/Ess, Gemeinde Esslingen, Württemberg, "Unterstützungsliste für durchreisende arme Israeliten,1871-1880.

Signed: Representatives of the Jewish community of Esslingen." (9/9/1871).[23]

The purpose of such requests was, apparently, to force *Wanderarmen* to make do with a single payment, and to encourage them to leave the community as quickly as possible. Accordingly, the Jewish communities collaborated with local authorities in order to rid themselves of the beggars as quickly as possible. This can be deduced from a request, written by the board of the Jewish community of Esslingen to its members: "The community of Esslingen is astounded at the low amount of money budgeted by the police for Jewish paupers. The community board therefore requests that community members raise their contributions, even beyond the regular payment of yearly membership dues."[24]

The wording of this letter makes it clear that every pauper, Jewish or non-Jewish, who arrived in the community's jurisdiction, was permitted to turn to the police for charity. The Jewish community wanted to exploit this situation by forcing the police to support the *Wanderarmen*, thereby alleviating its burden. Nevertheless, the community leadership's concern that the sums would not suffice forced it to turn to its members for additional help.

Although non-German settlements also dealt with beggars and *Wanderarmen*, I did not find any testimony in German archives of Jewish *Wanderarmen* receiving government aid. And yet, it is clear that occasionally, particularly in small villages, the Jewish communities collaborated with local authorities. How were the payments made? The Esslingen community's letter does not provide a clear answer to this question, leaving us to wonder if the community

---

23   *C.A.J.P* Esslingen, "Unterstützungsliste".
24   *C.A.J.P* Esslingen, "Unterstützungsliste".

supplemented the police payments or if the *Wanderarmen* were paid twice: once by non-Jewish authorities and once by the Jewish community board.²⁵

As mentioned above, the transition from individual charity to centralized charity was not sudden. It is very likely that both forms existed simultaneously for some time, with *Wanderarmen* begging from door to door while at the same time receiving institutional charity. And while these two forms of support did not necessarily contradict one other, it is certainly true that the centralized approach was the result of an effort to reduce individual charity.

During this transitional phase, the community boards were very critical of community members who refused to take part in the shared burden of centralized charity. The members, in turn, claimed that they were already giving direct charity to Jewish beggars and therefore could not afford additional payments. In some regions, a number of Jewish communities in the same district collectively raised welfare funds for Jewish *Wanderarmen* under their jurisdiction. However, some of the communities located within the regions of these collective welfare initiatives refused to take part in them. The following protocol, from the Esslingen's community's board meeting, illustrates the situation well:

> In its last meeting, the Jewish community board discussed the refusal to contribute to the fund for paupers. It was surprising to find out that some of the communities [in the region] have taken such a decision, i.e. avoiding their charitable duties. Some of them do not know that we deal with 3,000-4,000 paupers a year, 800 of whom stay in our community. Many of them, of course, also reach you [the other communities in the region]. If each and every one

---

25   *C.A.J.P* Esslingen, "Unterstützungsliste". September 12th, 1871.

of us were to donate enough money to support between six and eight paupers, he would suffer little [financial] damage. Should he refuse, the paupers will fill the streets, and this would surely not advance Jewish interests. The Jewish community board demands serious investigation into the matter. Furthermore, it instructs the poverty funds to continue transferring the sums as soon as possible. It is decided that Mr. Linderman will deal with the issue of donations.[26]

The exact timing of the transition from individual to centralized charity is of utmost importance, for it teaches us about the period when the polarization between established Jews and the new arrivals came into being. As long as there is evidence of frequent house-to-house begging, we can assume that the transition was not yet completed. So, for example, writes a member of the Jewish community of Esslingen to the community board, expressing his annoyance over the fact that community members continue to give direct charity to *Wanderarmen*: "Those people [*Wanderarmen*] even go so far as to enter [private] houses."[27]

The transition to centralized charity had its difficulties: Communities were often made destitute because of the *Wanderarmen*. For centralized charity to replace individual charity, it had to be broad enough to prevent the *Wanderarmen* from turning to Jewish homes to complete it. An example of this dilemma can be found in a charity file, dated 1897, of the Jewish community of Regensburg, which suggests, among other things, that door-to-door begging was still common in the late 1800s. In 1897, a privately funded charity for *Wanderarmen*, an organization called "Charity and Hospitality," was active in Regensburg, aiming to centralize charity for *Wanderarmen*.

---

26   *C.A.J.P* Esslingen, "Unterstützungsliste". November 20th, 1871.
27   *C.A.J.P* Esslingen, "Unterstützungsliste". November 20th, 1871.

Earlier, in 1881, the organization still ran two active funds for this purpose.[28] The fundraising was not carried out continuously, so that the organization occasionally turned to its members for additional funds.[29] In 1885, for example, the organization sent its members the following message:

> The cash register is empty. We ask for funds to be raised, even in modest sums. At the moment, we are in need of fewer funds, for it is winter, and there are fewer beggars. We ask for the funds to be collected during the *Aliyah la-Torah* [during the Shabbat prayer service, when the weekly Bible section is read]. From now on, we shall collect funds for this aim once a year. We have decided to eliminate all door-to-door begging. We are adding a list to this letter, and ask you to note your contribution. Once we have succeeded in putting an end to the phenomenon of door-to-door begging, we shall publish the names of the donors. Signed: The Community Board.[30][31]

The collection of funds was ad-hoc, occurring every time a centralized organization experienced difficulties in financing its activities. And yet, despite these initial attempts to cope with the problem in a centralized manner, the outcome was still lacking; as long as the organization failed to provide sufficient funds, it had no chance to succeed. The leaders of the Jewish community in Regensburg understood this, and accordingly requested that members increase their contributions:

---

28 *C.A.J.P* A/278, Gemeinde Regensburg, "Unterstützung armer und durchreisender Israeliten, 1879–1897", December 26th, 1881.
29 Ibid., dated December 26th, 1884.
30 Ibid., dated November 17th, 1895.
31 Ibid., dated November 17th, 1895.

The speed with which local Jews organized the transition from direct individual charity to centralized charity was the result, too, of the fact that the *Wanderarmen* were, as far as the community members were concerned, an acute encumbrance. The burden was not solely financial, for local Jews were also required to host and feed the paupers. As the strain intensified, local Jews became more willing to be recruited for joint activities. It was in this spirit that, in 1895, a local Regensburg Jew turned to the community leadership with the following offer: Every pauper staying in town shall be granted a free meal. During Jewish holidays, he shall be granted two free meals . . . such a person shall not receive more than one meal a week…I suggest a special fund for this purpose to be erected.[32]

A local Jewish family submitted a complaint concerning this very issue:

Foreign wandering Jews normally used to stay with us as guests on Fridays and on the Shabbat. As door-to-door begging has been all but eliminated, this practice should be cancelled as well. We are trying to ensure that these people turn to the Leidenheimer Restaurant on Shabbat and holidays. A righteous member of our community even offered his help in bringing this about. We ask you to donate funds for this cause.[33]

Although instances of door-to-door begging decreased throughout the years, the problem continued to exist, despite the concerted attempts to eliminate it, well into the 20th century, until just before the outbreak of the First World War. The 1890s, however, marked the end of the transitional phase, meaning that individual charity ceased to be considered a legitimate form of community

---

32 Ibid., dated November 16th, 1895.
33 Page form the fund registry of the *Wanderarmen* charity of Esslingen, 1871-1880. Ibid., dated November 16th, 1895.

charity. From then on, charity received through door-to-door begging was marginal when compared to centralized charity, the latter of which expanded with time.[34]

Beginning in the 1890s, many participants in the debate over the question of charity for beggars stressed the importance of the centralized solution, one reason for this being the concern of many Jews that non-Jewish charities, which were then growing at a steady rate, would exploit the Jewish beggars' destitution and convert them to their own faith. The fear of such an outcome, that the failure to expand the budget and the joint effort to deal with Jewish beggars would make the destitute Jews more susceptible to conversion, was a real concern to those tasked with confronting the problem.[35] The memoirs of Nachum Goldmann, who would later become the Chairman of the Jewish Agency's Executive Committee, prove that this fear was not entirely unfounded. Goldman recollects how, when he was in high school (ca. 1910), he used to attend gatherings of Protestant missionaries during which the missionaries tried to convince poverty-stricken Jewish immigrants to become baptized in exchange for material benefits.[36]

The change in the relationship between Germany's established Jews and the *Wanderarmen* was a long process, spanning a generation (late 1860s to the 1890s). In the beginning, greater emphasis was placed on direct individual charity. Simultaneously, as requests for charity increased in number, the emphasis was shifted onto joint

---

34 Jack L. Wertheimer, German Policy and Jewish Politics, The Absorption of East–European Jews in Germany 1868–1914. California University, 1978, p. 35.
35 *A.J.Z.* February 1867, p. 151.
36 Nachum Goldmann himself protested against this practice and warned other Jews of it. Nachum Goldmann, *The Autobiography of Nachum Goldmann*, New York: Holt, Rinehart and Winston. 1969, p. 24.

efforts, initiated by regional and community charitable institutions. Charity for *Wanderarmen* required a joint regional effort, but its results and success rate differed from region to region. And yet, the process took place all over Germany at the same time, albeit with local differences of a few years. Although the examples cited above are from Bavaria, it can be assumed that the transition from individual to centralized charity had been completed by the 1890s in other parts of Germany, as well. As a result, the hitherto personal relationship between the charity giver and the recipient slowly diminished, with the former increasingly relying on institutions to fulfill what had once been his personal duty. From now on, institutions, not individuals, would grapple with the problem of *Wanderarmen*.[37]

---

37 For examples of regional charity activities, see: Ibid., p. 123–129.

CHAPTER 3:

CHANGE IN PERCEPTION

For German-born Jews, or Jews who had been living in the country for many years, Jewish beggars became a common sight beginning in the late 18th century. The way in which local Jews perceived their nomadic brethren underwent significant changes over time.

The disintegration of the direct bond between local Jews and *Wanderarmen*, brought about by the gradual consolidation of institutional infrastructure (set up to combat the *Wanderarmen* and, at the same time, to help them), was a crucial factor in this change, which found expression in the treatment of beggars and, more specifically, in the terminology local Jews used to describe them. The change, however, was not merely conceptual; in fact, it was reflected in verbal attacks against beggars and in the types of institutions set up to combat the *Wanderarmen*. This chapter will trace this process, aiming to show how the established Jewish minority in Germany became increasingly resolute and uncompromising with respect to the Jewish paupers.

The linguistic change signifies a fundamental shift in the attitude of one Jewish group towards another – that is, of Jews whose goal it was to become Germans towards the *Wanderarmen*, the latter of whom wandered through Germany seeking charity and a livelihood. This change in perspective, however, was not absolute. On the one hand, the traditional negative attitude towards *Wanderarmen* and beggars continued to exist, with these being portrayed as harmful to local Jewry. On the other hand, they were perceived as part of a much wider, and not exclusively Jewish, phenomenon. While the traditional standpoint viewed *Wanderarmen* as a real nuisance, a bone in the Jewish community's throat, the new way of thinking – slowly trickling down – viewed vagabonding as an outcome of the social and economic changes then taking place in German society. The *Wanderarmen* phenomenon, then, was seen in the context of the period and the economic and social changes then taking place.

The traditional stance triggered the foundation of local institutions and organizations whose sole aim was to distance the *Wanderarmen* from the Jewish communities. Examples of these organizations were local funds, operating in places affected by a "surplus" of Jewish beggars, or local charity institutions. The second attitude, however, regarded the *Wanderarmen* as victims or side effects of harsh economic changes, leading to the establishment of new social institutions set up to cope with the heart of the matter. The purpose of these institutions was to eliminate the phenomenon of vagabondism by creating new conditions that would ease the absorption of paupers and of those dependent on the charity of others. The solution consisted mainly of workers' colonies and workshops established as a direct response to begging and vagabonding.[38]

From the 1850s onwards, Europe in general – and Germany in particular – witnessed tremendous technological progress, especially in the field of transportation. Trains gradually became the most important means of transportation, as a result of which Germany was soon covered with a network of railroad tracks. Roads were also improved; and at sea, high-capacity steamboats made immigration a viable option for paupers. From the perspective of someone from the last generation of the 19th century, Europe became smaller, her opportunities more accessible. The economic boom, the emergence of new sectors, and the ongoing industrialization created new opportunities for those willing to migrate. Among the migrants throughout Germany were also beggars and *Wanderarmen* who had decided to try their luck in a different place. It was during this period, too, that country-to-country migration rose significantly. In Germany, new arrivals experienced little difficulty in entering the country, for the German government during the Second German Empire, i.e. after Bismarck's unification of 1871, was very tolerant of non-Germans wanting to live in the country. The economy, then quickly developing and in need of labor, goods, and capital, intensively encouraged the mobility of all strata of society, including Jews (as a sort of prototype of migrant workers).[39]

---

38   More on this issue: see chapter 7.
39   On the number of *Wanderarme* in Germany see: S. Boos, "Die Beseitigung der Wanderbettelei. Eine schwierige Aufgabe der heutigen Judenheit", in *AZJ*, July 31st, 1872, p. 48-53.

Under these circumstances, the sight of beggars and migrant paupers passing through communities became a common one in Germany. Jews in general, and *Wanderarmen* in particular, ceased to move from place to place on foot, as they had done in the past, even under the strict movement restrictions characteristic of static European society until the 1850s. Beginning in the 1860s, they started using modern transportation – trains and steamers – on a wide scale.

How did established German Jews react to this phenomenon, the scope of which they had never experienced? From then on, their criticism regarding the arrival in their communities of poverty-stricken Jews intensified. Again, it is important to remember that *Wanderarmen* were not a marginal phenomenon but, rather, a large wave that threatened to drown Jewish communities in burden and in debt. "The beggars allow themselves to travel by fourth-class carriage," reports an article written in 1872 for the *Allgemeine Zeitung des Judentums*,[40] the main voice of liberal Judaism in Germany (hereafter referred to as AZJ). The article goes on to express the fear that a wave of Jewish beggars will soon approach Jewish communities. The writer complains that "the vagabonds' professional begging has become a common sight not only in the East, but also in Germany proper."[41]

In 1879, local Jews defined the problem of *Wanderarmen* as, mainly, "the beggars' problem," still failing to place the issue in a larger context. Only later did they recognize that economic and social factors were responsible for this new phenomenon. By century's end, however, this growing awareness found expression,

---

40 Translated: General Newspaper of Judaism.
41 S. Boos, "Die Beseitigung der Wanderbettelei. Eine schwierige Aufgabe der heutigen Judenheit", in *AZJ*, July 31st, 1872, p. 606.

Chapter 3: Change in Perception

as the following examples, all taken from Jewish publications of the period, will illustrate.

An article published in the bulletin of the German-Jewish umbrella organization, the *Deutsch-Israelitischer Gemeinde-Bund*[42] (*the DIGB*), in 1879 describes Jewish beggars in the hitherto common way, i.e. in a condescending and attacking manner:

> The presence of beggars, paupers, and vagabonds is a testament to how unhealthy and disastrous Jewish society has become. We have to organize to fight this phenomenon vigorously. The professional Jewish beggar moves from place to place, and local funds cannot solve the problem. A solution is only possible once the communities instruct their members to stop giving charity to beggars and poor passersby. Local paupers should be given [charity] only according to [the community's] means. Every person looking for a job who can prove that he is a skilled worker will receive financial support from the community's poverty fund. Those who are on their way elsewhere will only receive a ticket for the ride, handed to them by a representative of the community at the train station. Beggars will not receive a ticket unless they intend to return to where they came from. In certain cases, it will be necessary to turn to the police, who will act against them [the beggars]. Charity will be given only once a year, except in the case of local paupers [who are entitled to more]. Loafers, door-to-door beggars, and those who turn out to be swindlers are not to receive charity of any kind.[43]

In the 1870s, Jewish beggars were still portrayed in the same negative way:

> The damage caused by *Wanderarmen* is spreading like a cancer. They encourage laziness and other immoral begging-related types

---

42 Translated: Federation of German-Jewish Community.
43 *Mitteilungen des D.I.G.B.*, November 1879.

of behavior... The reasons for this phenomenon were the pogroms of the past. However, the *Wanderarmen* continued to exist afterwards as well, due to the poverty prevailing in their countries of origin. These types of behavior are not worthy of forgiveness.[44]

Wanderarmen were, during these years, still regarded as organized gangs of *Gauner*. Voices raised on this issue usually expressed anxiety, fear, and the suspicion that *Wanderarmen* were an organized, disciplined group whose sole intention was to deceive the very people trying to help them. An article written by a member of a poverty organization, published in the AZJ, reflects this prevailing fear:

> The beggars give a false impression of their real situation. They can be compared to a group of soldiers standing on a stage, hence creating the impression that a whole army is standing in front of you. This is an organized and even disciplined group. If we do not organize, then we surely will not be able to deal with them and other paupers. *Wanderarmen* have existed for some time now. Therefore, one has to thank every organization funded to protect individuals from them. Everybody knows that beggars living during the era of the railways are not content with just charity funds, but, in addition, also ask private individuals for charity. They even have a stock exchange of sorts in which they exchange names [of generous donors].[45]

This description – of *Wanderarmen* convening regularly to update one another on places and people – was not unusual. In order to create a negative attitude towards *Wanderarmen*, detailed and elaborate portraits of them were created:

---

[44] Boos, "Die Beseitigung der Wanderbettelei. Eine schwierige Aufgabe der heutigen Judenheit", in *AZJ,* July 31st, 1872, p. 605.

[45] Rosalie Perles, "Über fremde Armenvereine", in: *A.J.Z.*, 1897, p. 453.

As they gain experience, they also add disabled and blind people to their group. They forge documents and wander around for a long time in order to reach private houses. They declare that they had been expelled from Russia, and this word – "expelled" – works its magic: For them, this is an inexhaustible source of income.[46]

The *Wanderarmen*, especially those among them who had migrated to Germany from neighboring countries, noticed the disdain. According to them, the attitude of German Jews was worse than that of local German authorities. In the 1870s, for example, local Jews complained about poverty-stricken Jews arriving from Russia, at a time when this was happening in relatively low numbers, and, therefore, was far from being a "national calamity." In Jewish newspapers available outside of Germany, young Russian Jews were explicitly warned to avoid entering Germany. These publications highlight the extent to which these two groups (German and Russian Jews) were detached from each another, arguing that it would be preferable to suffer economic and political hardship at home than to migrate to a country where the local Jews would not only refrain from helping the arrivals, but, also, actively harass them in order to dissuade them from entering the country. Russian Jews who did enter Germany complained about local Jews trying to make their stay unpleasant. Others were at the receiving end of derogatory names like "Polish pig" or "Russian pig."[47]

Although we should avoid generalizations about German Jewry and its stance regarding the *Wanderarmen*, it is safe to say that the prevailing spirit was one of animosity; organizations, public comments, expressions used in newspapers and magazines – all point in this direction. What were the reasons for this public hostility

---

46   Rosalie Perles, "Über fremde Armenvereine", in: *A.J.Z.*, 1897, p. 454.
47   Ha-Maggid. Volume 7. 1881.

towards Jews entering Germany from neighboring countries? The crux of the matter lies in the local Jews' fear that the migrants would impede the process of Jewish emancipation and the integration of Jews into German society.

There were also objective differences between the two groups, differences pertaining to culture, behavior, dress, personal appearance, livelihood, and lifestyle, all of which contributed to the fear, felt by many German Jews, that the Jewish migrants would challenge their achievements. The local Jews further feared that the influence of *Wanderarmen* would lead to the collapse of the fragile relationship, the result of years of work, between Germans and Jews; that the foreigners would highlight the differences between them and their German neighbors; and, finally, that the paupers' numbers, personal appearance, and other characteristics (unique head covers, long side curls, black coats, and sociolects) would attract the attention of non-Jewish neighbors and local governments. The presence in Germany of those migrant paupers from Russia and Poland, even if brief, was evidence of a segregated group within Germany, of a self-inflicted ghetto. It was, accordingly, the awareness of this threat that defined the attitude of German Jews towards those from Poland and Russia. The extent to which the relationship between these two groups deteriorated is evident from a booklet published in 1891 by Rabbi Leon Wolf, a German Jew who was also known as "the stepchild of German Jewry." In his pamphlet, he argued that the source of German anti-Semitism was Jewish immigration to Germany (a popular claim at the time). Wolf based his premise on the allegedly negative traits of the *Ostjuden* (Jews from the East), which, in his view, justified the anti-Semitism they experienced. The same Jews, so Wolf further argued, were not particularly interested in social activities, with even the rich among them not bothering to help the weak and needy. In addition, he claimed that the situation of paupers in Russia was much better than that of their counterparts in Germany. A poverty-stricken Russian knew, according to Wolf, how to arouse pity, feeling no shame at using any means to accomplish his aims. It is an established fact, so the booklet argues, that Russian *Schnorrers* are already flooding the streets of Germany's large cities.[48]

In 1899, German Jewry still regarded the *Wanderarmen* as gangs of scoundrels, swindlers, and beggars, making no distinction between non-German and German-born Jewish beggars. However, spokespersons of German Jewry did not completely ignore the circumstances that had created the perplexing phenomenon, not just within the Jewish communities, but also (especially after the1880s) within German society, examples of which include the frequent economic crises that befell Germany between the unification of 1871 and the outbreak, in 1914, of WWI. These crises contributed to the rise of poverty and unemployment, which forced those affected to leave their homes and move from city to city in search of economic opportunities, employment, and food.

Jewish newspapers of the period, however, still adhered to the traditional viewpoint regarding *Wanderarmen*, making no attempt to connect their growing numbers to the new reality in Germany. An example of the inability, or unwillingness, to place this issue in the wider context can be found in an article published in the AZJ on December 15, 1899. Although the author, David Kirschfeld, distinguished between different groups of Jewish beggars in Berlin, he still blamed them for the problem and portrayed them

---

48 Ha-Maggid, Volume 19, 1884, and volumes 29-30, 1891. Quoted in: Shimshon Kirshenbaum: *ha-Hagira ha-Yehudit le-Russiya ve-Polin be-Rev'a ha-aharon shel ha-Meah ha-19*. [The Jewish migration to Russia and Poland in the last quarter of the 19th century]. Dissertation. Hebrew University of Jerusalem, 1959, p. 266-267.

in a caricature-like way, through which a reader would think that the beggars would stop at nothing in order to pocket a few coins. Kirschfeld writes, half-jokingly:

> In Berlin, there are two kinds of Jews: Those that are *Schnorrer* for themselves and those that are *Schnorrer* for others. In regards to the former, there are a few sub-categories: those who are ashamed to be poor, those who are not, traveling beggars, *Medinegeier* [country-walkers], and "fundraisers" [Jews who collected money, supposedly for charity funds, but who often pocketed the money]. There are those who manage their business meticulously and who collect coin after coin. The large-scale beggars try to get a hold of 10-Mark or 20-Mark banknotes. Some carry *Bittschriften* [written petitions] with them or give them to others in their name [so that the others can beg on their behalf]. Some paupers are hard to categorize, and are known, even amongst the *Schnorrer*, as *Sha'atnez* [or "mixed fabric"]. The *Sha'atnez* will stop at nothing to achieve their aims. All they want is to work as little as possible, and to scrounge as much as possible, so that they can sustain themselves without effort and worry.
>
> The most inferior amongst the beggars are the ones going door-to-door, equipped with documents explaining their reasons for begging alms. These documents are so tattered, filthy, and stained with oil, that no person would dare touch them. Instead, he prefers to reach into his pocket and to give the beggar a coin. He is lucky if the beggar disappears without starting to scream at the entrance to the house, so loudly that the walls start shaking. More elegant and pleasant are those dealing in "large-scale begging." These beggars aim for gold coins, and they carry with them a fundraising book with different initials, like A.B.-20, L-10 [the numbers represent the sums they supposedly received, the letters the names of the donors]. If you check these numbers and letters and compare them to the handwriting

of the beggar, you will find an extraordinary resemblance. Dealing with these people is embarrassing: They ask for gold coins, and once you tell them that this is impossible, these gentlemen will continue to be nice and pleasant. They will, then, explain to the donor that they are willing to compromise and accept regular coins…

Some have tried to make an even better impression by turning, in writing, to private organizations and funds. These writings ["petitions" in the original] were initiated by third parties who make a business of petition writing, collecting for the service 50 Pfennig from each beggar. The beggars later find out that they have been conned, for the organizations and funds recognize the handwriting of the "petition-producers" and, usually, do not need to investigate long before rejecting the petition out of hand. Another category is the "bypassing beggars" [beggars who stay in a community for a short period of time]. Not only does the community receive them warmly, it also supports them and allocates a yearly budget of 8,000 Mark. Were these people really travelling [i.e. leaving the community], it would be advisable to give them even larger sums. However, they stay in Berlin—a city that cares for them with so much affection…[49]

Jewish communities felt harassed by beggars to such an extent that in the district of Württemberg, for example, the synagogue committee (*die königliche israelitische Oberkirchen-Behörde*) decided to turn to the Jewish communities of the region and to ask them for a detailed report of harassment by beggars: "In light of harassment by Polish Jews, we asked the community to submit an account of the harassment and its scope."[50]

---

49 *A.J.Z.* December 15th, 1899, p. 591–594.
50 *Hauptstaatsarchiv Württemberg, Stuttgart,* (HW)E46 BOE 803, "Belästigung der israelitischen Bevölkerung durch polnische und ostpreußische Juden", April 27th, 1874.

Beginning at the onset of the 20th century, the attitude towards *Wanderarmen* worsened. Voices criticizing welfare – and even calling for its revocation – became louder and louder. It is interesting to note that these calls were uttered at a time when the charity funds and organizations were already functioning on a wide scale. In 1905, for example, a representative of the Nuremberg Jewish community stated the following regarding the treatment of *Wanderarmen*:

> Is it not our duty to help change this situation [i.e. whereby nomads and beggars regularly bother the Jewish communities], even if it means turning to the police? I hereby declare that in my opinion, every criminal [!], no matter what his religious affiliation, will be punished for his deeds... These energetic juveniles can find employment in Hungary much more easily than here. However, they prefer lethargy.[51]

In other cases, the remarks were more moderate, since some had second thoughts about refusing to give charity to Jews. A report, also dated 1905, from the city of Metz states the following:

> The funds [those dealing with *Wanderarmen*] share great responsibility. When we hand out charity to passersby, we share the blame and recognize our part in a bad deed, encouraging these juveniles to live a life of laziness and idleness.[52]

At a meeting of representatives of Jewish communities in Germany, which was convened in Cologne in 1905 in order to debate the issue of Jewish beggars, one representative defined them as "our *enfant terrible*." He claimed that the new generation of beggars, unlike their predecessors, were "immoral, swindlers, and vengeful creatures...While we cannot tar everyone with the same brush, there are still a great many of them who are not worthy of

---

51 *Mitteilungen des D.I.G.B.*, October 1905, p. 45.
52 *Mitteilungen des D.I.G.B.*, October 1905, p. 46.

what they receive. A thick book can be written about the ways they [the beggars] meet in hostels and develop methods there to extract money from private funds."[53] The same representative added that, "These people are sharp and devious, just like us."[54] Most of the descriptions of *Wanderarmen* characterized them as omnipotent swindlers, as deviant, impertinent "survival artists." Willhelm Neumann, one of the heads of the ZJW in Berlin, wrote the following in his proposal for a change in the manner in which communities dealt with *Wanderarme*n:

> The beggars act like businessmen for all intents and purposes. They take the train and get off at every possible station, approaching the poverty funds and asking for charity. Funds should only be given to those *Schnorrer* you actually know. That way, a just distribution can be guaranteed.[55]

These statements were not uttered in a vacuum. In some cases, those who uttered them were not just paying lip service to the prevailing attitude, but, rather, calling for the implementation of concrete action, even be it "unsociable." An example of this comes to us from city of Bochum, where, in 1904, a representative of the local Jewish community reported encouraging signs of the community's efforts to control the begging problem:

> Professional begging has almost completely stopped. What helped us here was the law prohibiting beggars from asking for alms outside their place of residence. We do not give support to paupers who

---

53 *Mitteilungen des D.I.G.B.*, October 1905, p. 112-113.
54 Ibid.
55 Wilhelm Neumann, "Reform des jüdischen Wanderunterstützungswesens Berlin", 1910, p. 5-6. Quoted in: Ernst L. Löwenberg, Aus zwei Quellen. Quoted in: „Jakob Löwenberg: Excerpts from his Diaries and Letters", in: Leo Beack Institute Year Book, 1970, p. 206.

come to us from other places with communities [Jewish communities with sufficient financial means]. We do not support peddlers, for a peddler earns his bread through his business.[56]

Despite the tough line evident in these and other records, local Jews in Bochum still supported the arriving beggars, if only to prevent them from harming the community. In 1905, in fact, the Jewish community of Bochum gave charity to 1,256 people.[57]

As mentioned earlier, it was in the 1890s that members of Jewish communities stopped giving money to door-to-door beggars, at least in a direct manner. At the same time, local Jews consolidated a clear and decisive line of action vis-à-vis foreign Jews, which led, among other things, to the foundation of institutions whose purpose it was to deal with the growing problem. This new arrangement was very different from the traditional charity system, the latter of which emphasized the moral-religious reasons for giving charity. And it was during this period, too, that German Jews founded an organization whose declared intention was to tackle the problem of *Wanderarmen*. The name of the organization, founded in Frankfurt a few years later, indicates not only the intentions of its proponents, but, also, a change in "battlefront" tactics: "The Association for the Struggle against Nomad Beggars."[58] This radical approach to the problem of *Wanderarmen* embedded itself in large swaths of German Jewish society during the late 19th century, creating an atmosphere in which a very clear distinction was made between German-born *Wanderarmen* and those from abroad. Moreover, the problem was discussed almost exclusively in the context of foreign elements; German-Jewish paupers were mentioned only implicitly, if at all.

---

56 *Mitteilungen des D.I.G.B.*, October 1905, p. 50.
57 Ibid.
58 *C.A.J.P*, TD-1133, "Verein zur Bekämpfung des Wanderbettelns."

Chapter 3: Change in Perception

The years leading up to the foundation of the ZJW marked a turning point in the way German Jews explained the problem and related to it: After most of German Jewry had accepted the uncompromising stance regarding *Wanderarmen*, other voices made themselves heard, voices that sought to identify the circumstances that had forced thousands of beggars to seek charity from Germany's Jewish communities. The proponents of this line explained the paupers' behavior not as a matter of character flaws, but as the outcome of the period's economic reality. This new line of thinking was even evident in Wilhelm Neumann's proposal, but he nevertheless denigrated the phenomenon, as if it had no connection to external circumstances:

> The main reason for nomad begging is not political persecution, but, rather, economic…Who does not know of the phenomenon of German women looking for their missing husbands? The current situation, one in which people exploit natural disasters, fires, and other tragedies to receive charity, is flourishing: People fake documents and do anything to receive alms. Therefore, one must check their documents, banishing the forgers immediately and warning others of their presence. Among beggars, the number of forgers is high …Many of them fake marriage documents with "spouses" they have only just met, living a life of debauchery and recklessness in different hostels and dilapidated sheds. On fast days, with everyone's consent, they gorge on fatty meals. Those who just days before had claimed to be blind are suddenly able to travel, by themselves, on trains. And when they approach the charity funds, they appear in the company of their wives and children…Is this not damning proof of the beggars' immoral behavior? Therefore, it is not surprising at all that the [Jewish] beggars' colleagues – the

Christians – join them in their ways. These we find under "non-Jews" in the blacklists.[59]

The change in attitude towards *Wanderarmen*, as indicated by Wilhelm Neumann, was apparent by the end of the 1880s, when migration within Germany became widespread. At the center of this new attitude was the recognition that the *Wanderarmen* were part of a new socio-economic phenomenon, one that was then occurring in all of Germany. Established Jews recognized that the charity-seeking nomads were different from their predecessors of the first half of the 19th century, and that the circumstances had changed completely. The new kind of nomadism was of unprecedented scope and dimensions, and although the reasons behind it were similar to those behind the wave of nomads who had wandered through Germany before Jews were granted freedom of movement, the *Wanderarmen* of the late 19th century constituted a social problem of unprecedented urgency. Later, during the years preceding WWI, those who tried to understand the problem relied more heavily on political and economic explanations, as a result of which a more forgiving attitude towards the *Luftmenschen* ("air people") found traction in Germany:

> The difficult times in trade and in the economy force thousands of people to migrate from Russia, Galicia, and the countries of the Balkans. Those are countries towards which Jews do not have a friendly attitude. Hundreds of destitute families return to us, even from England, France, and America. We should no longer castigate these *Luftmenschen*, who only 'wander around the world.' This

---

59 Wilhelm Neumann, "Reform des jüdischen Wanderunterstützungswesens Berlin", 1910, p. 3. Quoted in: Ernst L. Löwenberg, Aus zwei Quellen. Quoted in: "Jakob Löwenberg: Excerpts from his Diaries and Letters", in: Leo Beack Institute Year Book, 1970, p. 206. (on the "black lists" see ibid., p. 109-114).

kind of talking and shrugging will not solve the problems faced by these people. Nobody leaves the town he was born in because of mischievousness, the sole aim of which is to find his luck in a different country. A person who sells his valuables and leaves with his wife and children; a young person who leaves a hostile country because of psychological and physical enslavement – this person we must assist, if only with a warm meal and a place to spend the night, enabling him to continue on his way with renewed energy.[60]

Another prominent difference between the experiences of the early *Wanderarmen* (early 19th century) and those of the late 1800s and early 20th century was in the attitude they encountered from German Jews. In pre-emancipation Germany, *Wanderarmen* were an organic part of the socio-economic system, closely watched by the discerning eyes of the local authorities. Nomadism was accepted as a nearly inseparable part of society; as such, it never received undue attention, or at least not more so than other problems, like crime. The economies and societies of Europe were static during this period, making it difficult to travel and migrate. Only a minority did this, mainly people looking to complete professional training, seasonal workers in various sectors, "professional wanderers," and "anti-socials," the latter of which were unable to fit into society and live by its values. As the dimensions of the phenomenon were manageable during this period, coping with it was not difficult. When, however, the social and economic circumstances changed, so did the dimensions of the problem. At the end of the 19th century, German society was much more dynamic than it had been in the period discussed above, as a result of which grew an awareness of the direct link between nomadism and the socio-economic realities

---

60   *A.J.Z.*, "Herberge für jüdische Durchreisende", January 23rd, 1914.

that had created it. It was in this spirit that a representative of the Jewish community of Cologne said (in a speech delivered at a meeting of the DIGB) that "nomadism is a side effect of poverty."[61]

With the change in attitude came a change in the image of the Jewish beggar. As more people began to understand that unemployment was the main reason behind the growth of the *Wanderarmen* problem, the members of this group were increasingly seen as what they in fact were: unemployed nomads in search of livelihoods. Thus, it was the working capacity of *Schnorrer*, beggars, and *Wanderarmen*, rather than their alleged laziness, that became the main focus. Accordingly, new definitions of these groups entered the vocabulary. For example, when one now spoke of *Wanderarmen*, he referred to them as "Jewish craftsmen" or "Jewish laborers." Another new definition was provided by representatives of the Frankfurt Jewish community in 1905:

> There is now a new class of beggars, those who beg against their will. These are craftsmen whose number increases every day. They are people who are simply unemployed. It is not customary for Christian employers to employ Jews, and the Jews themselves, being underemployed, are not in a position to share what little they do have with other Jews. I request [and turn to the representatives of other Jewish communities] to enable Jews to produce their own cloths and to offer them work.[62]

A clearer distinction was made by the representatives of the Jewish community of Cologne, who divided the *Wanderarmen* into two distinct categories: "local nomads" and "nomad craftsmen." The local nomads were defined as people of German origin who, unable

---

61 *Mitteilungen des D.I.G.B.*, October 1905, p. 50-52.
62 *Mitteilungen des D.I.G.B.*, October 1905, p. 52.

Chapter 3: Change in Perception 67

to support themselves or their families, had to turn to the *Schnorrer* lifestyle in different parts of Germany. Regarding members of this group, it was recommended that they be permitted to stay in their place of residence and that they receive charity there. In the event that the local Jewish community was not able to provide the aid, larger neighboring communities were asked to help out – as did the community of Cologne, which provided charity to the *Wanderarmen* of the surrounding towns and villages. A representative of the community of Cologne spoke out in favor of this system, arguing that it was both moral and profitable – profitable in the sense that the larger communities would be able to share the burden of supporting paupers. The second category consisted, as mentioned above, of nomad craftsmen: "These are craftsmen who were employed in the past, who have meanwhile found employment, or who will do so soon. They should be looked after during the interim period, and workshops to employ them should be built.[63]

A great deal of attention was, during this period, focused on finding solutions for skilled laborers, forced by unemployment to leave their homes and try their luck elsewhere. Among these solutions, already attempted in non-Jewish German society, were "labor settlements" and "workshops" that provided unemployed Jews with a source of income, if only for a short period. Such places paid the laborers a wage, a wage that the laborers could save and later use in the absorption process.[64]

In conclusion, it is necessary to emphasize that during the period analyzed here the image of the "wandering Jew" changed continuously. The essence of this change was the transition of the

---

63 *Mitteilungen des D.I.G.B.*, May 1905, p. 112-115.
64 More on organized solutions to this issue, see Chapter 7 and chapter 10.

beggars, *Gauner*, and *Schnorrer* of the first half of the 19th century to the *Wanderarmen* – the immigrant paupers, craftsmen, and nomad laborers of the 1890s and onward. The classification of *Wanderarmen* into different categories was carried out by their contemporaries, using common concepts and ideas of the time. Both new terms and previously known ones were used to describe *Wanderarmen*. At times, old and new terms were employed simultaneously when describing the same group of nomad paupers, this in spite of the fact that the group described underwent significant changes, and in spite of the fact that the old terms were no longer applicable. By following the course of the definitions, we have been able to determine a) the essence of those changes as they applied to the *Wanderarmen* and b) the period in which they took place. These changes, however, were not purely conceptual; in fact, they signified the collapse of the individual charity system and the transition to centralized charity, from begging door-to-door to seeking charity from institutions. As mentioned above, this process was accompanied by a negative attitude towards the *Wanderarmen* and a deepening alienation between the nomads and the local Jews. Later, after the 1890s, the treatment of *Wanderarmen* improved, as it was recognized that the beggars were not "at fault," that their destitution was a byproduct of external circumstances. Once this happened, the development of institutional frameworks accelerated significantly, founded by local communities and by national Jewish organizations, all of which aimed to aid the *Wanderarmen* and, at the same time, to protect local Jews from their presence.

The move towards organized welfare, which replaced the traditional, direct relationship between those who sought charity and those who gave it, had further implications. The need for a support system, one that would support a large number of foreign Jews, led to the expansion of community institutions and frameworks. New organizations were established, new lines of actions were consolidated, but additional resources were needed. Community members became increasingly involved and cooperative, mainly by holding positions in the new organizations and by financing activities. It is quite paradoxical to note that it was during the period of Jewish emancipation and integration into German society that Jews became more involved in their own communities.

Foreign and German Jews moved from community to community; some managed to settle, but many others were constantly on the move. The need to support them forced the communities to look inwards, preventing, or at least delaying, German Jews from leaving their ghettos, a key element of the emancipation. The springboard offered by German society was not initially used by local Jews, for they needed to solve their own problems before they could focus on integrating into German society. It can also be argued that the development of infrastructure in the Jewish communities was an "anti-assimilating" activity, or, at least, one that postponed assimilation. Strengthening and expanding the organizational framework of the community – in other words, exceeding its traditional functions – strengthened the gravitational pull of Jewish community institutions and services. As a result, many Jews chose to stay in their community and to benefit from its services, in particular from services not related to religion. As a result of the fact that non-Jewish German institutions often did not provide the array of services available in Jewish communities (charity, old-age homes, hospitals, and various educational opportunities), Jews became, for lack of alternatives, dependent on their community. Many of these services were secular (charities, hospitals and loan organizations), and although it would have been possible to receive them in non-Jewish communal frameworks, the improvement and expansion of Jewish charity organizations restrained those who otherwise would have left the community, thus postponing the process of Jewish integration into German society. Beginning in the early 19th century, but mainly since the 1850s, Jewish communal institutions lost much of their authority, as a result of which many Jews left their communities and entered secular, non-Jewish society. Some kept their ties to the communities, others left permanently, and still others left for specific reasons,[65] but it is clear that many more would have left their community had it not been for the communal framework (including welfare).

By the end of the 19th century, the communities had consolidated their services, most often by simply adapting to circumstances (as opposed to planning ahead). An increase in overall population movement and, in particular, a rise in the Jewish population created a series of issues that demanded immediate attention. As a consequence, the non-mediated relationship between veteran members of Jewish communities in Germany and foreign Jews (beggars, foreign paupers, and other non-German Jews) was lost, with institutions taking over what had once been the responsibility of individuals. Acting as middlemen between local Jews and those from abroad, the institutions contributed to the collapse of relations between the two groups. For the *Wanderarmen*, and especially for

---

[65] A detailed discussion on Jewish and non-Jewish charity systems can be found in: Ahron Bornstein, *Mi-Kabtzanim le-Dorshei Avodah: Yehudim Navadim be-Germania 1869-1914* [From beggars to employment seekers: *Wanderarme* in Germany 1869-1914], doctoral dissertation, Tel Aviv University. Tel Aviv 1987, p. 180-231.

those from neighboring countries, the ensuing implications were grave, as the wandering Jews were now strangers not only in the eyes of the Germans, but also in the eyes of local Jews.

CHAPTER 4:

CHARACTERISTICS OF WANDERARMEN

Who were these *Wanderarmen*? What were their numbers, their ages? How did they move from community to community? Was the number of men among them high? And what role did the women play? Extant statistical data, most of which I have culled from the account books of the clerks who were responsible for handing out charity, enable us to answer some of these questions and to pinpoint some prevailing characteristics.

History, in order to be written accurately, requires documentation. The protagonists of history often provide these themselves, shedding

Chapter 4: Characteristics of Wanderarmen

light on and illuminating the period by leaving behind documents, written memories, or other material; through their point of view, we see historic events in the context of the period. The protagonists of our story, however, did not leave behind much written material. Available first-hand testimony – and it, too, is scarce – was written from the point of view of the charity givers, rather than that of its recipients, the latter of whom were too busy fighting for their physical survival, for their everyday needs, and for a basic, albeit meager, income. Occupied with the ordeal of being on the move, the result of either economic hardship or anti-Semitism, those who depended on charity were unable to write memoirs or testimonies.

The period covered here is relatively long, making it difficult to provide a representative snapshot or to precisely trace the developments under discussion; accordingly, we can only describe general trends, developments, directions, and outlines. Furthermore, we are dealing with a widespread phenomenon of nomadism, which means that we must examine as many locations as possible. Here, too, the source material leaves much to be desired: As of this writing, few statistics are available on the regions of Germany during this period, forcing us to make extensive use of those sources that have been preserved. The outcome of such an examination has often substantiated the research assumptions. As it turns out, a comparison of the different communities proves that the phenomenon under discussion repeated itself, as a result of which we can determine general trends even in places about which the records yield little. Another issue with which this chapter will deal is the question of whether it is even possible to group the *Wanderarmen*: Were they different, for example, from local German Jews? Were there demographic differences between the two groups? A general analysis of the group will answer this question in the affirmative.

Furthermore, it will show that the two groups influenced each other. Will it show that the groups more and more resembled each other?

The size of groups passing through communities

First of all, it is important to point out that our calculations regarding the number of beggars and *Wanderarmen* in the years between 1869 and 1914 are based on official numbers provided by charity funds all over Germany. The charity funds collected the numbers from border control stations and from communities of various sizes (small, medium-sized, and large). We have almost no information regarding the scope of individual charity given to beggars by members of the Jewish communities. Although the existence of this unmediated system of giving charity is significant in estimating the number of Jewish paupers moving between communities in Germany, it cannot be used in estimating the charity sums.

Due to the combination of individual and centralized charity, and due to the lack of official numbers, it can be assumed that the actual number of *Wanderarmen* was significantly higher than that which appears in the official statistics of the relevant organizations. Although some charity recipients apparently benefited from both forms of charity – official and individual – the data in this chapter relates only to those who approached the former. It is very difficult to estimate the number of Jews who received charity in other ways, but, as mentioned earlier, the very existence of individual charity throughout this period proves that the number of *Wanderarmen* who passed through Jewish communities was larger than the official documents indicate.

Chapter 4: Characteristics of Wanderarmen 75

In order to estimate the exact number of *Wanderarmen* in Germany, it is necessary to collect data from all charity funds and institutions and, through it, to arrive at the number of charity recipients. However, as this data is neither complete nor chronologically continuous, we have to settle for the existing data while at the same time inferring information regarding areas about which we do not possess data. By so doing, we will identify general demographic patterns through constant patterns in the areas we have data on.

Most of the available information is from Jewish sources. Although the Germans did conduct statistical surveys on the number of foreign Jews in Germany, they did not concern themselves directly with *Wanderarmen*. Official German statistics dealt with the number of non-German Jews (those without German citizenship) staying in Germany at any given time, but not with the movement of Jewish paupers or with the manner in which they received charity from Jewish communities. It was only when the *Wanderarm*en clashed with Germans, either with citizens or with the authorities, that they aroused the interest of German institutions.

The existing data on *Wanderarmen* is problematic in other ways, frequently not stating how long a Jew stayed in Germany, whether or not he tried to emigrate from or settle in the country, and how long he intended to stay. Although Jewish organizations recorded the *Wanderarmen* who received charity, we are left to guess about what happened to them afterwards: where they settled, how they were absorbed (if at all), etc. These and other questions will remain unanswered, for we are dealing with a large, unpredictable group.

The only attempt to determine the number of *Wanderarmen* was carried out by Jakob Segall, the editor of the *Zeitschrift für*

Demographie und Statistik der Juden (hereafter ZDSJ), a Jewish publication on Jewish demographics and statistics; published in Berlin, the ZDSJ is chock-full with information about Jewish communities in Germany. However, Segall's data, which he collected from the Central Bureau of Charity for *Wanderarme* – active in Berlin beginning in October 1910 – applies solely to the organization's activities, shedding no light on the preceding period. Segal states this clearly:

> Unfortunately, we have very little information regarding the number of *Wanderarmen* in Germany during the period before WWI. The publications of several charity organizations and of the Central Bureau of Charity for *Wanderarmen* offer limited data on the period following it. Therefore, we cannot give a complete answer to this question.[66]

In order to calculate more precisely the number of *Wanderarmen* in a certain year, it is necessary to combine data from different charity funds. Although the ZJW, Berlin's central organization for *Wanderarmen* charity, dealt with the issue of numbers since its founding, most of the data it collected was not preserved, as a result of which we do not know the exact number of *Wanderarmen*. Using data collected by local charity funds, we can estimate more easily the number of charity applicants on a regional level; lacking chronological order and uniformity, however, the data is not very helpful in an attempt to compare the number of charity funds over an extended period of time. Nevertheless, we know, for example, that the charity fund in the city of Bochum dealt with 825 *Wanderarmen* in 1881, with 1,083 in 1890, with 2,884 in 1900, and with 1,948 in 1905; later, the number of Jewish paupers supported by this

---

66 Jakob Segall, „Wandarmenfürsoge in Deutschland bis zum Jahr 1914," in: *Zeitschrift für Demographie und Statistik der Juden (ZDSJ)*, 1924, p. 69.

fund decreased, so that in 1912 it supported only 643. The city of Frankfurt a.d. Oder supported 1,385 *Wanderarmen* in 1883, 1,174 in 1890, 2,884 in 1900, and 3,254 in 1900; there, too, the number of charity seekers decreased (1,687 in 1912). In Leipzig, 721 people received charity in 1873 and 1,417 in 1914. In Berlin, the number of charity recipients was 3,316 in 1894 and 6,228 in 1911, a rare example of a rise in Jewish paupers on the eve of WWI. The data from Bavaria, similar to that from Berlin, points to a significant number of *Wanderarmen* before WWI: There, the number was in the several thousand per year, with indications of a rising trend.

By studying cases where we have data pertaining to the same year, we can find out which city was the most attractive to *Wanderarmen*. For example, in the period between April and December of 1913 (eight months), 43,000 *Wanderarmen* received charity, with the "most attractive" cities being Berlin (6,250), Cologne (4,000), Leipzig (3,952), and Hamburg (2,034). In Danzig, however, only 60 people received charity that year, in Freiburg only 39.[67]

This data, collected by the Berlin-based ZJW, enable us to categorize the charity-seekers according to sub-groups, as a result of which we are able to learn of special types of *Wanderarmen*: First, there were the local poor (*Provinzarme*), or Jews who lived permanently in the territory of their host community. Another sub-group, the *Auswanderer*, were Jewish migrants who were about to move overseas. The ZJSD made a clear distinction between *Wanderarmen*, i.e. Jewish paupers moving within Germany, and those whose intention was to immigrate.

Yet another sub-group, the "returning *Wanderarmen*" (*Rückwanderer* in German, they appear frequently in different

---

67 Ibid., p. 69.

records), was composed of foreign Jews who intended to pass through Germany on their way home, usually in Germany's neighboring countries. Most of these "returning *Wanderarmen*" were not German-born, and German Jewry feared that they would place, while traveling "home," undue strain on the German-Jewish charity system, a system that already had difficulties providing basic services. The definition of the charity seeker, however, was not always as detailed; very often, all charity seekers were referred to simply as *Wanderarmen*.

Records from places that upheld these distinctions indicate that the charity seekers were normally *Wanderarmen*, not *Provinzarme*. In Frankfurt am Main, for example, there were 31 *Provinzarme* (2.6%) and 1,627 *Wanderarmen* (70.7%) in 1913. In cities like Breslau, Stettin, and Thorn, more than half of all charity applicants were *Rückwanderer*.

The low number of *Provinzarme* is misleading, for the records only count those *Provinzarme* who were provided for by regional charity funds, funds that normally provided for Jews who were not members of the community. The remaining *Provinzarme* received aid through Jewish community institutions. Accordingly, we can state that their numbers were in fact much higher than the records indicate.

The main problem for the researcher, as noted before, is to find a community whose records include dada on more than one year (as is the case with Jakob Segall and his statistical yearbook on Jewish Berlin), for it is only through studying a sequence of years that one can analyze a development or a trend. A good example of this can be found in the books of the Würzburg Jewish community's charity fund. The community archive, a large part of which has been

Chapter 4: Characteristics of Wanderarmen 79

preserved, contains the charity fund's books for – and this is quite rare – nearly three decades (1865-1893). This source is especially significant, for it is the only one from the period that offers continuous data regarding our topic. The books recorded not only the names of the *Wanderarmen* who passed through the city and received charity from local funds, but also their places of origin, ages, family status, amount of charity received, and other information that struck the clerk as noteworthy.

The Würzburg community's documentation system, in effect (without interruption) until 1893, allows us to determine the exact number of applicants to the fund. The system was also very strict, enforcing the rule that non-resident paupers receive aid only once a year. In order to enforce this rule, the recording clerks generally entered the applicants' names in two separate registries: in the official registry and in an alphabetical index of names; the former was organized by week (chronologically), the latter alphabetically. This way, community officials made sure that an applicant would not be able to apply for aid twice in the same year. Every pauper asking for aid had, first of all, to identify himself. The clerk would then open the alphabetic index and see if the applicant's name was listed there; in the event that it was, he would check when the applicant had last received charity.

Unlike the Würzburg register, Segal's statistical yearbook makes it impossible to determine the frequency of charity applications, not to speak of the number of years beggars were registered as charity applicants. And as names are classified only be chronology (that is, they appear in chronological order) in Segal's yearbook, it is difficult to determine who was a returning charity applicant to the same fund. If one were to check whether a certain person received additional aid, and when, one would have to compare data related to thousands of names from the same charity fund, a methodological problem that is exacerbated by the fact that data are often missing from the records. The funds do, at times, list this information. The charity fund of Posen, for example, included this data in 11/1910: out of 472 charity recipients, 76 (16%) had received aid from the same fund prior to the recorded application; for 58 (12%), this was the third application, and eight had applied more than three times.

Beginning in 1874, clerks from Würzburg (where, as mentioned, a non-Würzburg resident was permitted to apply for charity only once a year), recorded the names of applicants who had received aid in the past. A sample of *Wanderarmen* receiving charity in Würzburg (between June, 1884, and June, 1886) reveals that 43% applied for aid only once, 23% twice, and 17% between three and five times. Another 17% tried to receive charity between six and eight times, some of whom returned each year with astonishing regularity. In other words, some of the *Wanderarmen* staying in Germany returned to the Würzburg charity fund on a regular basis, if only to receive a few bowls of soup. This indicates their dire economic situation and the absence of a centralized system of social aid. Another explanation, however, states that, being "foreign" Jews, the paupers were not associated with any Jewish community, making them entirely dependent on the funds.

The "Foreigners" in Germany

In dealing with this phenomenon, one in which large numbers of foreign Jews made their way, nearly unhindered, through Germany, we must answer several questions. How could the *Wanderarmen* move from community to community without the German

Chapter 4: Characteristics of Wanderarmen

authorities intervening? How was it possible that members of this group – economically weak, unable to sustain themselves – enjoyed such freedom of movement and activity in Germany of the Imperial period? The answer to these questions lies in the socio-economic situation in Germany, especially that which prevailed in the country from the 1890s onwards. The economic crisis of the years 1873-1895 was followed by a decade of prosperity in agriculture and industry, increasing the demand for laborers in all sectors of the German economy. Although the workers enjoyed mobility, the need for labor was so great that it became necessary to recruit foreign workers. This was particularly true of Prussia, where most of the seasonal workers (*Saisonarbeiter*) in agriculture were foreigners.[68]

Beginning in the late 1890s, the number of foreign workers in Germany increased significantly. They constituted the most important group of migrants, and were absorbed gradually into the labor market. In order to keep updated estimates regarding the number of foreigners residing in the territory of the Reich, German authorities conducted occasional population polls. One such poll, conducted in 1871, counted 270,000 foreigners in Germany. By 1910, this number had increased by nearly five-fold, to 1,259,880 foreigners. Most of the foreigners had come from Poland (from the territories of "Congress Poland," or "Russian Poland"), others from Galicia.[69]

In the industrialized areas, the need for manpower was acute, as a result of which the number of foreign workers there rose

---

68 Johannes Nichtweiss, *Die ausländischen Saisonarbeiter in der Landwirtschaft der östlichen und mittleren Gebiete des Deutschen Reiches 1890–1914*, Berlin 1950, p. 27.
69 Klaus J. Bade, *Vom Auswanderungsland zum Einwanderungsland? Deutschland 1880–1980*. Berlin, 1983. p. 29–30.

noticeably. Statistics from the region of Rheinland-Westfalen, where industrialization and modernization developed rapidly, indicate that, in 1861, only 16 Polish citizens lived in the area, all in the city of Düsseldorf; in 1890, however, more than 30,000 Polish citizens lived in Rheinland-Westfalen. The Polish population continued to grow during the following 20 years, so that, in 1910, the region was home to 300,000 Poles. The migration of foreign workers from Eastern to Western Europe, characteristic of industrialization, grew because of many reasons, among them wages, professional advancement, and general working conditions, all of which were better or more plentiful in Western Europe.[70]

German policies regarding foreigners in general, and foreign Jews in particular, changed according to political circumstances. When it was in the interest of the government to act in favor of foreigners, the migrants were treated sympathetically, experiencing few problems. This was the case in the 1890s, when Germany signed a series of agreements, mainly trade agreements, with its neighboring countries. At other times, however, foreigners were treated with hostility by German governments, an expression of which was expulsion from Germany, a policy that had been in effect since the 1880s. In 1881, for example, 600 Russians were expelled from Prussia, most of them Jews. It was during the 1880s that this trend intensified, with the authorities reasoning that expulsion was necessary in preventing the "Polinization" of East Prussia.

The Prussian government justified expelling Jews in paragraph 71 of the Law regarding Jews, dated July 23, 1847. This law prohibited

---

70 Hans–Ulrich Wehler, *Krisenherde des Kaiserreichs 1871–1918,* Göttingen, 1970, p. 219–220.

non-German Jews from taking on official functions in German-Jewish communities without a permit from the government's Office of Religious Affairs. In the same vein, German employers were prohibited from employing Jews who lacked local residency rights (*Heimatrecht*). The German constitution of 1870 permitted the expulsion of foreigners, if based on justifiable grounds. As justification, governments argued that Jews did not assimilate into life in Germany, and that negative and criminal elements were among them.[71]

German Jewry's response to the expulsion of foreign Jews was in line with its attitude towards *Wanderarmen*: Local Jews did not lift a finger to prevent the expulsions, and sometimes even actively supported and encouraged it. In 1886, for example, a number of Jewish leather merchants from Leipzig signed a petition in favor of expelling Jewish leather merchants from Russia who had entered the city and competed with local merchants.[72]

A key factor in the decision to expel a foreigner, Jewish or not, was whether or not he had received charity from an official source. In the event that he had received charity, the institution that provided it was entitled to demand the expulsion of the foreigner. If his origins were not known, the charity institution had to contact the police and ask for its assistance in removing the foreigner. The law stated that one should refrain from expelling a stranger who was in Germany for a limited period of time, or if he, or one of his family members, was sick.

---

71 Mascher, Das Staatsbürger Niederlassungs– und Aufenthaltsrecht, Potsdam, 1868. P. 10. Also: ha–Meggid, issue 35, 1884.
72 *Hamelitz*, issue 44, 1886.

The provision also recommended that women with German citizenship who were married to foreigners not be expelled. These women, however, could expect to be expelled, for, by marrying a foreigner, they had "adopted" his citizenship. The provision further stated that Germany was not to expel those whose native countries would later expel them, and that an expellee was not to be sent to a country to which Germans were immigrating (the United States, for example).[73] An expulsion had to be coordinated with the relevant border control station; when necessary, the expellee was accompanied by an escort from the charity organization or, in the event that the police had initiated the expulsion, from the police. (Expellees of this category were called *Ausländerlästige*, i.e. bothersome foreigners.)[74]

Deportations of foreigners from Germany continued in the years 1885-1886. Of those banished from the country, the largest group consisted of Polish citizens expelled from Prussia. The expulsions were part of a more general "Germanization" policy, common in certain regions of Germany (mainly Prussia), the aim of which was to purge the Reich of foreign elements. This policy, originating in anti-Polish and anti-Semitic thought, was authorized by Bismarck.[75]

---

73 Ernst Grässner, Erich Simm, Das Armenrecht, Eine systematische Darstellung sämtlicher das Armenrecht betreffenden Rechtsmaterialien, Berlin, 1914, p. 421–422.
74 Ibid. p. 424.
75 On the expulsions, see: Robert Koel, "Colonialism inside Germany: 1886–1918," in: Journal of Modern History, September 1953. Joachim Mai, Die preußisch–deutsche Polenpolitik 1885–1887, Eine Studie zur Herausbildung des Imperialismus in Deutschland, Berlin (Ost), 1962.

Helmut Neubach, Die Ausweisung von Polen und Juden aus Preußen 1885/6, Wiesbaden, 1967. Barbara Vogel, Deutsche Rußlandpolitik, Düsseldorf, 1973, p. 87–103.

Throughout the 1880s, the number of expelled foreigners amounted to 40,000 people, half of them Jewish.[76]

The policy of expelling foreigners, however, was not consistent, In spite of the large number of expulsion orders issued in Prussia, the authorities turned a blind eye to the massive immigration of Jews to Germany. In the 1880s, more than 13,000 Polish citizens continued to live in Prussia. Prussian authorities never published statistical data on the number of expellees, which is why we can only estimate. Researchers estimate that 30,000 foreigners were expelled from Prussia during this period, one third of whom were Jewish. In the 1890s, the expulsions continued in East Prussia and, albeit on a smaller scale, in other cities and regions, among them Hannover, Sachsen, Braunschweig, Dortmund, and Western Prussia. Another series of expulsions took place in 1905, this time directed against refugees from Russia who had fled the ravages of the Russo-Japanese War or the Russian Revolution, settling in Berlin, Breslau, and Königsberg. Of these, the Prussian parliament decided to expel 10% of those who had settled in Berlin. In the years leading up to WWI, another wave of expulsions swept Germany, forcing 200 Jewish cigarette workers to leave Berlin.[77]

Most of the expulsions did not originate in the same policy. In most cases, decisions were made on the local level, sometimes arbitrarily. Considerations regarding expulsions also depended on the needs of the local workforce, with the main interest being economic. Beginning in 1890, for example, the authorities enforced strict supervisory regulations on foreign workers (especially those from Poland), in order to prevent them from leaving their

---

76 The statistics are according to ZDSJ, June 1912.
77 Jack L. Wertheimer, German Policy and Jewish Politics, The Absorption of East–European Jews in Germany 1868–1914. California University, 1978, p. 71–87.

employers without finishing the very projects they were recruited for.⁷⁸ Foreign Jewish paupers who tried their luck in Germany were certainly aware of what would befall them should a German clerk implement the official expulsion policy. Theoretically, the danger also existed for foreigners who had stayed in Germany for a long time; even those who had lived in the country for over 30 years were not immune from it, for the policy was directed at people without a German passport. We know of cases in which veteran foreign workers – those who had lived in the territory of the Reich for decades – were expelled without recourse.

Although The German Citizenship Law of 1871 took a stringent approach vis-à-vis the foreigners, it nevertheless enabled them to receive German citizenship. The law stipulated that German states would decide when to grant citizenship to their foreign workers. There were several ways through which one could attain citizenship: service to the country in the framework of a church or a synagogue community; owning a house or property (which would enable the owner to provide for others); and, for foreign women, marrying a German spouse. In certain places (for example, in Saxony), one had to be a resident for 30 years in order to become a citizen. It is important to remember, however, that foreigners were subject to restrictions imposed by local governments. A foreigner was required, by law, to register with the local police upon entering a community, and communities were entitled to refuse that foreigner entry.⁷⁹

---

78 On additional considerations in the German expulsion policy, especially towards Jews, see: ibid., pp. 67–90.

79 The exact wording of the Law and its interpretation can be found in: Rudolf E. Huber, *Dokumente zur deutschen Verfassungsgeschichte, Nr. 192*.
In: P. Altman, *Die Verfassung und Verwaltung im Deutschen Reiche und Preußen*, Bd. 2, Berlin, p. 97–98.

During times of hardship, foreigners who intended to move to Germany did not take the possibility of expulsion into consideration, choosing instead to focus on their prospects for success. Furthermore, as was mentioned earlier, Germany was largely sympathetic towards migrants, especially towards temporary laborers; and it was even more sympathetic towards Jews, who could rely on families or on charity from Jewish communities.

CHAPTER 5:

A DEMOGRAPHIC SURVEY OF WANDERARMEN OCCUPATION

Is there a way to categorize the *Wanderarmen* by occupation? Did they intend to earn an income, or were they moving from community to community only to beg and to seek the charity of others? By determining, how, exactly, the *Wanderarmen* supported themselves before becoming nomads, we can find at least a partial answer to these questions.

Many *Wanderarmen* went from place to place searching for income. Therefore, it is important to analyze the group thoroughly

Chapter 5: A Demographic Survey of Wanderarmen Occupation

and to determine which, if any, occupations were common among its members, and how these occupations compared to those practiced by Germany's established, veteran Jews. The answers to these questions are significant, as they show – if indeed it is possible to characterize the occupational structure of this group – that we are not dealing with an esoteric group at the fringes of society, but, rather, with a group whose members were reacting to challenges and trying to improve their lives, employment, income etc., even if that meant living like vagabonds for an extended period.

Data on the employment of *Wanderarmen* can be found in the records of many Jewish charity funds, which required charity recipients to disclose personal information, including occupation and trade. Many of the funds allocated charity only to those who were able to work, and it is clear that most of the recipients had earlier learned a trade. The above-mentioned records, which are often continuous and which list the charity recipient's trade and where he had acquired it, enable us to categorize the *Wanderarmen* by occupation. Some of the funds collected the information and passed it on to the central office in Berlin, where it was edited statistically. It is preferable, however, to use the original records, for the statistical summaries rarely elaborate on the way in which the calculations were made and on the underlying data.

In cases in which we have direct data relating to the fund's activities, we can analyze the occupational background of the *Wanderarmen* with greater accuracy, especially if the data are continuous (i.e. covering a period of time without interruption). A good example of this is the charity fund of Würzburg, where a significant amount of data has been preserved, and where, in contrast to other charity funds, one can find many similarities. The sample I took from the Würzburg data – the fund recorded the names and demographics of tens of thousands of charity recipients – points to a similarity between the occupational backgrounds of "mobile" and "stationary" Jewish paupers, most of whom had worked in an unspecified branch of trade. Using the Würzburg data, it is possible to reconstruct the demographics of one charity fund's clients, as well as to determine if the trends indicated by the data compiled in Berlin (at the central bureau) also existed in Würzburg. The Würzburg fund is especially significant, for it covers several decades (1866-1893), thus enabling us to follow changes over a significant chunk of time. And although these changes were experienced by a limited group, it is still possible, through them, to learn a great deal about the *Wanderarmen*.

The following table categorizes those who approached the fund in Würzburg according to occupation:[80]

Table 1: Occupations of Wanderarmen (Jewish charity fund in Würzburg)

Occupation	1866-1871	In %	1881	In %	1891	In %
Salesman and Assistants	11		16		21	
Merchants	26		27		2	
Peddlers	–		1		3	
"Businessmen" and Mediators	3		2		1	
Total in Trade	40	51.9	46	62.2	54	46.5
Artisans	8		8		11	
Carpenters	2		2		8	

---

80 Staatsarchiv Hamburg (S.H), Nr 9225 „Statistik über die Grenzbüros".

Chapter 5: A Demographic Survey of Wanderarmen Occupation

Occupation	1866-1871	In %	1881	In %	1891	In %
Bakers	1		1		2	
Cigarette Workers	1		1		1	
Tailors	4		4		2	
Bookbinders	6		1		5	
Shoemakers	3		2		8	
Butchers	1		3		8	
Waiters	–		–		1	
Total in Handicrafts	26	33.8	20	27.0	46	39.6
Laborers	3		–		3	
Day workers	–		–		1	
Servants	2		1		–	
Teachers and Rabbis	5		6		12	
Painters	1		1		–	
Total	11	14.3	8	10.8	12	13.9

Analyzing this table, it becomes clear that most of the *Wanderarmen* were involved, in one form or another, in trade: as peddlers, small merchants, or mediators. *Wanderarmen* also worked as assistants to merchants, as salesman, and as grocers. Until 1871, 50% all *Wanderarmen* worked in trade; the percentage remained the same during most of the decade, rising slightly in 1881.

By 1891, however, *Wanderarmen* were increasingly turning to artisanship. Using local data, we can conclude that it was during this period that the group experienced significant changes in occupation, wherein blue-collar labor and artisanship slowly replaced trade.

This trend was apparent by 1893, when 60% of the applicants to the charity fund stated their occupational background as artisans. It is notable that many *Wanderarmen* worked in occupations that would later be in high demand in the industrializing German economy.

Additional data, taken from the Jewish charity fund of the West Prussian city of Stettin, confirm this trend, i.e. the decline in trade and the rise in artisanship. In September 1910, 42% of charity applicants had a background in trade; two years later, 35%. On the other hand, the percentage of *Wanderarmen* with a background in artisanship rose from 41% in September 1910 to 51% in 1911.[81] Likewise, data from the *Wanderarmen* charity fund in Bochum (North Rhine-Westphalia), indicates the ascendancy, during these years, of artisanship. With Bochum located at the heart of a developing industrial zone, it can be assumed that the Jews arriving there attempted to integrate into the local labor force. In Stettin, 40-50% of charity applicants were artisans and workers; in Bochum, 65%.

The Bochum numbers represent the highest percentage of artisan *Wanderarmen* in all periods, at least among those who were documented. The second most popular *Wanderarmen* occupation in Bochum was trade (21%). As for trade and labor (17%), it was divided into many sub-groups.[82] In order to determine if this data indicate a new direction in the manner in which *Wanderarmen*

---

81 C.A.J.P, R-IS, WR-993, Würzburg, „Tagebuch der israelitischen Wanderunterstützungskasse".

82 The data of the charity fund of Bochum are dated November 1910, and are as follows: 341 artisans (48%), 119 laborers (17%), 105 salesmen (15%), 40 merchants (6%) 23 artists (3%) and 77 skilled workers (11%). Quoted from: *Staatsarchiv Hamburg* (S.A.H.) 9225: "Statistik über die Grenzbüros". Nr. 355-356.

Chapter 5: A Demographic Survey of Wanderarmen Occupation

sought and earned a living, we must compare their occupational backgrounds to that of local German Jews. Population censuses in Germany point to the fact that the percentage of Jewish merchants was higher than in the overall population: Both national and regional data (from Bavaria, particularly Munich) show that nearly half of all merchants in Germany were Jewish. In 1895, 56% of German Jews were employed in trade, a number that changed only slightly during the following years (50% in 1905 and 1907). The numbers in Bavaria were similar: 54% in 1882 and 55% in 1895 and 1905. The city of Munich was no exception: 56% in 1882, 49% in 1895, and 45% in 1907.

When comparing the occupational division of local German Jews and *Wanderarmen,* it becomes apparent that the latter were much more involved in both artisanship and blue-collar labor: While at least 40% of all employed *Wanderarmen* belonged to these two groups, often less than 20% of local Jews did. In Munich, for example, only 13% of local Jews were employed as industrial laborers in 1882, and only 11% of local Jews in all of Bavaria. Later, these numbers increased to 16% in Munich and 15% in all of Bavaria (still less than half of the number for *Wanderarme* in this field). The number of local Jewish industrial workers also rose in Prussia from 10.8% in 1882 to 22.5 in 1907. In other words, even among local Jews, the percentage of industrial workers rose significantly in this period. When looking at the numbers for the entire Reich, this trend is clearly apparent: In 1895, 19% of all employed Jews in Germany were industrial laborers; in 1907, 23%.

The following tables which pertain to the end of the 19th century until the first decade of the 20th, categorize local German Jews by occupation, especially in Bavaria, where Würzburg is located:

Table 2: Occupations of Jews in Germany (by percentage)[83]

Occupation	1895	1905	1907	1907 (non-Jews)
Agriculture	1.43	1.35	1.30	33.06
Industry	19.30	21.80	21.40	37.30
Trade	56.00	50.00	50.56	11.12
Unskilled and self-employed	16.80	19.26	19.40	11.25
Public Service	6.14	6.50	6.50	5.70
Servants	0.37	0.46	0.40	1.57

Table 3: Occupations of Jews in Bavaria (by percentage)[84]

Occupation	1882	1895	1905
Agriculture	9.71	3.85	2.10
Industry	11.76	13.33	15.02
Trade	54.47	55.07	55.00
Unskilled and self-employed	19.84	22.00	21.56
Public Service	4.16	5.60	6.00
Servants	0.15	0.15	0.32

---

83   ZDSJ, 1910, Heft 11, p.65.
84   ZDSJ, 1910, Heft 11, p.82.

Chapter 5: A Demographic Survey of Wanderarmen Occupation

Table 4: Occupations of Jews in Munich (by percentage)[85]

Occupation	1882	1895	1905
Agriculture	–	0.2	0.1
Industry	12.9	15.7	15.1
Trade	56.8	49.5	45.0
Servants	0.3	0.1	0.3
Public Service and Free Occupations	7.4	7.2	10.4
Unskilled Labor	22.6	27.3	29.1

Table 5: Occupations of Jews and non-Jews in Prussia[86]

Occupation	1882		1895		1907
	Jews	Christians	Jews	Christians	Jews
Agriculture	1.2	34.6	1.3	28.9	1.0
Industry	10.8	34.9	18.8	42.9	22.5
Trade	57.0	9.6	54.5	13.0	55.2
Public Service	17.7	5.8	5.9	5.5	6.6
Unskilled and self-employed	11.5	8.8	16.9	2.3	14.2
Servants	2.8	6.5	2.6	–	–

---

85 ZDSJ, 1905, Heft 10, p.86.
86 Felix Theilhaber, *Der Untergang der deutschen Juden*, München, 1911, p. 118.
For a detailed analysis of German Jewry's occupational structure, in comparison to the non-Jewish population and according to occupational stratification in the large cities, see: Segall, Jacob: *Die beruflichen und sozialen Verhältnisse der Juden in Deutschland*. Berlin, 1912, p. 26-30.

Data from the Würzburg charity fund illustrate the relative growth of artisans and laborers among *Wanderarmen*. It is, however, important to point out that the change was the result not only of the new reality members of this group confronted in Germany, but also of the occupational structure that existed in their countries of origin. Indeed, data from Galicia and Austria-Hungary reveal that the occupational divisions in these areas were very different from those in Germany; the divisions are important to our study, for many of the *Wanderarmen* in Germany came from Galicia and Austria-Hungary. According to data from Galicia, 29% of the employed were categorized as working in industry. In Austria, 28.7% of the employed were categorized as such, and the number of merchants there was significantly smaller than in Germany: 43%, as opposed to the 40% employed in agriculture and industry. Undoubtedly, this was a component in Austria's greater productivity during the period.[87]

In spite of the fact that laborers and artisans were included in the same framework, there is a fundamental difference between the two occupations' dependence on the charity system. The laborers who approached the charity funds for *Wanderarmen* had been salaried employees in the past, and intended to become integrated as such. Their source of income had depended on external funds (employers), and so was the welfare they became dependent on after losing their income (Artisans, on the other hand, had been self-employed, and, thus, responsible for their funds themselves). The situation of laborers of non-German background was particularly dire, as no institution was required to support them, even if they did encounter economic hardship. German laborers, on the other hand, were entitled to payments, albeit meager, granted to them by certain

---

87   ZDSJ, 1905, Heft 8, p.2.

welfare laws (applying only to citizens). Artisans received better treatment, for they, unlike the laborers, were more easily able to find part-time work performing odd jobs, as a result of which they were less dependent on the charity system.

A more detailed account of the occupations held by *Wanderarmen* can be found in the data of South German charity funds. The fund of Nürnberg-Fürth, for example, details the occupations of all those who applied for charity in 1911; it is interesting to note that here the percentage of peddlers was significantly higher than elsewhere – together with the merchants, they represented 50.6% of all applicants to the charity fund, as opposed to 40% in other funds; according to the data, too, the number of "unskilled workers" was larger in Nürnberg-Fürth, the number of laborers and artisans smaller. Comparing the data of this charity fund to that of another such fund in the same region (Würzburg), we notice significant differences.[88] The relative number of peddlers approaching the Nürnberg-Fürth fund was higher than that of peddlers approaching other funds.

It is important to note here that all of the above data are based on self-representation: Jews defining themselves as merchants were often de facto peddlers, or traveling salesmen carrying very little merchandise with them (It is therefore questionable if a more objective source would have classified them as merchants). In addition, it is important to note that at the time (1911), South Germany was still less developed industrially than the rest of the country. This might explain the low number of (industrial) laborers in the region. Bavaria, which lagged in the industrialization process, attracted fewer laborers and skilled manpower than did other regions, perhaps explaining the underrepresentation of these occupations in the Nürnberg-Fürth charity fund.

---

88   While this is true, it is important to remember that the earlier mentioned data from Würzburg relates to a different era – 1890.

Another development was the increasing availability of jobs in religious instruction and in other occupations pertaining to Judaism: *Shochet* (kosher slaughterer), *Chazzan* (cantor), etc. Due to Jewish migration within Germany, many Jews from small communities found themselves in large cities, as a result of which the growing communities found it necessary to expand their infrastructures. There was a demand for such workers in East Prussia; although the communities there had lost many members as more and more Jews left for the western parts of the country, their numbers were later replenished by the arrival of foreign Jews, making it necessary to refill positions connected to the Jewish community. Accordingly, *Wanderarmen* who expressed an interest in positions of this kind were absorbed more easily. It is possible, however, that many *Wanderarmen*, seeking to be absorbed by a Jewish community, misrepresented themselves as *gabbaim* (synagogue managers), religious teachers, or *shochetim* (kosher slaughterers).

The occupational stratification of the women was very different from the men's. What little data we have on the topic indicates that most women were either unskilled or, in cases where the recipient's occupation was not known, classified as such. Almost half of all female applicants to the Würzburg charity fund between 1879 and 1893 were categorized as unskilled laborers (46.5%), followed by saleswomen and peddlers (25%), and by artisans and industrial workers (7.8%). Data taken from unofficial lists indicate a similar division: Here, too, the largest groups were unskilled workers – this group included women who did not work – and beggars, followed (in size) by saleswomen, female artisans, and laborers. Comparing this data to that which pertains to Jewish women in Germany during the period, we find significant differences in employment numbers: In 1882, only 15.94% of Jewish women in Germany were employed, as opposed to 21.97% in 1895 and 30% in 1907.[89] According to the data, then, unemployment was more common among local Jews than among *Wanderarmen*.[90]

Young and Energetic: The Age Structure of *Wanderarmen*

Data regarding this period enable us to determine the age structure of *Wanderarmen*, to clarify whether it was permanent, and to identify its characteristics. As mentioned earlier, most of the data on this topic originates from the records of local charity funds and from the central bureau of statistics in Berlin. And although the data was collected in different, but far from all, regions of Germany, it is nevertheless possible to discern certain trends.

The earliest data concerning the age division of this group can be found in the Würzburg charity fund. Data covering the years between 1866 and 1894 indicate that the average age of *Wanderarmen* steadily fell during this period. Until 1871, for example, the largest age group was of those aged between 40 and 50, i.e. middle-aged people, for the large part married with children. During the same period, those over 50 were well represented among charity applicants to the Würzburg fund, at approximately 33%; and those younger than 20 years of age constituted 15% less than the largest group (40-50). A decade later, the number of *Wanderarmen*

---

89 Segall, Jacob: Die beruflichen und sozialen Verhältnisse der Juden in Deutschland. Berlin, 1912, p. 78.
90 ZDSJ, 1905, Heft 4, p.3.
   For data on Jewish women's occupations see: Segall, Jacob: *Die beruflichen und sozialen Verhältnisse der Juden in Deutschland*. Berlin, 1912, p. 78. On the division in Würzburg see: C.A.J.P, Würzburg, „Tagebuch der isralitischen": S.H., „Statistik uber die Grenzburos."

over 50 had shrunk to 25%, dwindling further, between 1882 and 1891, to 17%. The 40-50 age group, as mentioned above, had been the majority group before 1871, after which it was replaced by the 20-30 year-olds, i.e. young people who, in their prime, had left their homes in search of income; this age group constituted approximately 24% of all *Wanderarmen* until 1881, and approximately 33% by 1891. Simultaneously, the number of those younger than 20 years of age also increased. In all, the number of those younger than 30 increased significantly, so much so that they constituted nearly half of all *Wanderarmen* between 1881 and 1889. Foreign Jews, then, were "new blood," lowering the average age of Jews in Germany. However, we should qualify this statement by pointing out that this was a general development in Germany, not limited to *Wanderarmen* or to Jews. It is, then, not surprising that records from the charity fund in Stettin, in West Prussia, attest to the same development: There, half of all *Wanderarmen* were aged 30 or younger.[91]

It is difficult to draw clear conclusions from this case, as we lack data from previous years. The trend, however (the younger average age of *Wanderarmen*), also existed in other places: In the town of Halberstadt, in Saxony, 70% of *Wanderarmen* applying to the local charity fund in 1911 were under 40, and approximately 50% under 30.[92]

There is a clear link between the location of the charity fund and the age composition of those who applied to it for relief. In industrial areas, for example, the demand for workers was high; accordingly, we can assume that they attracted younger *Wanderarmen*. Records from charity funds in industrial cities buttress this argument: In the city of Bochum (which was, during the first decade of the 20th

---

91 Staatsarchiv Hamburg (S.H), Nr 9225 "Statistik über die Grenzbüros".
92 Staatsarchiv Hambrg, "Zentralstelle für jüdische Wanderarmenfürsorge".

century, at the height of its process of industrialization), 64% of all applicants to the charity fund in 1910 were under the age of 30.

Statistics on *Wanderarmen* in Germany for the year 1914, all of which are based on data from the central charity organization in Berlin, show that the vast majority were young people. When we compare their age composition to that of settled German Jews, we see that the age differences were significant. In 1882, more than half of all *Wanderarmen* were in the 20-40 age group (in Würzburg, this group made up 51.05% between 1882 and 1892, and in Stettin, 53.2% in 1909).[93]

The average age of the local Jewish population, on the other hand, was significantly higher. In Berlin, for example, the 20-40 age group constituted only 37.8% of the Jewish population. This group was even smaller in Hamburg, constituting 34.2% of the Jewish population there in 1905; that same year, non-Jews of the same age group constituted 35.6% of the city's total population. In conclusion, it can be argued that a comparison of local Jews and *Wanderarmen* almost always shows (very clearly in 1905) that *Wanderarmen* were, on average, significantly younger than local Jews, as a result of which their ranks were continuously rejuvenated. For these and other reasons – their foreignness, their dress, their lifestyle – the young *Wanderarmen* were more noticeable than local Jews.[94]

Gender Division amongst the *Wanderarmen*

When we talk about *Wanderarmen*, we mainly think about men. What role did women play in this group? Were women a dominant

---

93 Jacob Segall, „Wanderarmenfürsorge in Deutschland," p.70.
94 ZDSJ, 1910, Heft 2, p.31.

force, or did they only rarely go on this journey by themselves (and if then, only to join their husbands)? What was the ratio of men to women? Finally, did women approach charity funds as well, and in what numbers?

In order to identify certain attributes of *Wanderarmen*, we must rely on data pertaining to the issue of gender. Data on the gender of those who applied to charity funds, for example, help us to determine whether the *Wanderarmen* acted as individuals or, rather, as families, just as it helps us to determine if the men preceded their families, if the number of women was equal to that of the men, and if children played a role in the process.

Unfortunately, we do not possess much data on the representation of men, women, and children among the *Wanderarmen*, with what little we do have pertaining mainly to the years leading up to WWI. Earlier data is problematic from a scholar's perspective, as the manner in which the funds documented information is not known to us. For example, did a family applying for charity only register the name of the head of the family, or was it required to list every member? Despite this methodological problem, we do have enough data from which we can draw conclusions about *Wanderarmen* families, albeit in a limited manner (limited, that is, to the locations and periods covered by the records).

Although the ratio of male to female applicants to the charity funds varied according to location, it was, usually, the men who made up the bulk of applicants. Statistics show, however, that the proportion of children and women was higher in East Germany, specifically in border cities, as families tended to move there together. In Breslau, for example, women and children constituted, respectively, 17% and 11.27% of those who were registered at the fund. In Soldau,

19% of charity applicants were children. In other places, however, applications from women and children were marginal: In Bremen, men were in the overwhelming majority, at 92%. On average, women made up between eight and 14% of applicants to charity funds. Segall's data from 1913 data point to a high percentage of women in the cities of Breslau, Frankfurt a. Main, and Königsberg; in Königsberg, the higher number of female applicants was the result of the fact that foreign Jewish women often frequented the clinic there. In Touraine, Katowice, and Danzig – through which *Wanderarmen* often passed to and from Germany – women would often wait for their husbands, which explains why the number of female applicants to charity funds was high in those cities, too.

Interestingly, the closer the fund was to Central and West Germany, the fewer were the women and children registered there. One explanation for this might be that *Wanderarmen* families found more support in funds located closer to the border or in the areas they had migrated to. It is, of course, obvious that single men were able to navigate the ordeals of migration more easily than did families. For this reason, men constituted the vast majority of charity applicants to funds located far from the borders. On average, 77% of all *Wanderarmen* who received charity were men, 90% in some funds. The fact that charity funds mainly supported men shows that the motive behind migration was economic. Had it not been so, the charity allocated to men, women, and children would have been more equal. This uniqueness of this gender composition is most obvious when we compare it to the gender divide among foreign Jews who had already settled in Germany, and to the gender divide among local Jews.[95]

---
95 Jacob Segall, „Wanderarmenfürsorge in Deutschland," p.70.

Comparing Eastern European Jews and *Wanderarmen*, we find significant differences among them regarding the gender division: Only 55% of Eastern European Jews were men, similar to the proportion among German Jews (in 1910).[96] The number of men was higher among non-Jewish migrants to Germany: For example, 60% of all Catholic migrant workers were men. Jacob Segall, who analyzed the demographics of Eastern European Jews migrating to Munich, found that, between 1880 and 1910 (a period of massive immigration to Germany), the male majority among foreign workers steadily shrunk. In 1880, 60% of all foreign workers in Munich were men (63% in the 1890s), but by the 20th century women made up 43% of this group. These numbers indicate a migration pattern whereby the men migrated first, with the women joining them at a later stage.[97] In addition, the data mentioned above indicate that the *Wanderarmen* were different not just from local German Jews, but also from foreign Jews who had settled in Germany. There were significant differences between *Wanderarmen* and local Jews (both foreign-born and German) regarding gender representation. As did their age demographics, this made the *Wanderarmen* stand out among the Jewish population.

The Origins of *Wanderarmen*

The historiography of German Jews rests on a widespread assumption, according to which Jewish paupers, beggars, and *Schnorrer* were all *Ostjuden*, i.e. Jews from Eastern Europe. Although

---

96 The data were taken from documents regarding the Jewish population in Munich. See: Jakob Segall, Die Entwicklung der jüdischen Bevölkerung in München, 1875-1905", Berlin, 1910, p.48-49.
97 J. Werthheimer, German Policy, pp.209-211.

Chapter 5: A Demographic Survey of Wanderarmen Occupation 105

it is difficult to prove how firmly entrenched this assumption was, a variety of sources indicate that it was very widespread. Accordingly, it is necessary to study the origins of the *Wanderarmen*.

Analyzing the origins of a member of this group, it is necessary to emphasize not just his native country, but also his route within Germany. Usually, "origin" indicates the migrant's first home, "route" his migration within the country. Although charity funds and institutions documented the origins of their applicants, they were rarely able to do the same for the applicants' route within Germany. It is, however, possible to reconstruct routes by looking at the overall map of charity organizations.

Using the funds' records, we can pinpoint the geographic origins of most *Wanderarmen*. For reasons that are not clear to us, it was customary for Jewish charity funds to detail the origins of each applicant. The recording of such information was, most likely, standard procedure – as was the recording of other bureaucratic information – for there is no evidence that a certain place of origin would have benefited an applicant.[98] The debates preceding the establishment of charity organizations (and those that took place afterwards) did not reveal any bias towards *Wanderarmen* based on their place of origin, be it Poland, Hungary, or Russia. It can, thus, be assumed that the interest in an applicant's place of origin mainly served the statistical endeavors of the ZJW.

It is difficult, however, to determine the exact origins of the *Wanderarmen*, for we are relying on information given by applicants to the charity funds, the latter of which were not able to verify the charity seekers' statements. It is, for example, obvious that in the

---

[98] Official documents of the time usually included first and family name, age, place and occupational background.

period during which Russian Jews were expelled from Germany, not many *Wanderarmen* rushed to identify themselves as such. On top of this, we face two additional methodological problems: a) the fact that many countries did not then issue passports to their citizens, making it relatively easy to submit false data to charity funds, and b) that the funds recoded an applicant's country of birth but not the place from which he had traveled to the fund or the amount of time he had spent as a *Wanderarmen*. In order to answer these questions, albeit in a limited manner, we must rely on local data.

The ZJW gathered much data, pertaining to 1914, on the origins of the *Wanderarmen*. Data collected from charity funds close to Germany's borders reveal that most of the applicants came from neighboring countries. For example, the majority of applicants to funds close to the Russian-German border were Russian Jews. A report summarizing all German charity funds (it did not state the applicants' proximity to their respective countries of origin) tells us that *Wanderarmen* from Russia were the largest group, constituting 54.8%; of these, most could be found in the cities of Cologne, Frankfurt a. Main, Königsberg, and Posen. *Wanderarmen* whose place of origin was the Austro-Hungarian Empire, on the other hand, mostly came to Bremen, Breslau, Hamburg, Leipzig, Dresden, and Freiburg, constituting 30% of all *Wanderarmen* in Germany.[99] There were, in addition, a few places where *Wanderarmen* of German origin were represented, like Bochum (21.6%), Bremen (31.8%), Kassel (14.9%), Frankfurt a. Oder (17.8%), Fürth, and Hannover (18.3%).[100]

---

99 It has to be pointed out here that the data only refers to applicants to charity funds in the year 1914.
100 Jakob Segall, "Wanderarmenfürsorge in Deutschland," p.72.

Chapter 5: A Demographic Survey of Wanderarmen Occupation

Most of the existing data on this topic, which pertain to local charity funds, were collected by the ZJW and organized statistically by Jacob Segall. It should be pointed out that it is usually not possible to verify Segall's data, for much of the original local data were lost. Würzburg, however, is an exception: Using a sample of the original statistics compiled there, which covers an extended period, we will be able to categorize the *Wanderarmen* according to country of origin. As Würzburg was located in Germany's South, it mainly attracted Jews from Austria, Bohemia, and Galicia. German applicants to this fund, however, constituted the largest group (nearly 50%). Surveying Segall's data, we discover that at no other point did German *Wanderarmen* constitute so large a chunk.

We must not accept these findings unconditionally, for it is often difficult to identify place names. For example, the fund sometimes recorded an applicant's city, and not the country, of origin; and as cities in different regions often share the same name, these omissions complicate our calculations. In order to avoid the possibility of an incorrect calculation, I chose to leave out applications in which the charity seeker's country or region of origin was not clearly stated. When unable to find a place name in the atlas, I used the name suffix (mentioned in the application), which often helped me to determine its geographic location.[101]

As mentioned above, the Würzburg data point to a far higher representation of *Wanderarmen* of German origin than existed in other cities. It is possible that the data, provided by the *Wanderarmen* to the fund, confuses place of birth with the city (or town) from

---

101 I was able to identify the countries of origins of many charity applicants with the help of a detailed historical atlas: Andreas, Allgemeiner Handatlas, Vierte Auflage, Bielefeld, Leipzig, 1904. Steiler Handatlas, Zehnte Auflage, Gotha, 1926/1927.

which the applicants had just arrived. Likewise, it is possible that many non-German applicants who had lived in the country for a long time prior to applying claimed Germany as their country of origin. Excluding from our calculations applicants whose stated country of origin cannot be verified, we arrive at the conclusion that most of the applicants to the Würzburg fund were from Poland, followed by Galicia and Bohemia.

Data from the Würzburg fund also enable us to identify the origins of German-born applicants. And yet, despite the available details, it is difficult to draw conclusions regarding the areas in Germany from which *Wanderarmen* came from, as they, too, are commonly referred to as "other," with "other" referring to places that could not be identified, places that were not listed, or places that were listed but that the applicant did not identify. Still, the data indicate that most of the fund's German-born applicants came from Bavaria (where Würzburg is located), followed by Hessen (bordering Bavaria), Prussia, and Silesia.

We must also keep in mind that the funds often insisted on treating applicants who were, for all intents and purposes, German (applicants who had lived in the country for decades or since early childhood) as Polish, Hungarian, or Russian. Furthermore, it is not possible to tell from the data how long an applicant had stayed in Germany prior to applying, and to what extent he had been absorbed. Other places, as well, had a high percentage of German *Wanderarmen*: Data from eight charity funds in Saxony show that, on average, 20% of applicants were of German origin (and never less than 15%). The number of *Wanderarmen* of Austrian origin was the largest in Saxony, a region that borders Bohemia, Austria, and Galicia. As a result of the fact that the funds did not record the date on which applicants had entered Germany, it is difficult to determine criteria stating when a Polish Jew, for example, had ceased to be considered a foreigner (after having lived in Germany for a certain time).[102]

We can also categorize *Wanderarmen* according to language. Language, as an important factor in the absorption process, is no less significant than country of origin. But, here, too, the funds (or the applicants) often left out this key piece of information. In Austria-Hungary, for example, the funds recorded neither the mother tongue of the *Wanderarmen* nor their additional languages. Data from Hannover, on the other hand, indicate a clear preference for German-speaking *Wanderarmen*, who constituted approximately 50% of charity recipients there.[103] Similarly, the Bochum charity fund had a large number of German-speaking applicants (56% in 1910). This is especially significant, for the countries of origin represented there were not limited to those in which German was the primary language; in 1910, the Bochum charity fund supported 118 Germans, 239 Austrians, 202 Russians, and 76 "others."[104]

The Routine of Wandering

How did *Wanderarmen* choose their path? What were the distances between stations? When did the funds feel pressure?

---

102 The eight communities were Annaberg, Bautzen, Chemnitz, Dresden, Freiberg, Leipzig, Plauen and Zitarre. See: S.H. Statistik über die Grenzbüros".

103 For a report on Hannover, see: A.H. Statistik über die Grenzbüros.

104 Also in Hannover, the number of German-speaking *Wanderarmen* constituted about half (1910/1911), see: S.H. Statistik über die Grenzbüros".

And was there a connection between the patterns of wandering and political events, or were the motives solely economic? Answers to some of these questions can be found in the records of charity funds that continuously documented their applicants. The Würzburg fund is one such example, covering the years 1866-1894: In 1869-1870, 1,500 *Wanderarmen* received charity there yearly; in the 1870s, this number decreased to fewer than 1,000 per year. It is interesting to note that in the years 1874-1879, i.e. during a period of economic crisis in Germany, the number of applicants to the charity fund in Würzburg did not increase; in fact, fewer applicants approached the fund during these years of scarce income opportunities and worsening conditions. During times of economic growth, on the other hand, the number of charity applicants rose. These findings point to an important fact: that economic hardship was not always the reason behind nomadism. Rather, the opposite is true: It was during times of economic growth and the establishment of new employment opportunities that the number of *Wanderarmen* increased.

The data also contradict those who claim that the migration of Jewish paupers was caused exclusively by either political hardship, persecution, oppression, pogroms or by the economic hardship they experienced in their countries of origin. Rather, there were additional reasons for Jews to migrate to Germany: the economic changes of the German market created sources of income as well as employment opportunities, (which often coincided with socio-economic hardship in the migrants' countries of origins). Either way, it is clear that the Jewish charity funds played a central role in making a large and long-term *Wanderarmen* work force necessary (as the funds' capacities would soon be exhausted).

Another indication of the economic, as opposed to the political, nature of the *Wanderarmen* phenomenon in Germany can be found in the distribution of charity applicants according to month: Certain patterns repeated themselves at certain months on a regular basis (with no connection to specific one-time events). Such findings, if based on continuous data, illustrate the socio-economic patterns of German Jewry (and Jewry in neighboring countries), as it shows the cyclic nature of economic patterns, rather than the much less predictable nature of political circumstances.

Surveying the Würzburg fund, we discover that the number of applicants increased during certain months: June, July, and August were always peak months. In 1866-1880, for example, the average number of charity applicants was 100 in June, 152 in July, and 101 in August. This trend also applies to 1881-1893, when, on average, 228 applicants received charity in August and 190 in June. The slow months were in the winter. In the years 1866-1880, the number of charity applicants in November, December, and January was approximately half (75 applicants on average) of that during the summer months. In 1881-1893, too, significantly fewer applicants applied during the winter months: 144 in December, 226 in July. These numbers prove that *Wanderarmen* used the charity systems continuously, but on a different scale and according to economic need, which changed according to season. In the summers, the demand for labor was higher, causing more movement among the *Wanderarmen*; those who were unable to find employment during the busy summer months turned to the charity funds. Data from the Würzburg fund confirm that these are patterns of a long-term socio-economic trend.[105]

---

[105] The data are based on the Würzburg charity fund documentations from the years 1866-1894, see: C.A.J.P, Würzburg, "Tagebuch der israelitischen".

Table 6: Charity Recipients from the Würzburg *Wanderarmen* Fund

Month	1866	1867	1868	1869	1870	1871	1872	1873	Monthly Average
January	71	78	111	101	128	45	65	39	79
February	75	113	94	101	146	43	49	60	85
March	74	94	128	125	162	54	43	45	90
April	59	70	69	95	111	38	40	35	64
May	93	143	100	155	118	49	55	44	94
June	158	122	158	193	152	77	40	48	118
July	116	196	192	244	256	103	79	73	157
August	73	173	191	178	241	124	84	62	140
September	55	148	118	147	160	79	58	52	201
October	82	75	116	129	80	76	47	32	79
November	33	24	111	110	119	84	48	45	71
December	63	99	128	128	66	60	49	45	63
Total	972	1335	1516	706	1739	832	657	580	103

Chapter 5: A Demographic Survey of Wanderarmen Occupation

Month	1874	1875	1876	1877	1878	1879	1880	Monthly Average
January	54	82	54	57	71	53	117	69
February	36	84	63	56	59	48	134	68
March	58	90	55	57	58	45	168	75
April	47	64	45	88	62	40	127	67
May	43	95	85	88	81	70	156	88
June	30	101	117	96	87	76	195	110
July	48	114	137	140	129	139	124	118
August	39	107	140	124	92	85	264	121
September	49	102	112	57	79	106	199	86
October	93	74	104	76	75	60	163	92
November	90	61	60	71	71	–	112	75
December	69	41	72	45	41	102	121	72
Total	656	101	1044	955	895	842	1880	89

Month	1881	1882	1883	1884	1885	1886	1887	1888	Monthly Average
January	143	133	149	missing	147	117	130	135	136
February	111	138	165		128	132	125	145	134
March	159	143	177		141	131	165	120	148
April	103	161	121		88	116	132	132	121
May	185	189	170		115	153	147	151	158
June	218	187	228		247	155	162	186	
July	228	213	267		235	213	204	237	228
August	262	235	259		135	213	224	291	231
September	157	213	123		141	192	124	115	152
October	171	144	147		161	116	128	100	138
November	147	159	162		165	152	152	151	155
December	120	145	159		124	107	121	133	112
Total	2004	2060	2157	–	1827	1827	1841	1896	159

Chapter 5: A Demographic Survey of Wanderarmen Occupation

Month	1889	1890	1891	1892	1893	Monthly Average
January	150	115	112	109	112	119
February	194	112	82	118	111	123
March	125	110	128	144	156	132
April	147	98	73	94	95	101
May	166	149	144	195	missing	163
June	192	223	261	236		163
July	192	223	261	236		228
August	212	202	207	249		217
September	158	136	178	194		95
October	137	142	116	130		131
November	117	140	128	147		113
December	114	128	136	90		117
Total	1866	1730	1867	1905	–	142

A detailed analysis of this data, which covers a long period, reveals an interesting fact: It was in April that the number of charity seekers reached its nadir. One possible explanation for this trend is the fact that the Jewish holiday of Passover which, presumably, the *Wanderarmen* spent with their families, meaning that they were less likely to approach the funds, usually falls on this month. This is further proof that internal considerations were far more influential in the lives of charity seekers, and that it was not always external pressure or political events that turned Jews into *Wanderarmen*. It was in the fall, too (during the Jewish month of *Tishrei*), that fewer Jews approached the funds, most likely the result of the abundance of Jewish holidays during this month (Rosh Hashanah, Yom Kippur, and Sukkot). It is, however, more difficult to verify this connection, as the charity funds' documentation was based on the Gregorian calendar (whereas the Jewish holidays are based on the Jewish calendar). And while Passover almost always falls on April, the *Tishrei* holidays do not always fall on the same corresponding month of the Gregorian calendar.

By using data taken from the statistics available in German population censuses, we can verify the similarity between Jewish and non-Jewish patterns of migration. Through it, we can also analyze internal German migration by month, just as we did above. During the period before WWI, non-Jewish migration reached its lowest level in February and stayed that way until April, when it reached its peak and the numbers doubled. In the following months, internal migration once again began to dwindle, so that the numbers for July and August were even lower than those recorded before April. These patterns differ from those that apply to Jewish *Wanderarmen*, who, as mentioned above, turned to the funds in peak numbers in July.

Chapter 5: A Demographic Survey of Wanderarmen Occupation 117

Non-Jewish migration numbers rose in October, with the coming of winter.[106] [107]

The reason for this seasonal fluctuation in numbers of migrants (Jewish and non-Jewish) was related to the job market and to other developments that required one to move: the expiration of a rental contract, the military draft, and the nature of occupations performed by migrants. Among Jews, there was a higher percentage of self-employed and merchants, people whose occupations were not tied to specific seasons and who were not forced to leave their homes for extended periods.[108]

Did Jewish charity applicants stay in the same regions? It is difficult to answer this question, for the charity funds strictly adhered to the law prohibiting an applicant from applying for charity more than once a year. After the applicant had received charity from the fund, he would "disappear" from the list for a year, and it is therefore difficult to determine whether or not he continued to receive charity. The data, however, provide a partial answer. The Würzburg fund, for example, shows that the number of charity applicants fluctuated from month to month. In 1871, 843 *Wanderarmen* received charity from the fund: 45 in January, 43 in February, 54 in March, 38 in April, 49 in May, 77 in June, 103 in July, 124 in August, 79 in September, 76 in October, 84 in November, and 60 in December. These numbers prove that the movement of *Wanderarmen* was widespread, and that the number of charity recipients changed from

---

106 C.A.J.P, Würzburg, „Tagebuch der israelitischen".
107 The data are from 1900, with July being the basis of measurement (July = 100). The division is as follows: January-79; February-71; March-99; April-135; May-104; June-91; July-100; August-94; September-109; October-153; November-92; December-75.
108 Rudolf Heberle, Fritz Meyer, Die Grosstadte, S.178.

month to month. From this, we can deduce that charity applicants did not stay in the region; had they done so, the numbers recorded by the charity funds would have been more constant.

In addition to these patterns, which repeated themselves each year and over an extended period, there were also external events that contributed to the fluctuating rates of nomadism. For example, we can identify a clear connection between the charity applicants in Würzburg and the political persecution and pogroms suffered by Polish and Russian Jews. When a series of pogroms broke out in Tsarist Russia in 1881-1882, the number of applicants to Jewish charity funds increased all over Germany, from 1,879 in 1881 to 2,004 in 1883. It should be noted, however, that there had been an increase in applicants in 1880, prior to the pogroms, and that the average number of charity applicants did not rise drastically after the pogroms of 1882. Therefore, we can assume that while the pogroms certainly increased the pace of Jewish migration from Eastern Europe to Germany, it was not the sole explanation for it. Furthermore, charity funds in cities removed from the borders with Russia and Poland (like Würzburg) experienced an increase, albeit a smaller one, of *Wanderarmen* from those two countries. The main indication, though, that the *Wanderarmen* phenomenon stemmed from economic – rather than political – circumstances is the fact that most of the paupers migrated without their families. Although political factors influenced the growth in numbers, they had little to do with overall patterns.

Using records from several funds, records in which the paupers' next stop were noted, we can estimate the distances traversed by *Wanderarmen* from station to station. A report from the Magdeburg charity fund, for example, indicates that most of the city's *Wanderarmen* in 1910/11 had arrived from nearby cities, within

Chapter 5: A Demographic Survey of Wanderarmen Occupation 119

a radius of 150 kilometers. They had arrived from Hannover (67 people), Minden (three), Frankfurt a. Main (three), Schonbeck (two), Potsdam (two), Kassel (two), Berlin (two), Münster (two), Leipzig (two), Stettin (one), Brandenburg (one), and Budapest (one). Most of the applicants to the Magdeburg charity fund had arrived from Hannover, which is situated 140 kilometers to the west of the city. Some came from nearby cities, e.g., Schönbeck (25 km), Dessau (60 km), and Brandenburg (80 km), and still others traveled greater distances: Hildesheim (130 km), Leipzig (110 km), and Potsdam (100 km). Excepting a few statistically irrelevant cases, no one had traveled more than 150 km in order to reach Magdeburg; these exceptions include Hamburg (200 km) and Wechsel (200 km).

The data reveal another important piece of information: most of the *Wanderarmen* in Magdeburg came from larger cities. Magdeburg is a smaller town, but it is strategically located between Berlin and Hannover (in the West), and between Berlin and Leipzig (in the East). We further learn from the fund's records that most *Wanderarmen* continued on their way to Berlin afterwards. Magdeburg's charity applicants were sent to the following funds: Berlin (75 people), Leipzig (11), Brandenburg (nine), Halberstadt (four), Hamburg (three), and Hannover (three).[109]

A report from Hannover, also dated 1910/11, confirms the findings of the Magdeburg fund; according to the latter, 418 of the city's 1,129 *Wanderarmen* had arrived from Magdeburg. Similarly, the Magdeburg welfare fund mentions that the majority of its applicants had come from Hannover. In absolute numbers, however, only 67 *Wanderarmen* arrived at the Magdeburg fund. It is unclear why this number was so small, but possible answers could be that

---
109 Staatsarchiv Hamburg, „Statistik über die Grenzbüros".

some of the migrants arrived later, or that some, changing their routes, never arrived at the fund.[110]

This demographic analysis of the Jewish *Wanderarmen* has highlighted several of their distinguishing traits: There were many of them in Germany, and their presence there turned into a widespread phenomenon in many communities. The paupers' mobility and the system established to deal with them emphasized the phenomenon and made it easy to identify. A sample analysis of the demographic data shows that the *Wanderarmen* were younger than veteran German Jews, and that 90% were unmarried males; among veteran local Jews (both German-born and migrants), on the other hand, the gender distribution was almost equal. Surveying the data, we also discover that the occupational structure of *Wanderarmen* society was very different from that of settled Jews (locals and migrants): The proportion of laborers and craftsmen among *Wanderarmen* was considerably larger than among settled Jews, the number of merchants significantly smaller. Furthermore, it can be argued that the paupers' demographic structure influenced that of settled Jews, and that certain *Wanderarmen* patterns (age structure, for example, or changes in occupation) existed among settled Jews. Identifying and understanding the structure of this group is important, for in it we can find the changes that would in later years confront German Jewry.

---

[110] The designated destinations of Hannover's charity recipients in 1910/11 were: Berlin (542 people), Magdeburg (418 people), Kassel (21 people), Hamburg (nine people), Bochum (111 people) and other (28 people). See: Staatsarchiv Hamburg, "Statistik über die Grenzbüros".

CHAPTER 6:

GERMAN JEWS AND THE FIGHT AGAINST WANDERARMEN AND BEGGARS

There were approximately 1,000 Jewish communities in Germany in 1900, some of which could barely gather a *minyan* (prayer quorum of 10 men) for *mincha* (the daily afternoon prayer) while others had an abundance of organizations, synagogues, committees, factions, and sub-factions (with the ensuing rifts and disagreements). The multiplicity of Jewish communities shows the extent to which Jews were spread out geographically. The distance between communities, coupled with the fact that shared religion was sometimes the only common denominator between members of different communities, exacerbated efforts to unite all German communities under a single framework. In Germany, almost all Jewish communities operated independently, with the exception of Württemberg, where the communities were united under one framework (Even in Württemberg, however, it was local government policy, rather than the Jewish communities, that initiated the unification).

German Jews did not hurry to establish a central organizational framework that would impose its will on individual communities. It could very well be that the communities refused to unite, or that the distances between them had bred independent communities who knew how to manage their own affairs. Whatever the case, it is clear that there was no real reason to unite the Jewish communities.

It is reasonable to assume that the *Wanderarmen* issue, a shared problem, would have united the communities. In fact, the pressing problem not only failed to do so, but (at least in the beginning) actually led to further alienation and the cessation of joint efforts and activities. Needless to say, this delayed the solution to the *Wanderarmen* problem.

In order to effectively deal with the growing number of *Wanderarmen* in Germany, local Jewish communities needed to cooperate. The manner in which the problem was dealt with went through three phases: the local level (at first, efforts to deal with the paupers were carried out locally), at the regional level, and, but only later, through a national framework. This chapter will focus on the communities' joint efforts in regards to the *Wanderarmen*, covering the period between the early 1870s and WWI, the period during which a national umbrella organization (dealing with *Wanderarmen*) was established in Germany. Later in the chapter, I will discuss the actions and surveillance methods of the organizations set up to deal with the *Wanderarmen*. Founded on July 29, 1869, the DIGB (*Deutsch-Israelitischer Gemeinschafts-Bund*, or German-Jewish Union of Communities) was a central Jewish organization that aimed to deal with Jewish beggars in specific and *Wanderarmen* in particular. The DIGB, which became permanent only after it numbered 100 Jewish communities, was the first nation-wide Jewish umbrella organization set up to deal with the *Wanderarmen* (or, as the organization called it, the "affliction of begging"). After the Second German Reich was established in January 1871, the DIGB continued to operate, but it was not officially recognized by the state. A year later, in 1872, the DIGB chose Leipzig as its headquarters, only to move to Berlin later that same year. By then, it had become Germany's largest Jewish organization. At its peak, it counted 1,200 communities as its members, published a number of publications, subsidized Jewish education, and was active in social welfare. Its leadership was not elected, but, rather, chosen by a small circle of affluent Jews.[111]

Even before the foundation of the DIGB, Jewish communities had tried to supervise the *Wanderarmen*. In Berlin, for example, efforts of this sort were already made in 1850, with the purpose of determining who really needed welfare, and when to stop it.[112] However, it was only with the foundation of the DIGB that attempts to deal with the *Wanderarmen* on a national level were made. Immediately after its establishment, the organization placed the

---

111 The DIGB's first president was Moritz Kohner, followed by Samuel Kristeller and Jacob Nachod. See: Jehuda Reinharz, *Fatherland or Promised Land* (Michigan: University of Michigan. 1975), p. 1–11.

112 Willhelm Feichenfeld, Jüdische Wohlfahrtspflege in Berlin, Beilage zum Bericht für die Großloge für Deutschland, Berlin, 1909, p. 5.

issue of Jewish beggars and *Wanderarmen* at the top of its agenda and publicly announced its intention to combat them.[113] The *Allianz* organization, founded in 1860 by French Jews, worked to prevent Eastern European Jewish paupers from entering France. In October, 1869, representatives of *Allianz* and the DIGB met in Berlin and agreed to establish a joint fundraising committee for the purpose of preventing Jewish paupers from Eastern Europe from entering Germany.[114]

The DIGB convened representatives of Jewish communities to consolidate a joint program that would reduce the hardship caused by the *Wanderarmen*. At first, the DIGB instructed the communities to stop giving charity to Jewish beggars (*Schnorrer*), and it did not hesitate to approach the police when it was unable to deal with certain cases.[115] It was in 1872 that the DIGB began to focus increasingly on the struggle against *Wanderarmen*. An observer in Heilbronn described the escalation of the problem as such (the circular is dated 1872):

In recent years, the *Wanderarmen* phenomenon has increased in scope and become a national calamity. The welfare and charity these people have been receiving not only did nothing to alleviate the situation, but, rather, exacerbated the problem. Most of the charity seekers are either single men at the prime of their lives, and thus able to work, or foreign children who are of school age. Our organization has existed since 1862. In the last few years, it has

---

113 See: *Israelitisches Familienblatt* (from now on referred to as IFB) from May 10th, 1917.
114 Ismar Schorsch, Jewish Reaction to German Antisemitism. 1870–1914. N.Y./London, 1972, p. 24.
115 Siegfried Brandt, *Die Wohlfahrtseinrichtungen der jüdischen Gemeinde Berlin,* Dissertation, Universität Köln, 1923, p. 162.

given charity to 1,825 individuals, to the amount of 2,414 Guilder [German currency at the time]. Our efforts are supported by the local organization dealing with paupers and by private individuals. Our aim is to deal with local, "embarrassed" paupers rather than with [professional] beggars. We also try to deal with those coming from countries without an education system and from countries that do not allow Jews to move and settle freely. For this purpose, it has been decided to open a center in which these people will be taken care of, thus reducing the number of those roaming the streets.[116]

Harassment (or perceived harassment) by Jewish beggars increased during these years in many regions of Germany, and the demand that they be dealt with was often expressed in the Jewish press.[117]

There is evidence that in the 1870s the problem of Jewish beggars also concerned German authorities. For example, a letter sent to the Foreign Office in Württemberg states that "recently, there is news of an increase in the phenomenon of Jewish beggars coming to this region. It is necessary to use every possible means to stop this. Destitute and unemployed Jews who are residents of the German Reich [unlike their foreign brethren] should receive charity, but the local population should be helped in defending itself against these people.[118]

In other regions of Germany, too, Jews were harassed by beggars, with the former demanding a solution to the problem. However, institutions that were able to deal with *Wanderarmen* did

---

116 S. Boss, "Die Beseitigung der Wanderbettelei", p. 647–648.
117 Calls to fight *Wanderarme* can be found in the official journal of the liberal–Jewish AZJ, for example in the following years: 1869: p. 940–942, p. 1021–1022. 1870: p. 40–41, p. 387. 1872: p. 605–607, p. 623–625.
118 H.W., "Belästigung der israelitischen."

not exist then, and it was necessary to establish them. Committees, all of which aimed to deal with the *Wanderarmen* problem, were set up in communities both large and small. In April 1873, an envoy was sent to every community with laws and regulations pertaining to charity. It was noted in the report that every community had the right to decide whether or not to establish a charity fund, and whether or not it would provide accommodation for beggars within its territory. The communities were required by the DIGB to put an end to the traditional way of giving charity, in which a pauper approached Jewish homes and asked for alms. It was decided that only those who were physically unable to provide for themselves would receive charity, that a special fund would provide loans for use in future periods of distress (*Vorschußkasse*, i.e. advance fund), and that communities that did not maintain a fund for foreigners would establish one. The declared aim of all these funds was to make begging a "less profitable business." And so, the new system of giving charity was designed with the aim of enabling communities to supervise strictly the manner in which it was given. Funds were asked to give aid only after scrupulously examining each charity applicant – his destination, his family status, his economic status, and his documents. The DIGB demanded that welfare organizations cooperate on the *Wanderarmen* issue, also recommending that, in the event that a community lacked the resources necessary to deal with *Wanderarmen*, it unite with a neighboring community for this purpose. The first objective was to eliminate begging as an economic activity, as a source of income. The leaders of the DIGB believed that making it difficult for *Wanderarmen* to beg from door to door would force them to look for alternative sources of income. In a letter dated September 9, 1871, sent to the local police by Jewish community representatives from the city of Esslingen, we read the following: "The Jewish community wants to eliminate the begging of Jewish paupers from Galicia, Hungary, and other places, and would like to inquire whether the local police can assist."[119]

Already at the start of these joint discussions, some expressed the opinion that, in addition to dealing with *Wanderarmen*, it would be necessary to eliminate the causes of poverty. In dealing with the problem of poverty, long-term actions were emphasized, for the objective was to guarantee that a class of permanent welfare recipients would not come into being. To this purpose, it was suggested that the support system would also include the children of *Wanderarmen*: "First and foremost, our concern is about orphans and children of paupers. We have to care for these children, for their education and learning, so that they will succeed in finding employment later on. It is necessary to establish funds that will grant them loans, to be paid back at the appropriate time."[120]

Another article published in the AZJ in 1872 and dealing mainly with the attempt to find a solution for the *Wanderarmen* problem in Germany, argued that many Jewish communities in Germany did not have an organized welfare system, and that the initiative had come mainly from affluent Jews. "Now, we have to ensure that even small donations will be used for welfare."[121]

Despite this and other expressions of goodwill and joint intentions, most communities still lacked the infrastructure necessary to establish the recommended system of charity, especially after the 1880s, when begging reached an unprecedented level. In Bavaria, however, the foundations for such a system had been laid earlier. In the city of Fürth, for example, an organization that aimed to

---

[119] *A.J.P., Esslingen,* „Unterstützungsliste."
[120] S. Boss, „Die Beseitigung der Wanderbettelei", p. 624.
[121] S. Boss, „Die Beseitigung der Wanderbettelei", p. 624.

remove beggars and *Wanderarmen* from the city was founded in 1874; its regulations became the basis for other organizations of this kind until WWI.[122] *Wanderarmen* from Galicia and Russia passing through Bavaria sped up the establishment of a regional welfare center in the mid-1870s, with the member communities committed to giving charity only through funds founded in the cities of the region: Ansbach, Augsburg, Bamberg, Fürth, Nuremberg, and Würzburg; smaller communities, too, were required to adhere to the regional organization's regulations.[123] The success of the Bavarian regional fund led to its expansion and to the establishment of similar institutions in other regions,[124] and its regulations were distributed among other Jewish communities in order to help them establish their own welfare funds. So successful was this fund, in fact, that it eventually extended its influence to Dresden in the East, to Kassel and Fulda in the West, to Magdeburg and Hannover in the North, and to Coburg in the South. Regional funds were established in the cities of Dresden, Leipzig, Magdeburg, Hannover, Kassel, and Erfurt. It was recommended that only *durchreisende Arme* (passing paupers, or beggars who moved from community to community without settling) were to be granted charity; if any money was left over after the *durchreisende Arme* were taken care of, it would be given to paupers who had settled in the fund's jurisdiction. An additional recommendation was that the funds aid Jewish merchants in financial distress, helping them to reach their destination.

---

122 Other parts of Germany also had precedents: In Leipzig, since 1872 (and possibly before), a similar institution had been successfully working to diminish the numbers of beggars.

123 An example of the regional fund's scope: In the first year of the Fürth fund, a sum of 14,000 guilder was paid as an advance payment on *Wanderarmen* charity. See: Jakob Segall, „Wanderarmenfürsorge in Deutschland," p. 59.

124 On regional organizations, see: S .H., „Statistik über die Grenzbüros," p. 123–127.

Outside of Bavaria, the ideas of the regional fund were not unanimously accepted, nor was its recommended plan of action. Only a few Jewish communities joined the central organization, among them Erfurt and Leipzig. Other communities, like Dresden, supported the program but did not bother to implement it; and still others, like Braunschweig and Kassel, openly and vehemently opposed joining the organization.

Although the idea of a centralized welfare organization was not implemented to its full extent during these years, it did gain momentum at the local level. In Hannover and Bremen, for example, local organizations were set up to aid the poor (even those who were not members of the community), beggars, and *Wanderarmen*. Organizations dealing with foreigners were not a new phenomenon in the Jewish communities of Germany: Testimonies from the early 19th century mention the steps taken by local Jewish authorities in regard to *Wanderarmen*. These testimonies also came from Bremen, a popular destination for *Wanderarmen*, especially for those who planned to leave Germany; there, charity efforts were organized and funded by the local Jewish community. A charity organization called *Die heilige Brüderschaft* (the holy brotherhood) conducted regular charity work in Bremen during the 19th century. The year of its founding is not mentioned in the records, but we do know that, in 1882, another organization for the support of *Wanderarmen* was founded in the city, offering sleeping arrangements, food, money for travel expenses and, in some cases, employment referrals. The Jewish community of Bremen also dealt with victims of the pogroms in Russia, many of whom had fled to the city; in Bremen, a special committee was established for the purpose of aiding the foreigners.[125]

---

125 Ibid.

Until the 1890s, it was possible to identify signs of activity on the local level. In places in which the pressure on the local population was particularly burdensome, an infrastructure for charity organizations was laid, their tasks clearly defined. In 1872, the AJG wrote the following: "In Magdeburg and Bonn, organizations are successfully achieving their three objectives: supporting local paupers, supporting paupers of the region, and supporting *Wanderarmen*."[126]

The reports collected by Jakob Segall's indicate that, by the 1880s, German Jews had not yet merged their regional activities into one strong, centralized institution, although efforts aimed at doing so continued intensively. In 1884, the DIGB decided to use the framework of the Jewish communities in dealing with the *Wanderarmen*. During this period, there were disagreements regarding the necessity of taking a firm stance on the *Wanderarmen* problem and regarding its solution. Many communities refrained from taking a stance, content with worrying only about removing paupers from their town or city, as a result of which the decision to take joint action was postponed. In October 1891, members of different charity committees, in Germany and abroad, gathered in Berlin to discuss a solution to the *Wanderarmen* problem. The conference, however, only highlighted the extent to which these organizations were unwilling to cooperate.[127]

This topic occupied every meeting of the DIGB in the years 1892, 1894, and 1896, at which point it was decided that joint action was urgently needed. Although several joint efforts did not result in the establishment of a central organization, they did serve as the impetus behind the establishment of regional organizations. Such

---

126 S. Boss, „Die Beseitigung der Wanderbettelei," p, 606.
127 Stenographischer Bericht über die Delegiertenversammlung zur Beratung der Hilfsaktion für die russischen Juden, Berlin, October 20 and 21, 1891.

Chapter 6: German Jews and the Fight against Wanderarmen and Beggars

was the case after a convention in Frankfurt a. Main in 1894, when representatives of the Jewish communities of Frankfurt, Wiesbaden, Mainz, Mannheim, and Heidelberg, as well as from smaller communities, decided to fund an organization whose purpose was to reduce the number of *Wanderarmen* in the region.[128]

We have determined that every central organization established during these years dealt with this issue in one way or another. The CV, or *Central-Verein deutscher Staatsbürger jüdischen Glaubens* (Central Organization for German citizens of the Jewish faith) is a good example: Established in 1893, it became, as did the DIGB, an important umbrella organization for German Jewry, succeeding, during its 45 years of activity, in establishing a presence in every region of Germany (by establishing committees, convening meetings and general assemblies, and nominating representatives). In 1911, the CV maintained six nationwide organizations (*Landesverbände*).

The CV, which was established in response to the wave of anti-Semitism unleashed by the *Konservative* party in the 1880s and 1890s, later assumed the political role of representing German Jewry. The organization sent representatives to the German Foreign Ministry in order to oppose granting Russian Jews unrestrained entry into the territories of what was then the Second German Reich, and even went so far as to demand that the government adopt a tougher stance on the issue of *Wanderarmen*. In the 1890s, the CV was successful in Saxony, Braunschweig, and Dortmund, but it was only in 1905 that government policy pertaining to Jewish migrants became more stringent, resulting in the expulsion of a large number of Russian Jews. In 1908, however, the CV began to focus on the violation of Jews' rights and the discrimination against them; accordingly,

---

128 Jakob Segall, „Wanderarmenfürsorge in Deutschland", p. 59.

the organization worked tirelessly to prevent the expulsion of Jews without German citizenship from Germany, evidence of which was its vocal defense of cigar workers in Berlin and of Jews who had left Russia. But even before the CV decided to act on behalf of Russian Jews, it had done so on behalf of German Jews. Between October 1891 (the organization's funding date), and January 27, 1898, the CV worked on behalf of 195,034 people.[129] [130]

The conference organized by the DIGB in 1898 decided upon joint courses of actions to be taken by the organizations under its supervision, rules that were later adopted by organizations dealing with *Wanderarmen*, *Schnorrer*, and beggar populations. These rules distinguished between three categories: the able-bodied, those who were unable to work, and the sick, the last of which approached the funds for medical reasons. It was decided that the able-bodied would receive a *Jahreskarte* (a yearly ticket) with which they would approach the funds; that the disabled (or those unable to work for other reasons) would receive help from the communities' regular welfare institutions; and that communities were forbidden from giving charity to permanent beggars or to those who falsely presented themselves as *alte Gelehrte* (old men of wisdom, i.e. rabbis).[131]

The numerous debates leading up to the establishment of a nationwide organization for *Wanderarmen* led to the creation of a special committee whose purpose it was to publish its findings on the matter (1889). The committee concluded that all existing welfare

---

[129] The CV published a magazine called *Im Deutschen Reich*. See: Yehuda Reinharz, *Fatherland or Promised Land*, p. 37, 57.

[130] The CV also dealt with Russian Jews entering Germany, which enabled the DIGB to be available to deal with welfare, charity, and community social work. See: Jack L. Wertheimer, *German Policy*, pp. 162–164.

[131] Willhelm Neumann, "Reform des jüdischen," p. 5–8.

institutions should be united; that regional organizations should be established in regions in which they did not yet exist; that Jewish *Wanderarmen* crossing the borders into Germany should be arrested and returned to the country they had come from; that those who did not behave properly should be documented; and, finally, that a Jewish workers' colony should be established in Weißensee, next to Berlin.[132]

Despite these tireless efforts, the Jews of Germany had still not, by the early 20th century, been able to consolidate their efforts and activities. Regional divisions and lack of experience were the reasons for this failure, and there were even some who claimed that organizations like the CV and the DIGB, organizations which supposedly represented German Jewry, were not authorized to speak on behalf of all German Jews, rendering their efforts insignificant.[133]

In 1900, the DIGB convened a meeting in Berlin, suggesting a new idea: dealing with Jewish poverty not by giving paupers money, but, rather, by offering them professional training.[134] Later, at a convention of Jewish community representatives in 1902, it was reported that the *Wanderarmen* situation had not changed. As a result, the convention decided to establish border offices, the aim of which was the supervision, from the time they entered Germany, of foreign *Wanderarmen*. The representative from Munich, Dr. Werner, suggested nullifying the clause in the poverty commission's regulations whereby paupers were able to receive charity once a year. Werner argued that paupers regularly approached the funds

---

132 See: Jacob Toury, "Organizational Problems of German Jewry, 1893–1920," in LBIYB, 1968, p. 10.
133 Ibid., p. 59.
134 AZJ, No. 18, 1901.

on the exact date of their first receiving aid, exploiting their right to charity by waiting not even one extra day before drawing from the fund.[135]

The problem of Jewish door-to-door begging was partially solved in May 1901, when the *Hilfsverein der deutschen Juden* (Aid Organization of German Jews) was established. Its activities centered on two main issues: migration and education. This enabled the DIGB in Berlin to focus on dealing with *Wanderarmen* all over Germany. The *Hilfsverein*, also called *Ezra* [Hebrew for aid], had objectives fundamentally different from those of the other Jewish aid organizations, with its two main goals being humanitarian activities and German patriotism. In 1905, the Prussian ministry of the interior officially recognized *Ezra* as the official agency dealing with migrants passing through Germany on their way overseas. The organization was to improve the spiritual, moral, and economic situation of Jews in general, and Eastern European Jews in particular. Similar organizations operated in France, Austria, and England. In a public statement issued after its founding, *Ezra* announced that it would take upon itself the duties of welfare, education, and the development of agriculture and craftsmanship while cooperating with other countries and spreading German language and culture. The organization stressed the importance of culture as a political instrument, and further believed that the only way to free those Jews who had not experienced the emancipation was through German education (*Bildung*). *Ezra*'s leadership did not see any contradiction between its Jewish philanthropic aims and German interests, arguing that they were identical and complementary. Among its leaders were liberal Jews like Paul Nathan, as well as a number

---

135 AZJ, No. 10, 1902.

of distinguished Jewish scientists and businessmen, among whom were also Orthodox Jews.[136]

Ezra did not change the existing methods (those employed by other organizations), and operated according to the existing patterns. Between 1904 and 1914, *Ezra* supported 210,771 Jews, all of whom were passing through Germany on their way to the ports from which they would depart overseas.[137] These were years of increasing mobility for migrants, among whom there were also poverty-stricken Jews. In the years 1904-1913, approximately 200,000 Eastern European Jews passed through the Rhine region. Although many of them were on their way to America, their short stay in Germany put pressure on charity funds and Jewish welfare organizations.[138]

The Years Leading Up to the Central Organization: The *Wanderarmen* Problem Worsens

In debates urgently convened by the DIGB, community representatives, hoping to convince the DIGB to implement joint

---

[136] On this issue, see also: *Hilfsverein der deutschen Juden, Festschrift anlässlich der Feier des 25–jährigen Bestehens des Hilfsvereins.* Berlin. 1926. Arthur Goldschmidt, „Zur Geschichte des Hilfsvereins der deutschen Juden", in *ZDSJ,* No. 3–6, 1927. Steven Aschheim, *Brothers and Strangers,* pp. 37–38.

[137] On this issue, see: *Ha–Melitz,* issue 266, 1901. Quoted in: Moshe Rinot, *"Hevrat ha–Ezra le–Yehudei Germania be–Yetziah u–be–Maavak"* [The German *Hilfsverein* for Jews departing and struggling], Jerusalem, 1971/2, p. 22–29. Mark Wischnitzer, "To Dwell in Safety", p. 113.

[138] E.G. Löwenthal, Angewandte "Zedaka", Von jüdischen sozialen Einrichtungen im Ruhrgebiet in den letzten 150 Jahren. 1963. p. 592.

action, reported that the *Wanderarmen* problem was worsening. Dr. Lambrecht of Nuremberg described the situation as follows:

Data from the large cities show that, every year, 2,800 people receive welfare. This number might surprise some of the people present here. In Frankfurt, 2,375 people asked for welfare last year [1902]. This number does not include welfare applicants with a Russian passport. The numbers for Munich and Nuremberg are similar. If we were to take into account that peddlers do not appear in the funds' records, and that they also received small sums, the number would be even higher. These bothersome people make a living off selling worthless merchandise. This, too, is a form of begging, as the peddlers do not have a trade permit for the merchandise they sell while moving from place to place. Once caught by the police, they turn to support funds and ask them to pay their fines. Here in Bavaria, we have seen "gypsy wagons," including *Wanderarme* families of children, adolescents, and their parents. Fifteen to twenty people live in each wagon. The youth grow up without education. Regarding their morals – there is no reason to describe this to you, ladies and gentlemen.[139]

> In 1904, German-Jewish communities felt that the pressure from *Wanderarmen* had intensified. A report from Nordhausen states the following:

The *Wanderarmen* phenomenon has grown to immense proportions in the last years. Two thirds of the people asking for welfare are barely able to survive. They try to plunder communities' funds by presenting forged documents or false information. It is our responsibility to act on behalf of the beggars, and not just by giving them money; we have to think of other ways.[140]

---

139 *Mitteilungen des DIGB.*, October 1905, p. 44–45.
140 Ibid., p. 46.

In order to overcome the problem, it was suggested that communities distinguish between German and non-German beggars:

> No German [Jewish] beggar, and there are 500 of these, will receive any form of welfare. Regional funds have to care for their people. In the event that the funds lack the necessary resources, it is the responsibility of the larger communities to help out. It is necessary to provide [the charity seekers] with work, not alms. Regarding those between 50 and 80 years of age, there is nothing to be done anymore: They are accustomed to a life of loitering and vagabonding.[141]

In 1905, with the organizational framework expanding, it became necessary to deal directly with *Wanderarmen* and their families. The representative of Nuremberg described the activities of his local branch as follows:

> In the last months, we sent five girls and five boys to educational institutions. And even though their parents are illiterate, their children are talented. In the case of one family, we supported them with a sum of 1,000 Mark for a whole year. Another family, who has two boys studying in Berlin, is supported by one of the sons, who is 17 years old and works as a gardener.[142]

While in the larger cities charitable organizations steadily consolidated their responsibility for and supervision of the paupers, the volume of applicants to the funds of smaller communities intensified, some of whom turned to the smaller funds after receiving charity in the larger nearby cities. The representative from Cologne reported that "in recent years, our *Wanderarme* budget has not grown. However, the small communities around us complain that beggars are increasingly turning to their funds."[143]

---

141 Ibid., p. 46.
142 Ibid., p. 48.
143 Ibid., p. 49.

The discussion surrounding the establishment of a centralized institution continued in 1905, and although every community was required to send a representative, not all did so. The deterioration of the *Wanderarmen* problem in Germany served as the basis for the comparison between Jewish and non-Jewish *Wanderarmen*: The Jewish communities complained that, in contrast to the resources available to Germans, theirs were scant. A publication from 1899 states the following: "The Jews are doing all that they can, and more, in dealing with the problem of 'door-to-door begging,' which breeds immorality, lies, and bad deeds. It is necessary to enable the paupers to lead independent lives, and it is [only] to this purpose that they should receive money."[144]

The Jewish community understood that there was no alternative to creating a joint, unified organization and to centralizing resources for joint action. On May 22, 1909, a committee convened to discuss the principles of establishing such an organization. The joint session marked a turning point, for it was then that the objectives and working methods of the organization were formulated clearly. It was decided that local paupers were to be supported within the frameworks of the communities they belonged to; that, should a community encounter difficulties in financing the support, the surrounding communities would help out; that able-bodied paupers would be required to work in special workshops established for this purpose; and that *Wanderarmen* were to move from place to place quickly, not staying in any one community for long.

Organizational procedures were also decided upon: Germany would be divided into 21 regions, with Berlin as their center. The fundraising would be carried out in such a way that small communities

---

144 Ibid., p. 17.

would allocate 20% of their budget to unexpected cases, 20% to regional organizations, and 60% to the central organization in Berlin. The committee also decided to establish additional regional committees. On June 26, new regional funds were founded in places that lacked a fund, with the central organization slated to begin its activities on October 1, 1910.

In South Germany, the centralized organization was yet to be completed. Many *Wanderarmen* continued to arrive in the region, for the funds in South Germany did not, unlike those in the North, meticulously review the applications of charity seekers. In Baden (South Bavaria), Alsace-Lorraine, and Württemberg, too few organizations were capable of centralizing the struggle against Jewish *Wanderarmen*. In Upper Silesia, a unique situation arose, as many *Wanderarmen* from neighboring countries arrived there only in order to receive financial support before returning to their countries of origin. It was suspected, however, that these *Wanderarmen* would not return to their countries of origin, and that they would continue to wander throughout Germany. Accordingly, the regional funds in Silesia were instructed to implement several rules: Every *Wanderarme* passing through the region was required to return to his place of origin by using the shortest possible route; paupers from abroad were to receive support with the purpose of enabling them to continue on their journey (of these, some entered Germany for medical purposes, others requested permission to migrate from Germany, and still others returned to their countries of origin)[145]; and young and able-bodied applicants were to be offered work in the framework of labor workshops. It should be noted that none of

---

145 See: Wilhelm Neuman, Die deutsche Zentralstelle für jüdische Wanderfürsorge, Seperat–Ausdruck aus dem Monatsbericht, Januar 1913, p. 103–105.

these suggestions came into being *ex nihilo*, and that the process had been consolidated earlier, by community frameworks tasked with the responsibility of dealing with non-local charity applicants.

Criticism of the intention to establish a central organization was still being heard on the eve of the organizations' founding, in 1910. The opposition's stronghold was South Germany, as a result of which the Bavarian organization did not, at first, join the central body; voices demanding that the southern organizations join the central organization in Berlin continued to be heard later on. In 1913, Willhelm Neuman, then deputy secretary of the central organization of the communities of Bavaria, Württemberg, Baden, and Elsaß-Lothringen (neither of which was associated with the central organization in Berlin), requested that the member communities exert their influence on local communities and funds, and persuade them to establish support organizations for *Wanderarmen*, thus enabling the central organization to, as it required of itself, circumscribe all of Germany: *das ganze Deutschland soll es sein* ("It shall be all of Germany").[146]

The reasons for the objections to the centralized organization are not apparent from the sources. However, some of the remarks and actions of local organizations indicate that the objections were based on the suspicion that a central organization would not be able to solve the problem. And so, even though the issue demanded joint action and centralized leadership, an all-encompassing (encompassing all of the regions of the Reich) organization was never established in Germany. There were those who used social arguments to buttress their opposition, claiming that the objective of a centralized organization was to promote the interests of the

---

146 Ibid., p. 4.

affluent at the expense of the poor. Others raised concerns about the bureaucratization of the system, suspecting that the people appointed to official positions would become cold, calculating clerks.[147]

In my opinion, the objections of the South German communities stemmed from the differences between the non-Jewish welfare system in Bavaria and that which prevailed in the rest of the Reich. Non-Jewish *Wanderarmen* were treated differently in Bavaria than in other parts of Germany: In contrast to Prussia and other regions, where a solution to the *Wanderarmen* problem was regularized in 1907, Bavaria acted according to its own system. It is, accordingly, possible that the reason behind the Bavarian Jewish organization's refusal to join the central organization in Berlin stemmed from the fact that doing so would have meant forever severing itself from Bavaria's non-Jewish welfare system, which was independent from the welfare systems in the rest of Germany.

---

147 IFB from July 14, 1910.

CHAPTER 7:

CENTRALIZED SOLUTIONS TO THE JEWISH *WANDERARMEN* PROBLEM: MECHANISM, DEPLOYMENT, AND SPHERES OF INFLUENCE

After the foundation of the ZJW in October 1910, the Jewish *Wanderarmen* issue was dealt with in a centralized manner. The ZJW tried, from the outset, to delegate authority to regional organizations, aspiring to expand the system into regions in which charity organizations were not active. The organization had to cope with a variety of challenges: On the one hand, it had to deal with German-Jewish *Wanderarmen*; on the other, and at the same time,

Chapter 7: Centralized Solutions to the Jewish Wanderarmen Problem 143

with foreign Jews entering Germany in large numbers. This was one of the reasons that the ZJW chose Berlin as its headquarters; from there, it was possible to delegate responsibility and overlook the activities of regional branches. In the beginning, the ZJW was headed by Dr. Martin Philippson, with Bernahrd Kahn acting as his deputy.[148]

The first paragraph of the ZJW's regulations stated that the organization was established at the initiative of the DIGB, in collaboration with the *Allianz*, the *Hilfsverein der deutschen Juden* and the German branch of *B'nai B'rith*.[149]

The main objective of the ZJW was to establish a network of regional funds that would focus their activities on clearly defined regions. These funds were called *Provinzialkassen* (provinces' funds); a network of regional funds called *Landeskassen* (funds of the Länder, i.e., Germany's states) served larger regions like Württemberg and Hessen, to name but a few. The central organization would, furthermore, deal with differences of opinions regarding the issue of foreign paupers and the welfare allocated to them on a local level. It was decided that the ZJW would focus on the *Wanderbettler* (nomad beggars) and on the *Rückwandererfrage* (the issue of returning migrants). The regulations defined precisely the organization's functions and areas of activity.[150]

---

148 Additional positions were filled by Hirsch–Halberstadt (secretary), Wilhelm Neumann (secretary), Julian Meisel (treasurer), and Max Beer (deputy secretary). See: Wilhelm Neuman, *Die deutsche Zentralstelle*, p. 1.
149 The ZJW established relations with 57 employment offices (*Arbeitsnachweise*) associated with B'nai B'rith. See: Wilhelm Neuman, *Die deutsche Zentralstelle*, p. 1.
150 *S.H.*, 9225/330, "Zentralstelle, Satzung der deutschen Zentralstelle für jüdische Wanderarmenfürsorge." In: Wilhelm Neuman, *Die deutsche Zentralstelle*, p. 3.

The main task of the ZJW was to collect and exchange information about the *Wanderarmen* population. It was decided that the information would be disseminated through articles published in the *Mitteilungen des DIGB* (the DIGB's magazine) and through a "blacklist" of seasonal beggars, i.e. a list distributed to all communities, containing the names of beggars who exploited the charity system. It was further decided that the central branch in Berlin would be responsible for supervising the activities of the funds: This would include supervising the establishment of facilities for beggars and *Wanderarmen* (workshops, employment offices, labor colonies, hostels for homeless *Wanderarmen,* and so on). Studying these regulations, it becomes clear that the organization aspired to put down roots and to control the entrance of *Wanderarmen* and foreign paupers into the Jewish communities of Germany. This involved developing stricter and more accurate methods of recordkeeping, supervision, public relations efforts, and budgeting.

The ZJW's new regulations expressed ideas that had been formulated earlier, in the regional gatherings of local communities. It was decided that the new organization would integrate representatives from existing organizations: *Ortsarmenkassen* (local poverty funds) and special funds for foreign paupers, as well as district and national funds; every three months, representatives from the local branches of these organizations sent reports to the central organization in Berlin, reports in which they detailed their work regarding *Wanderarmen* and the number of charity applicants who had approached their fund. In return, all members of the ZJW were entitled to receive funds from Berlin exceeding the amount the members could raise at the local level. Member organizations were required, as a condition for membership, to send the central organization one-fifth of their independent budgets. Most of the funding for local funds and organizations came from membership dues, donations, and from assets transferred to the ZJW, as well as from the ZJW's independent financial activities.[151]

The statute required the member organizations to participate in the annual general assembly, to which each member organization sent one representative. The larger organizations (the DIGB, the *Allianz*, *Ezra*, and *B'nai B'rith*) also took part in the general assemblies.

Even after the establishment of the ZJW, the local *Wanderarmen* funds continued to be of central importance. If a community did not have such a fund, the central organization in Berlin recommended establishing one:

Due to the prohibition on giving charity privately, it is necessary that every community establish a local fund, the revenue of which will come from its members. In spite of the fact that individual charity originates in religious-moral intentions, it nevertheless constitutes a serious obstacle to dealing with foreigners. The ZJW can refund sums spent on foreigners by the local funds. Should this principle be observed everywhere, a great amount of money will be accumulated, which will have a positive effect on the welfare system.[152]

Many communities maintained budgets for two distinct groups: foreign Jews and local paupers. In these communities, funds for the support of foreigners came from the same fund as those for local paupers. After the establishment of the ZJW, however, a new funding source was made available, and this was particularly helpful to communities that had not been able to bear the financial burden of increased welfare applications. The ZJW's objective was to

---
151 Wilhelm Neuman, Die deutsche Zentralstelle, p. 3.
152 Wilhelm Neuman, Die deutsche Zentralstelle, p. 2.

distribute resources equally, thereby improving the welfare system. It tried to achieve this aim by establishing regional and nationwide funds in as many places as possible. Accordingly, a small Jewish community whose members were unable, or unwilling, to support the Jewish paupers could from then on refer them to the nearest branch of the central fund, where the paupers would receive money and, afterwards, continue on their journey. Funds of this kind were active all over Germany, in every place where the *Wanderarmen* issue had necessitated joint action. Border stations were set up at central border crossing points through which migrant paupers passed on their way to Germany. These stations mainly dealt with migrants who were on their way to the ports (migrants who intended to immigrate), and although the objective of the border stations was to supervise the migration of *Wanderarmen* to Germany, they were, for all intents and purposes, welfare institutions. Jews passing through the stations received financial support, after which they approached the charity funds within Germany. Unlike official border offices and other institutions, like labor colonies and shelters, these border stations were part of an unofficial welfare system: *Wanderarmen* stayed there for extended periods and received charity. Compared to local funds and regional organizations, however, the stations were significantly smaller in both size and in scope of activities.

As early as the beginning stages of the joint effort regarding Jewish migrants and beggars, statutes regulating the manner in which the welfare system was to be run were drawn up. The fact that the paupers were constantly on the move made it crucial, from the outset, that the welfare system be guided by a uniform system of rules, and that these rules be applied by the different local funds. A lack of uniformity, in fact, would have created a situation in which paupers would flock to certain funds – more generous funds,

Chapter 7: Centralized Solutions to the Jewish Wanderarmen Problem   147

say, or those where charity was more easily obtainable – in large numbers. Furthermore, as was already mentioned in the late 1870s and throughout the 1880s, the main objective was to eliminate, or at the very least to diminish, begging and the traditional, direct charity system. In order to achieve these aims, Jewish beggars were to be turned away from private homes and sent to recently established poverty relief funds. By studying the statutes of the central organization in Berlin, as well as those of the regional branches, we can learn about the objectives of the organizations' leaders and the way in which *Wanderarmen* were received, treated, and financially supported.

Border Offices

Most Jewish beggars passing through Germany had arrived there from abroad. Therefore, the funds situated at Germany's borders were of utmost importance. As Germany had numerous and widely dispersed border crossing points, the ZJW deemed it necessary to determine clear, equal, and uniform criteria for distributing welfare; and as more and more took up the *Wanderarmen* issue, it became necessary to find a common denominator. In addition to funds established at the initiative of the DIGB, other organizations joined the charitable efforts, e.g., the one representing the *Hilfsverein*, which dealt mainly with migrants from overseas.[153]

---

[153] Organizations representing the *Hilfsverein* were active, among other places, in: Gollub, Thorn, Danzig, Myslowitz, Tilsit, Memel, Ratibor, Leipzig, Dresden, Stettin, Solda, Ostrowo, Poznan [German: Posen] and Insterburg. In addition, they were active in the port cities of Bremen and Hamburg. See: *S.H.,* "Zentralstelle, Anweisung an die Grenzbüros."

The instructions given to the border stations included detailed directions on how to question a charity applicant. The offices were instructed to act according to the regulations without exception. And so, every Jew entering these offices in order to receive welfare was questioned about his age, place of birth, place of residence, occupation, and number of children, after which he was asked to explain why he had left his home, what he intended to find in Germany, and if he had ever spent time in the country before; in the event that an applicant had, in fact, earlier visited Germany, he was asked to explain his reason for coming, leaving, etc. Finally, the clerks checked whether his documents were still valid and whether he possessed a valid *Auslandspass* (travel passport, literally "abroad passport").

Offices near the borders also encountered Jews entering Germany for medical purposes, or those who claimed medical needs as a pretext to enter the country. For this purpose, a doctor was stationed on-site to examine the applicants and to determine whether their ailments justified travelling to Germany. This examination was also conducted when the sick person was in possession of medical documents from his country of origin. At the border station, the doctor decided where to refer the sick person to and which treatments to recommend. In addition, the border stations checked whether the Jewish community to which the patient would be sent was, in fact, able to support him financially and provide him with welfare.

Many Jews tried to enter Germany on the pretext that a position was waiting for them at a Jewish community. Indeed, the situation in many Jewish communities – dwindling membership numbers, the aging and retirement of religious officials – made it necessary to seek employees from outside the community, often from abroad; for migrant Jews seeking to enter Germany and to be absorbed by a Jewish community, this was a convenient pretext, and all they needed to do was claim that they had been invited to fill a position in a community. In order to prevent easy access to the country, German Jews tried to verify the veracity of such claims by contacting the relevant community. What's more, the applicants often requested that Jewish organizations cover their travel expenses, which the organizations agreed to do only in cases in which the applicant could provide a letter of appointment. The organizations were attuned to the fact that many communities were unable to cover the travel expenses of their new employees and instructed the border offices (with which they left funds) to pay the expenses of those who were able to offer proof of their new employment.

The border offices were warned of people who presented forged peddler documents while intending to live in Germany as beggars. The regulations clearly determined who was to be rejected. For example, it was fairly common for women to try to enter Germany and to apply for charity on the grounds that they were looking for husbands who had, in fact, moved to Germany with the intention of establishing themselves economically before the arrival of their families. The funds were instructed to reject these applicants, and to accept only those who were able to offer proof of the husband's whereabouts. This policy intended to prevent a situation in which women would wander around Germany, especially those who were unable to prove that they could support themselves without depending on the charity system.

The instructions also warned against able-bodied workers who masqueraded as idlers or as unfortunates; against people who enriched themselves by collecting money for non-existent charities; against those who claimed that they intended to join their families or friends without being able to prove that they had been invited to do so; and against Torah scholars who offered to sell their books or those of others.[154] Furthermore, the offices were instructed to strictly enforce the rule that migrants from Eastern Europe who wished to enter Central Germany, South Germany, Alsace, and Switzerland prove their ability to provide for themselves while in Germany. According to the organizations, the failure to enforce this rule would result in Jewish communities being harassed and exploited, for the applicants would turn into beggars.

Border offices were instructed to verify an applicant's planned route and to make sure that he did, indeed, intend to arrive at the declared community. In order to ensure that migrants would travel to their destinations using the shortest route possible, and that they would not bother Jewish communities along the way, local branches of the ZJW tried to track the routes of charity seekers within Germany. Jewish community funds were warned of people who claimed that they were not familiar with Germany's railway network, a common pretext used to move from community to community: "A person lacking resources verifies his travel route before embarking on his journey, never choosing back roads or detours. Those who do use these routes – for example, those who travel from Berlin to Leipzig via Dresden – prove that the purpose of their traveling is begging."[155] According to the instructions issued to organizations, migrants used such excuses to avoid reaching the destinations assigned to them by the funds. Therefore, the funds were instructed to ask each applicant questions about the purpose of his journey, the duration of his stay, and the communities he planned to pass through.[156]

---

154 *S.H.*, "Zentralstelle, Anweisung an die Grenzbüros.

155 *S.H.*, "Zentralstelle, Anweisung an die Grenzbüros. Nr. 694, paragraph 6 of the document.

156 *S.H.*, "Zentralstelle, Anweisung an die Grenzbüros. Nr. 694, paragraph 8 of the document.

Chapter 7: Centralized Solutions to the Jewish Wanderarmen Problem 151

The border offices were instructed to be in constant contact with the central branch of the organization in Berlin, as well as with the organizations approached by Jewish *Wanderarmen* (Jewish labor workshops and colonies). The funds were required to provide, to the best of their ability, employment. In addition, they were also instructed to make sure that medical treatment be provided only to those who could prove that they were unable to receive the treatment in their place of origin. When medical treatment was approved, the patient was sent to receive it from the nearest specialist. According to the relevant instruction, "a person shall not be sent to receive treatment in Berlin if he can receive it in Breslau or Königsberg." The regulations stated that paupers who had reached their destitute state through no fault of their own, those who were unable to work, and those who received regular charity payments would receive (or continue to receive) charity, but that under no circumstances would they be permitted to continue wandering from community to community, and that they be returned to their places of origin. As mentioned above, the funds were warned of beggars, idlers, and owners of forged documents who masqueraded as Talmud scholars: "It is necessary that they be reminded of their responsibility towards their children, and that their immoral ways be pointed out to them. The Jewish mercy they were hoping to exploit is not blind. It is in this spirit that we also instructed the other poverty funds."[157]

Wanderarmen whose applications for charity had been approved by the fund set off with a signed and numbered envelope and a travel stipend, the amount of which was calculated according to the length of the pauper's planned route. The envelope contained an *Abfertigunskarte* (dispatch card) containing the following personal

---

[157] *S.H.,* "Zentralstelle, Anweisung an die Grenzbüros. Nr. 694, paragraph 9 of the document.

details: name, age, profession, family status, place of origin, place from which the applicant had reached the fund, and destination. All funds agreed to keep a "fund book" in which these details were recorded, and to make the information available to other organizations. In the ports of Bremen and Hamburg, the *Hilfsverein* placed its offices there at the service of the effort to deal with Jewish *Wanderarmen*, ensuring that migrants leaving for overseas would not exploit the welfare system. All *Rückwanderer* (returning migrants) were sent to their countries of origin by the border offices, but these paupers, too, received a travel allowance (calculated according to length of route) from the *Grenzkasse* (border fund). The instructions determined that only the destitute, women, the elderly, children, and those sent to the border offices by the regional funds of Germany were entitled to have their travel expenses to their city of origin covered.

The able-bodied were sent to the first station on the other side of the border. As the regulations pertained only to non-German migrants, it was decided that *Wanderarmen* from Germany's Eastern provinces (for example, Upper Silesia and East Prussia) would receive support, but not a *Wanderarmenkarte* (an identity card for *Wanderarme*). This was, presumably, done in order to stanch the flow of Jewish migrants from the East.[158]

After a meeting of the ZJW, held in June, 1911, the border offices were asked to make sure that *Wanderarmen* who had received charity at the border stations pass through all regional funds located on their route, thus facilitating close supervision. *Wanderarmen* naturally crossed borders, and many of those passing through Germany continued to other countries. As a result, the border offices, with the

---

158 On this instruction see: *S.H.*, "Zentralstelle, Anweisung an die Grenzbüros. Nr. 692.

Chapter 7: Centralized Solutions to the Jewish Wanderarmen Problem 153

help of the ZJW, communicated with similar institutions in other countries: "The organization communicates with other countries: Switzerland, Belgium, France, and Holland. A large movement [of migrants] exists in the cities of Basel and Brussels. The organization also communicates with the ports of Amsterdam, Rotterdam, and Antwerp." The purpose of these international connections with different organization was to supervise the route of *Wanderarmen*.[159]

The role of the border offices was dual: First and foremost, they acted as a *Vorprüfungsstelle*, a preliminary interrogation station where migrants were questioned and where it was decided whether they would receive charity. Second, the border offices dealt with what was called *Repatriierung*, or "return to homeland," i.e., dealing with migrants who were returning to their countries of origin and facilitating their return home.[160]

Many of the welfare applicants possessed different letters and certificates of approval documenting their status and recommending welfare. Regarding these, too, the instructions were strict, and it was decided to disregard *Armutszeugnisse* (certificates of poverty) and *Empfehlungsbriefe* (letters of recommendations), both of which were often presented by Jewish welfare applicants, unless they were issued by official community institutions or by state officials.

This issue needs further explanation: *Empfehlungsbriefe* and *Armutszeugnisse* facilitated, for those who possessed them, the process of receiving charity from the welfare organizations. Letters of recommendations were, throughout the 19th century, common in the Jewish communities of both Eastern Europe and Germany, and

---

159 Erster Rechentschaftsbericht der deutschen Zentralstelle für jüdische Wanderarmenfürsorge, January 28, 1912.
160 Wilhelm Neumann, *Die deutsche Zentralstelle*, p. 3.

I found evidence of their existence in the funds' records. In some cases, applicants to Jewish charity organizations claimed that they possessed such letters. These letters of recommendation were often called *Armutszeugnisse*, or "poverty certificates," even though they were not identical to *Armutszeugnisse*. The documents contained the name of the certificate owner, details about his past, family status, character, and features. In Jewish community archives, I found records of "poverty certificates" only in the period preceding 1880, records in which both *Armutszeugnisse* and *Empfehlungsbriefe* were clearly mentioned. The following, for example, is a letter (dated April 3, 1868) sent from Tilsit (present-day Sovetsk) to the local welfare committee of Königsberg: "I cannot provide for my family. I am 40 years old, at the height of my abilities, that is, and a father of three children. As I do not possess an *Armustzeugnis*, I have to rely on Mr. Feiler."[161] In his "And the Crooked Shall Be Made Straight," the late Israeli writer and Nobel Prize laureate Shai Agnon recounts the story of an *Empfehlungsbrief* written by the Rabbi of Buchach, a town in Galicia (present-day Ukraine) that was then under the rule of the Austro-Hungarian Empire. There is good reason to believe that Agnon's description is not just the fruit of his imagination, but, rather, an account of reality. The hero of Agnon's story, Menashe Chaim, becomes impoverished and, in search of income for himself and his wife, leaves both wife and home. For this purpose, he turns to a local rabbi to provide him with a letter of recommendation. Agnon describes how the document was written and, afterwards, the tragedy it brought about:

The rabbi saw that Menashe Chaim was in very great distress and took pity upon him. He puffed on his pipe, considered the matter, tested his quill, and began to put down on paper the various

---

161 *C.A.J.P*, Königsberg, „Notstand in Ostpreußen", 1868.

Chapter 7: Centralized Solutions to the Jewish Wanderarmen Problem 155

merits of this esteemed but needy person. And the rabbi wrote a testimonial letter, and in the letter the rabbi related how the man Menashe Chaim HaCohen was a resident of our city, how as long as he had been there he had known him to be a dear and honorable man, a man of wealth and pelf, upon whom the sun of success had once shone, for whom the wheel of fortune had recently turned, throwing him ten degrees backward, so that he has no means wherewith to provide food for his household. Now he has donned upon his face the veil of shame and has opened his hand to receive, to beg for help and compassion from the generous amongst our brethren, the House of Israel. I have therefore manfully girded my loins to recommend him in this missive scroll, and my hope, by the good Lord, is that by means of this he will find aid and salvation, that our brethren, the House of Israel, those among the people who offer willingly, will help him and treat him with the dignity he deserves and not dole out the bread of disgrace. And I request from our brethren, the House of Israel, the noble and generous of the nation of the God of Abraham, to receive this man with benign countenance wherever he goes and to bestow upon him according to his deserts. Of this it is said, "thou shalt sustain him," with dignity. For this good deed, may the Lord open the windows of Heaven for them and pour out blessings and success upon them till their lips weary of saying, "Enough." The rabbi signed his name to the letter, dating it the third day (corresponding to the third day of Creation that the Lord twice saw it was good) of the week during which we read in the Torah, "The Lord shall command the blessing upon thee in thy storehouses, and in all that thou settest thine hand unto; and he shall bless thee in the land which the Lord thy God giveth thee," in the year 5618 since creation. For added force, he blackened his seal in the flame of the candle and stamped the letter with his imprimatur. Then he handed the letter to Menashe Chaim, directing him to set out on his way, assuring him that wherever he would go, all would treat him with charity and loving kindness. And Menashe Chaim took the letter and left the building, his head reeling, his eyes swollen like two water skins filled with tears. He did not even glance at the lofty language as he did when he had dwelled upon wealth's heights and a poor man would come to him with a letter of introduction, when he would take pleasure in the honeyed sweetness of the rabbis' stylistic flourishes.[162]

Armutszeugnisse, which were very similar to the one described by Agnon, had already existed in Germany a few years previously, albeit on a much more limited scale: The Prussian Law of 1879 clearly defined the way in which *Armutszeugnisse* were to be used. Such a document was issued by the authority tasked with dealing with the problem, known as the *Armenverwaltung* (poverty administration), and given to paupers who were eligible for welfare from the state. The *Armenzeugnisse* included information on the applicant's occupation, financial situation, and family status, as well as a detailed account of the sums he had received from the *Armenverwaltung*. The conditions for receiving an *Armutszeugnis* were strict, which is why most people did not bother to apply even if they were in need of welfare; for example, the instructions dictated that, in order to be eligible for an *Armutszeugnis*, an applicant had to prove that he was without property or possessions, and that he was not able to financially support his family.[163] I did not find any evidence, in records pertaining to the poor in Germany, that the German "poverty certificate" was widely used in the German welfare system. The certificate was usually issued as legal evidence

---

162 C.A.J.P, Königsberg, „Notstand in Ostpreußen", 1868.
163 Ernst Grässner, Erich Simm, *Das Armenrecht*, p. 405–408.

for welfare seekers needing official documentation of their economic situation.[164]

The situation in the Jewish communities was fundamentally different: There, the paupers used the *Armutszeugnis* as a tool, a useful tool, in collecting money from private Jewish homes, as well as from the Jewish communities' charity funds. In addition, the certificate served as a "character reference," facilitating its owner's dealings with the welfare system. Many Jewish communities opposed the common practice of issuing *Empfehlungsbriefe* to *Wanderarmen*, claiming that many of the recipients were exploiting the situation. According to one testimony, many *Empfehlungsbriefe* were carelessly written and unreliable:

> One man came to me with an *Empfehlungsbrief*. I checked with the person who had written the letter and asked him: Do you know this young man? His answer: no. His justification [for writing the *Empfehlungsbrief*] was that the specific person seemed to be a good Jew, and that he was also a Talmud scholar. Similar things occurred many times.[165]

The Blacklists

The relatively large number of organizations, local funds, and offices supporting Jewish beggars misleads one into believing that the organizational framework was a widespread network, encompassing

---

[164] On the use of *Armutszeugnisse* for the sake of legal purposes, like contracts and usage in court, see: Ernst Grässner, Erich Simm, *Das Armenrecht*, p. 408. The German *Armutszeugnis* was also used to receive convalescence pay and discounts for train tickets. See: R. Kluge, *Handbuch für Armenpfleger*, p. 408.

[165] Mitteilungen des D.I.G.B., October 1905, p. 121.

even the most remote corners of Germany. However, the vast size of the Reich made it virtually impossible for an organization like the ZJW to effectively supervise local branches. Supervision was, however, conducted at the local level, especially in cases in which the funds suspected that they were being exploited by swindlers who managed to hide their assets and applied for welfare repeatedly. The very idea of strictly supervising charity applicants contradicted the idea behind granting it: It is, naturally, difficult to treat a pauper humanely, to offer him aid and to worry about his basic needs, while at the same time employing strict measures aimed at deterring him from abusing the goodwill of the charity providers. This dilemma was at the center of the Jewish charity system, which, although it defined itself as governed by a moral code of charity and by the religious commandments, also employed strict measures designed to protect the peace and property of the charity givers.

As welfare was handled on the Jewish level, the Jewish communities were solely responsible for its proper management, without any outside intervention (from German police or state institutions). The absence of an accepted authority (a nationwide Jewish organization tasked with dealing with this matter) that could have imposed its rule on local communities meant that it was up to regional institutions to enforce rules and regulations against those who either violated them or tried to damage the system. One of these initiatives was the "blacklists," the objective of which was the creation of a national database that would protect those who ran the charities from swindlers and exploiters. In this way, a system of documenting suspicious persons – those who tried to receive funds without meeting the organizations' requirements – developed in Germany. To be sure, the success rate of this supervisory method was low, neither improving the funds' effectiveness nor reducing the

Chapter 7: Centralized Solutions to the Jewish Wanderarmen Problem 159

number of paupers who tried to exploit the system. The "blacklist" system of *Wanderarmen* drew on the experience of South German funds, specifically on the strict supervisory method developed by a Nuremberg Jew named Martin Lebrecht. The system worked as follows: The first fund reached by a *Wanderarme* would issue him a card on which his final destination was recorded. Then, the fund would send the applicant's name to the central organization in Berlin and to the fund he intended to reach next. Several times each week, the Berlin organization would send the regional organizations information about abnormal activities in and exploitation of the welfare system, warning them of individuals believed to be exploiting the funds or presenting false information:

Every week, we distribute 4-5 lists [of the funds' welfare recipients] based on the reports we receive. These lists are sent to the regional funds. The funds report to us every week, with the exception of the funds in Berlin and Frankfurt an der Oder, which publish such lists every day. Listed are welfare applicants who are criminals, trying to deceive [the funds] by presenting counterfeited documents. In Frankfurt an der Oder, 10 percent of welfare applicants are criminals.[166]

Other data indicate that the ratio of *Wanderarmen* who presented trustworthy data to those who tried to cheat the system favored the dishonest applicants. This was especially true in Nuremberg: "In the city of Nuremberg, Martin Lebrecht's blacklist contained 1,300 names. This is an astonishing number, considering that [only] 6,000 people are receiving welfare."[167] Each "blacklist" consisted of an average of 10 pages on which were listed the names and routes of

---
166 Erster Rechenschaftsbericht der jüdischen Deutschen Zentralstelle für Wanderarmenfürsorge, from January 28, 1912, p. 10.
167 Wilhelm Neumann, *Reform des jüdischen*, p. 3.

Wanderarmen expected to deviate from the regulations. In addition, the lists gave detailed descriptions of swindlers of whom the regional funds should be warned. In order to improve efficiency, regional organizations were also required to report to local welfare funds about *Wanderarme* there.

We do not have sufficient data regarding the number of swindlers who appeared in the "blacklists," as many of these lists were either lost or destroyed. According to a relatively late source (1927), 233 lists were issued regularly until 1933 (after the establishment of the central organization in Berlin, once per month). In addition to these lists, there were 250 "blacklists" listing a total of 1,734 names.[168] Obviously, this estimate is far from accurate: In the state archive in Hamburg, I found that the "blacklist" for 1911-1912 (just one year) listed the names of 3,427 *Wanderarmen*. It should be noted, however, that we are here referring to those who tried to cheat the system, and not to those who applied for charity in accordance with the laws and regulations. The Hamburg lists were sent to funds all over Germany, and their wide distribution indicates the desire of the welfare system's leadership to combat the exploiters. The willingness of the funds to send to the central branch in Berlin monthly reports on *Wanderarmen* who breached the regulation indicates the success of the supervisory system. One observer had this to say of the system: "The blacklists are in high demand. Last year's lists reported 4,357 violators, but the number was actually 3,600, for several people appeared on the list twice."[169]

---

168 Bericht über die Tätigkeit der Hauptstelle für jüdische Wanderarmenfürsorge, in: Die Zeit, from April 1, 1925 till December 31st, 1926. Berlin: 1927. p. 11–13.

169 IFB February 21st, 1913.

Chapter 7: Centralized Solutions to the Jewish Wanderarmen Problem

On the other hand, to those studying these lists from the perspective of the period, it is frightening to think that Jews tried to hunt each other by creating police-type "wanted" lists the aim of which was to hunt down people suspected of deceiving the welfare system. Many of these "criminals" were actually desperate paupers left with no option but to turn to one of the Jewish funds for small amounts of money. And while supervision was necessary, the registration procedure alone made it very difficult to start with (additional measures reduced the number of accepted welfare recipients even more, and excluded many who needed it). One has to understand that the welfare system did not just cover a limited geographic region but, rather, a comprehensive system covering most of the areas Jewish paupers came from or went to. There is a colorful human element to these lists that depicts the population of welfare applicants and the humiliation and insult they endured from permanent community members when seeking aid. The lists also indicate a high level of suspicion, lack of trust, and even hostility towards the welfare applicants. This attitude was there from the outset, and hostility was directed against all welfare applicants: it was assumed, from the start, that the applicants were deceivers who were not in need of welfare. "These people even occupy our hospitals and pretend to be sick."[170] Others warned of *Wanderarmen* who masqueraded as teachers:

> The beggars claiming to be teachers are the most dangerous. For example, there was a self-proclaimed teacher named Wertheim from Magdeburg, who tried to receive welfare at different places. He was not known to any of the funds there [in Magdeburg]. We warn [the communities] of teachers or *gabbaim* [maintenance managers of synagogues]. Their recommendations should be treated with suspicion. We also warn of fellow Jews who arrive with ritual

---

170 *S.H.*, "Zentralstelle. No. 454.

objects and newspapers, presenting themselves as fundraisers for charities in the Holy Land.[171]

Who were these people? They were possibly criminals, possibly imposters, and possibly petty crooks who deviously tried to receive small amounts of money even if their economic situation did not justify receiving aid.

The lists are an inexhaustible source of information on the personal details of the *Wanderarmen*, including their detailed physical description – rare written sources that describe the *Wanderarmen* to the smallest detail. Each "blacklist" contained a page on which the names of those who broke the rules were listed. Below each name were a few defining characteristics, including unique physical characteristics, behavior, age, place of origin, route, and other identifying details. Here, for example, are a few entries from one such "blacklist":

Weizmann Chana; 35 years old; place of origin: Weiheim; profession: peddler. Recommended to expel her. Mishel Levalzter; from Kolomea [present-day: Kolomyia, Ukraine]; 78 years old; profession: teacher; arrived at the fund from Chemnitz.

Sholeyn Perlmutter; from Vishnitz; 41 years old; profession: painter; Comment: behaved impertinently. Felker, Esther; from Odessa; 48 years old; Acted with impertinence as well; expelled from Odessa, as she was a scoundrel.

The descriptions were short and to the point:

Salo Cohen, from Hannover, 61 years old, impertinent merchant, expelled.

Other descriptions included the reasons for removing someone from the fund:

---

171 *S.H.*, "Zentralstelle, Die schwarzen Listen". No. 8, 438, 542.

Vogelsinger Haim, Vishnitz, 70 years old, has 450 Mark on him; Goldstein Shmuel, from Bushina, 68 years old, merchant, is not [as he had stated] a 'believing' Jew.

The "blacklists" described many of the applicants as corrupt and lacking in character: "He acted impertinently and was expelled from the place." Others were described as swindlers who had presented false information to the fund: "He presented many false facts and tried to deceive everyone." Or, in a different case: "Guttman, Michael, baker, it was already noted in Chemnitz that he is a liar. Was sent back to his birthplace, Cologne, where it was determined that he was not completely sane, and that he shall move on."[172] This belief – that a person who wandered from place to place for income could not be sane – became widely accepted, and it is a fact that many *Wanderarmen* were considered to be either crazy or mentally unstable. Nomadism, according to this view, was evidence of mental illness, as a result of which some *Wanderarmen* were admitted to psychiatric institutions. A magazine on psychiatry mentioned the case of a Jew named Bernard Ahron whose name was difficult to pronounce: Ahron, a native of Berlin who had nine siblings, was institutionalized in 1890, after which he was repeatedly released and readmitted. Later, he was caught committing the misdemeanor of wandering around and begging.[173]

Others were portrayed as swindlers trying to profit from the train tickets they had received from the charity funds: "Goldman Isaac Hirsch was trying to sell his train ticket. We therefore confiscated it at the train station." According to the "blacklists," others lied

---
172 Zeitschrift für die gesamte Neurologie und Psychatrie, Volume 168. 1940, p. 65–111.
173 Zeitschrift für die gesamte Neurologie und Psychatrie, Volume 168. 1940, p. 65–111.

about their financial situation: "We expelled a few people since they were, indeed, persons of means." The welfare application of one woman was denied, as she had "refused to present us her money." Still others were described as idlers who refused to work: "[The application of] Reinech Joel of Sinzheim, 33 years old, was denied, as he refused to work, on the grounds that he was not willing to work for a wage of four Mark a day. He appears to be an authentic Social-Democrat."[174] Likewise, the Hannover fund reported the reaction of a Jew sent to work on behalf of the fund: "I would prefer my hand to be amputated than to work. There [at the labor workshop] others can work."[175]

The wording of the "blacklists" indicates a harsh and hostile approach towards professional beggars who tried to deceive the funds. A Jewish woman applying for welfare at one of the funds was described with disdain as someone who exploited her disability in order to make profit: "A blind woman by the name of Schnederson, who cannot write her name in any language, is walking around with a 13 ½ year old child named Barnard Baron. Through him, she tries to raise *rachmones* [mercy; in the original quote, the word appeared in Hebrew letters].[176]

Critics of Jewish *Wanderarmen* stressed the beggars' supposedly deficient behavior and low morals. A report from Hannover states: "During our dealings, we exposed people lacking any sense of honor, like this 16-year-old who stole in a few cities, among them Halberstadt, where he stole a Torah scroll. We found the stolen scroll and returned it to its rightful owner. Another young man, aged 19,

---

174 *S.H.*, "Zentralstelle, Die Schwarzen Listen." No. 86, 88, 211, 220, 220, 434, 478, 518, 579, 589 and 607.

175 Report of the "Committee for Dealing with *Wanderarme*" in Hanover–Braunschweig (1911). See: *S.H.*, "Statistik über die Grenzbüros", No. 9225.

176 *Mitteilungen des D.I.G.B.*, October 1905, p. 121.

received welfare [from us], which enabled him to go to Hamburg, where he turned to the railway mission. Afterwards he returned to us and asked for more welfare. We discovered his identity and did not grant him the remaining money he had planned to receive. A 40-year-old *Schnorrer* smuggled, in exchange for [a bribe of] two bowls of soups, his countrymen through the border to Germany. We have his photograph in our records, and know that he has been turning to Germany's funds for many years. He is expected to repeatedly turn [to welfare funds] over and over again."[177]

Testing the Welfare Seekers' Jewishness

The various attempts to deceive the funds show not only how desperate the applicants were, but also how strong was the gravitational force of the Jewish welfare system, which was spread out all over Germany. Another indication of this inclination was the large number of attempts made by non-Jews to pose as Jews and to benefit from Jewish welfare funds. We know of them from the "blacklists," which recorded the names of those who were caught. Lajos Kassák, the Hungarian poet, painter, and avant-gardist who spent the years preceding WWI as a *Wanderarme*, writes the following on his memoirs:

> [Emil] Szittya told me straight: 'I went through all the quarters. Now it is your turn. Do you know the Jewish funds?' 'How could I know them [I answered], I am not Jewish!' 'However, you surely are not the crown prince either, and no diamond will fall out of your crown if you were to receive two Mark from the Jewish funds. I will accompany you. The fund's counter is in the front room, you wait

---

177 For the Hannover report, see: *S.H.*, Zentralstelle.

until it is your turn, and then you say: 'I implore you, I am Jewish.' I was looking for a courteous way. 'And if they notice that I am not Jewish at all?' 'The people at the counter cannot determine if you are Jewish or not. If they ask you from where you came, say Hungary, from the village of Tiszaeszlár, that your whole family has been murdered, and that you were the only one who had managed to flee, that you are here now, and that you have no acquaintance or family.' This made the whole issue look better and I promised to cooperate.

The large room was full of bearded men with side curls. Everyone hummed, which made it sound like a beehive. The men talked to one other in Russian, Polish, and Yiddish, and they talked with their hands and feet… I later understood that some had fled pogroms in Russia and Poland, and that these were homeless people worthy of mercy. The majority were ragtag, knocking on doors every spring and returning to their families every fall with a small fortune. These were impatient, violent troublemakers who used their misery as if it were a holy artifact that needed to be displayed for all to see…The cashier spoke in German, and they answered in their ugly jargon. The line of people displaying their emotions was long. Afterwards, I stood in front of the small window. 'I am a poor Jew,' I stuttered unconvincingly. The words hurt my tongue. Under my jacket, my heart raced, as if it wanted to jump out of my chest. The hot air in the room almost made me choke to death. I did not dare look the cashier in the face. 'From where?' I recited what I was taught to say. My face was pale and withered. 'Oh yes, Tiszaeszlár, I know,' said the cashier and sadly sighed while placing the silver Mark coins in front of me. A tired Szittya waited outside the door. 'You have them?' he asked hesitantly. 'Yes,' I answered. 'I did something ugly, and I am ashamed of myself about this ugly act of stealing. If I did not know that you are the bigger crook of the two of us, I would tell you to spit in my face and to report what I did to the police.'[178]

The impersonators, however, did not usually encounter so little suspicion from the funds. Sometimes, the funds made it difficult for welfare applicants, exacerbating the application process. In addition to checking documents and clarifying the wanderers' intentions, the funds also tried to verify the applicants' Jewishness. For this purpose, applicants were asked to read a short section of the *machzor* (Jewish holiday prayer book) or the Torah (Hebrew Bible) in Hebrew. The Hungarian Kassák mentions this in his memoirs, telling the story of a friend of his who had to undergo such an exam when applying to a Jewish fund. And while Kassák's description is arguably accompanied by anti-Semitic overtones, it does contain a grain of truth regarding the methods of Jewish funds. Kassák, the Hungarian *Wanderarme*, advises his friend on how to deceive the Jewish funds and describes a personal experience:

> 'He is crazy! [The cashier responsible for handing out money at the Jewish fund] However, if you know how to present yourself skillfully, you will be able to line your pockets with a few Mark. His craziness is specific: He wants people asking for support to read from a book in Hebrew. If you only know a few letters, the money is guaranteed.' In the front room, two old men with side curls were sitting. I sat between them and observed them. Maybe I could learn something from their methods. But even though I tried to the best of my abilities, I could not understand their language. And when one of them asked me if I was Jewish, I interpreted this as a bad omen: If these two already noticed that I didn't belong to them, what would a third person say? A thin patriarch with a great beard showed his head

---

[178] Lajos Kassák, *Als Vagabund unterwegs, Erinnerungen*. Berlin, 1978, p. 81–88 (Translation of passage: Benjamin Rosendahl).

through the door. The two almost gave each other secret signs with their feet while running through the door. One of them returned to me after a brief moment. He growled something to himself, surely cursing his friend, while twirling his side curls, which hung like bottle openers. We waited maybe for fifteen minutes, at which point his friend came out of the room, and the second one swallowed with an inward sigh.

'What did he give you?' I asked the old man. '*Nu*, five Mark.' I expressed my excitement loudly: 'Five Mark!' '*Nu*, weren't we burned twice in Warsaw, wasn't my family slaughtered during the pogrom? If I could only tell you what had happened to my family! So what are five Mark, compared to all these catastrophes?' I knew the old man was not telling the truth, but I did not contradict him. I was too busy with myself. If the old man had gotten five Mark, maybe I, too, would not leave empty-handed. Then, it was my turn. I entered a large room with locked windows. A thin person, looking like a patriarch, stood in front of me. A special, holy atmosphere was in the room. The old man did not want to deal with me and sank into his chair. He quietly put his head between his hands. Time passed. Without his head moving, he asked me: 'And now, what happened?' 'Ah-ah-ah,' I stuttered, my eyes nearly jumping out of their sockets from the stress. However, not a single word left my mouth. When I had entered the room, I greeted the man in a normal way, but when I saw the big book, I knew I had to play dumb.... '*Nu-nu-nu*, this comic performance is really unnecessary,' he said. He came towards me until he stood in front of me. I felt that he pierced me with his look. 'Why did you come if you are not Jewish?' Without blinking, he continued: 'If you are Jewish, then read!' I raised my legs up, the same way geese do when walking on ice, and brought my hand to my forehead. I surely must have looked

Chapter 7: Centralized Solutions to the Jewish Wanderarmen Problem

ugly at that moment. I felt that all that was human had left me. I felt that for a piece of bread, I had humiliated myself with excuses far below self-respect. Then I began making incoherent sounds. He grasped my shoulder and pushed me out the door. 'Do you want to be a Jew? You are just a normal nomad! Can a Jew walk around with such gypsy hair?' He pushed me out of the room, but I did not want to be treated like this, like a little boy. I continued to pretend [being a poor Jew], started crying and weeping as if I had just been sentenced to death. This lasted for a long time, until the old man had had enough. He threw a 50-Pfennig-coin at me and said: 'Here you go, smarmy gypsy! And now get out before I arrest you!' I took the money and, next to the door, broke out in loud laughter. From outside I heard the old man cursing me. He can be as mad as he wants, I thought to myself; at least I have half a Mark. I had never worked so hard for a few Pfennigs. With a feeling of victory, I returned to my guest house.[179]

---

179 Lajos Kassák, *Als Vagabund unterwegs, Erinnerungen.* Berlin, 1978, p. 114–117 (Translation of passage: Benjamin Rosendahl).

CHAPTER 8:

REGIONAL ACTIVITY

The bulk of *Wanderarmen* welfare work centered on regional funds, as German Jews were not, during those years, able to establish an efficient, centralized organization. In addition, the country was large, making it all but impossible for one organization to supervise the movement of *Wanderarmen*. As a result, each region set up its own framework through which it dealt with the *Wanderarmen* problem. The regions differed from one another, with the main differences being the patterns and direction of migration experienced in each, and the degree to which each was desirable as a destination for beggars. This chapter will discuss the regional frameworks that shouldered the *Wanderarmen* burden, as well as the way in which these frameworks were organized. In spite of the differences between the regional organizations and funds, it is still possible to pinpoint a few defining characteristics that repeated themselves in several regions. For the large part, welfare activities were carried out by *Provinzialkassen*, i.e. regional funds. Located in central areas and amid major transportation intersections, the *Provinzialkassen* were responsible for supporting *Wanderarmen* who passed through the territory and those who had been referred to the fund by smaller towns and communities in the area. A regional fund required the surrounding Jewish communities to join it and to help finance its activities, to the best of the communities' abilities. In 1910, *Provinzialkassen* existed in the following regions: East Prussia (seat of the fund: Königsberg), West Prussia (Thorn), Pomerania (Stettin), Berlin, Brandenburg (Frankfurt a.d. Oder), Posen (Posen), Breslau-Liegnitz, Breslau, Sachsen-Thüringen (Magdeburg), Hannover-Braunschweig (Hannover), Westphalia (Bochum), Rheinprovinz and Birkenfeld (Cologne), Kassel and Waldeck Province (Kassel), Hessen-Nassau and Hessen Province (Frankfurt am Main), Saxony (Leipzig), Lothringen (Metz), with additional funds in the cities of Nuremberg, Hamburg, and Bremen.[180]

Similar to the instructions regarding *Wanderarmen*, which were published by the central organization in Berlin and sent to all border offices, the regional funds were instructed to give welfare only to those who held an *Abfertigunskarte* (clearance card). It was the funds' responsibility, too, to classify the applicants according to their work capabilities: Young and able-bodied *Wanderarmen* should be referred to workshops and offered employment, or be given a train ticket and funds in order to reach the next district's

---

180 Jakob Segall, "Wanderarmenfürsorge in Deutschland", p. 66.

fund. The funds given should never exceed the amount necessary to travel to the neighboring district's fund. If an applicant is able to prove that he will find work in a specific place, he should be directed there immediately by the regional fund.[181]

Funds were further instructed to adopt a strict approach when giving welfare, with the regulations stating the following: "It is prohibited to enable passersby to collect savings."[182]

The funds were not just responsible for welfare, however: Among their responsibilities was to ensure that *Wanderarmen* leaving the region would reach the next regional fund without deviating from their route. Suspecting that the unrestrained movement of *Wanderarmen* would enable the paupers to approach Jewish communities' institutions or, even worse, Jewish homes, the regional funds formed a network the aim of which was to supervise the movement of *Wanderarmen*.

The funds' range of duties also found expression in the way in which they paid attention to the smallest details regarding the migrants' itinerary. For example, the funds had clear instructions on what to do when they suspected that a *Wanderarme* might arrive at the next regional fund after the onset of the Jewish Sabbath, which commences on Friday night:

If a passerby arrives at the reception desk [of the fund] in the evening hours, when the offices are closed, he should be referred to a place of lodging. This will be noted in the *Abfertigungskarte*.

---

181 *S.H.*, 92251692, "Anweisung für die Provinzial–bzw. Landeskasse", ausgedruckt von der deutschen Zentralstelle für jüdische Wanderarme, Steglitzerstraße 85, Berlin. (Paragraphs 2–4).

182 *S.H.*, 92251692, "Anweisung für die Provinzial– bzw. Landeskasse" (Paragraph 5).

Regarding *Wanderarme* and *Rückwanderer* [returning migrants], if they are travelling on Friday or on the eve of Jewish holidays, it is necessary to see to it that they arrive before the start of the Sabbath or a holiday.[183]

The regulations of the Hannover regional fund teach us about the way in which the fund developed into a regional body responsible for the support of *Wanderarmen*. The regulations determined that all Jewish communities in the *Provinz Hannover* [Hannover district] and in the *Herzogtum Braunschweig* [Duchy of Brunswick] would be subordinated to the regional fund. The *Armenkassen* (poverty funds) of all Jewish communities in the Hannover and Braunschweig districts later decided to unite under an umbrella organization, establishing the *Provinziallasse für jüdische Wanderarmenfürsorge Braunschweig-Hannover* (regional fund for Jewish *Wanderarmen* welfare for the districts of Brunswick and Hannover). Headquartered in Hannover, the regional fund would be a member of the ZJW in Berlin, to which it would transfer 20% of its income. This would make the fund a *Verband* (association) of the ZJW. It was the declared aim of the fund to give welfare to *Wanderarmen* in an effective way, while at the same time to fight against *Wanderarmen* begging (door-to-door begging).[184]

Funds were responsible for the support of both foreign and local paupers, the latter of whom were given employment or, if necessary, money. The regulations determined that although the local paupers fell into the regional fund's jurisdiction, they were to be supported by the local, rather than the regional, funds. Foreign paupers, on

---

183 *S.H.*, 92251692, "Anweisung für die Provinzial– bzw. Landeskasse" (Paragraph 7).
184 *S.H.* 9225/665, "Satzung für die Provinzialkasse Hannover–Braunschweig für die jüdische Wanderarmenfürsorge" (Paragraph 1–2).

the other hand, would receive charity only from the regional funds, which were instructed to conduct comprehensive examinations of the applicants' physical abilities and "to give foreigners support only once a year."[185]

Each regional fund was required to have representatives in similar organizations of the region (workshops, employment offices, and border offices). Members of the funds were members of the Jewish communities in the area or members of *Ortsarmenkassen* (local poor funds) in the regional fund's jurisdiction. Membership was granted under the condition that 80% of the local funds' income, or of the small communities' income, would be transferred to the regional fund. In turn, the regional funds were required to send 20% of their income to the central organization in Berlin. It was also possible for individuals to become members of the regional funds, on the condition that they donate money each year. Other sources of income came from onetime payments of private individuals, various donations, interest on the fund's capital, and, in the event of deficit, from money sent by the central organization in Berlin. The fund was managed by a committee elected for a three-year term. The elected members, who were also registered as members of the ZJW in Berlin, represented the nearby Jewish communities and poverty funds. From the regulations of the Hannover–Braunschweig fund, we learn that the fund elected several functionaries (chairman, secretary, treasurer, and their substitutes), that decisions were made democratically, and that a mandatory general assembly was held once a year.[186]

---

185 *S.H.*"Satzung für die Provinzialkasse Hannover–Braunschweig für die jüdische Wanderarmenfürsorge".

186 *S.H.*"Satzung für die Provinzialkasse Hannover–Braunschweig für die jüdische Wanderarmenfürsorge".

Every member of the fund sent a representative to the assembly, and it was he who cast a vote on his organization's or community's behalf. Other representatives were also permitted to vote, but only on the condition that their local organization had transferred money to the regional funds (exceeding the amount required). Every additional annual payment of 100 Mark entitled an affiliated organization to send an additional representative – he, too, would cast a vote – to the general assembly. The limit, however, was 10 representatives per organization.[187]

The regulations further stated that the funds' activities would be audited every year, that any change to the regulations required a 75% majority vote, and that the same percentage was necessary if a regional fund wanted to leave the ZJW (on the condition that more than half of the fund's members took part in the vote).[188]

The regional funds were usually responsible for a clearly delineated area, but there were cases in which the funds were subject to nationwide organizations. These funds belonged to one of the *Länder* (states) within Germany. Although Germany had been established as a unified Reich in 1871, large sections of it were nevertheless partially autonomous, e.g., Bavaria, Hessen, and Baden. In these cases, the regional funds were called *Landeskassen* (state funds).

An example of how such a state fund operated can be found in sections 16 and 17 of the Bavaria *Landeskasse* regulations, which determined that all foreign paupers not belonging to one of Bavaria's Jewish communities "had personally arrived at the central fund in

---

187 *S.H.*"Satzung für die Provinzialkasse Hannover–Braunschweig für die jüdische Wanderarmenfürsorge" (Paragraphs 11–12).
188 *S.H.*"Satzung für die Provinzialkasse Hannover–Braunschweig für die jüdische Wanderarmenfürsorge" (Paragraphs 13–15).

order to receive support. These paupers are to receive support only once a year, excepting special cases. Several *Landeskassen* operated within the framework of *Ezra*.[189]

Despite the tendency to centralize activities, the regional funds and *Landeskassen* were still a minority among the funds, the majority of which were welfare funds that operated on the city or town level, allocating charity to those who arrived there. The *Ortsarmenkassen* constituted the smallest link in the *Wanderarmen* support system; originating from the community welfare system, usually from funds for the support of foreign Jewish paupers, the *Ortsarmenkassen* merged into the general charity system after the establishment of the ZJW, albeit keeping their independence. Due to a shortage in the budget for foreign poor, and especially after increases in applications, the local funds were not always able to financially support foreign Jewish paupers. In such cases, the applicants were referred to the regional funds in the area.

The regulations of the Worms welfare fund, where a special fund was established with the purpose of confronting the *Wanderarmen* problem, teach us about the way in which regional funds worked (similar regulations also existed in other place). The fund was part of a communal welfare organization whose aim it was to support local poor and to keep "door-to-door peddlers" away from Jewish homes. Members of the welfare organization were obliged to pay a biannual membership fee; a few members donated additional funds on an individual basis. In order to prevent members from giving charity in the traditional manner (in which money or food was simply handed to the beggar), the regulations required members to send their donations to the fund. Membership in the fund also granted social

---

[189] C.A.J.P, N.1 98/Ansbach, "Entwurf der Satzungen für den Verband jüdischer Hilfsvereine in Bayern, Armenkasse 1896–1914".

prestige, with the fund clearly stating (in its regulations) the order in which its members would appear in the annual report, if at all: Only members who donated more than 150 Mark per year were entitled to be mentioned in the report. The regulations further stipulated how the fund's money was to be invested; how the private funds, which were subordinate to the main fund, were to be managed; and how the money was to be distributed to the poor.[190]

Although Germany was home to many local funds during this period, we know little about them, for the local funds, unlike the regional funds, did not adhere to an organized accounting system. The funds' activities were part of the Jewish communities' continuous welfare work, and most of the data regarding the funds can be found in Jewish community archives. Extant archival material is scarce, however, making it difficult to determine the ratio between local poor (permanent residents of the communities supporting them) and foreign poor (temporary dwellers). In most cases, *Wanderarmen* turned to the regional funds only after the local funds were unable to support them. It can therefore be assumed that the local funds also dealt with *Wanderarmen* (as opposed to local poor).

The reality, of course, was far more complicated. The relationship among the ZJW, the regional funds, and the local funds was not clearly set: For example, in South Germany – especially in Bavaria – the system was not centralized. Accordingly, the division between local and regional funds was not always clear there. As a result, and despite the fact that the Nürnberg-Fürth fund was the most important fund in Bavaria, other funds, like the ones in Ausgsburg

---

190 Dokumentation zur Geschichte der jüdischen Bevölkerung: Die gemeindlichen Juden in ihrem privaten und öffentlichen Leben, vol. 3. Landesarchivverwaltung Rheinland–Pfalz (publisher), 1972. P. 341.

and Ansbach, were also crucial to the success of the welfare system in Bavaria. Regional funds in Germany differed from one another according to their financial standing and geographical location. Although the two frameworks within the Reich (Southern and Northern) shared common principles and organizational structure, it was not until 1914 that they united.

Local, Regional, and Nationwide Organization

Even after the establishment of the ZJW in Berlin, which tried to centralize the response to Jewish *Wanderarmen* in Germany, local organizations continued for the large part to bear the daily burden of dealing with the paupers. These organizations had been founded years before the ZJW, and had already attempted to centralize their activities in the 1870s. The process was gradual: First, a local organization was established to deal with *Wanderarmen* passing through the town, after which a few communities would unite their efforts in order to solve the problem on a wider geographic scope. For example, communities bordering a central city would cooperate and establish a joint organization, acting on behalf of all the communities involved. At a later stage, attempts were made to unite the local organizations into one large regional organization; an example was the central organization of Bavaria, which comprised all of the region's communities. Finally, the ZJW was established.

Although the existing records on regional funds deal with a relatively small number of organizations, there are striking similarities in the findings. For this reason, and working on the assumption that the same patterns also repeated themselves in places

Chapter 8: Regional Activity 179

about which we lack archival information, it is possible to use the existing records. Most of the surviving archival material relates to the funds in Bavaria, where the archives of the local organizations have been preserved, and to larger, independent cities like Hamburg and Bremen. Most of the documentation pertaining to the Kingdom of Prussia, however, has yet to be found.[191]

A number of communities in Bavaria established a charity framework for the poor and for foreign migrants as early as the 1850s, but testimonies regarding beggars in this area predate the establishment of an official framework by many years; as early as 1768, in fact, efforts were made to reduce beggary. In 1791, a man named Yosef Yitzhak of Guggenheim complained that the *Wanderarmen* situation was not any better than it had been during his father's time.[192]

Funds were usually established at the same time as the local welfare system, and only in communities that could bear the financial burden. Bavaria was the first of Germany's states to establish a regional fund that united several communities. The first organization of this kind was established in Fürth-Nürnberg, and it was also the first to publicly declare its intention to support foreign paupers and to fight against door-to-door begging. The organization's *Wanderarmen* report from 1875 describes the events leading up to its foundation:

---

[191] Conversations with scholars working there made it clear that only little material exists there.
[192] The name of Yosef Yitzhak (of) Guggenheim's book is: "Gedanken über Betteljuden und ihrer besseren, zweckmässigeren unmaßgeblichen Versorgung, quoted in: *S.H.*, 9225/123. See also minutes of the DIGB meeting, quoted in: *S.H.*, "Zentralstelle", October 1905.

The growing exploitation of private Jewish charity giving by local and foreign *Wanderarmen*, especially those from Poland, led local communities to establish, in 1861, a support organization for '*Wanderarmen* belonging to our people' [i.e., Jewish *Wanderarmen*]. However, despite all the energy invested, the organization was not able to cope with the bothersome problem of *Wanderarmen* and beggars. Welfare given to *Wanderarmen* was limited to the local level of individual communities, and the welfare system was not known to all of them [i.e., all communities of the region]. Accordingly, the Bamberg organization, led by Mr. Leonard Müller, convened a meeting in 1874 calling on similar organization to establish a central Bavarian organization, in order to act in collaboration against professional Jewish beggars. For this purpose, 60 representatives [of different communities] gathered on May 3, 1874, for a general assembly. The assembly decided to establish an alliance of organizations and authorized Dr. Ortenau of [the city of] Fürth, Dr. Yoseftal and Dr. Mehr of [the city of] Nuremberg to compose the organization's regulations and to apply their 30 years of experience. On December 13, the regulations were ratified at a general assembly led by Dr. Ortenau. The local communities ratified the regulations. [The city of] Munich later announced that, due to its remoteness, it would not be able to join the organization. It was decided that the regional organization would be established in the city of Fürth, and that the community board would ratify this in its assembly. At the same time, the organization called on every community in Bavaria, 250 in number, to join it. Most of the communities did so, excepting Aschaffenburg and the communities in its vicinity. After the establishment of the central office, all [member] communities committed to begin their activities on January 1, 1875. It did not happen. The process of joining the organization advanced sluggishly, as a result of which the organization suffered financial losses.[193]

The first organization was established in 1861, but the document clearly indicates that the communities had by then accumulated 30 years of experience in dealing with the Jewish *Wanderarmen* problem. From this, we can conclude that beggary was a common problem in Jewish settlements already in the 1840s. In February 1875, when additional communities joined the regional organization, the scope of activity grew:

> Thirty five neighboring communities joined the organization and thus enabled us to pay welfare and, in special cases, to grant support that was four times that of previous years. Altogether, the income from 35 communities totals 14,913 Florins and the expenses 13,606. Last year, 1,408 people received support, compared to 1,473 the year before that. In other words, the number of recipients was reduced by 65 people.[194]

The organization's funding depended on members' donations, compound interest, assets, and income from special fundraising activities. In order to achieve a maximal level of centralized organization, and in order to avoid double payments by the same members, other institutions in the Jewish communities – those, that is, that were located in the territory of the regional fund – were prohibited from giving charity to *Wanderarmen*; instead, these *Wanderarmen* were referred to the fund in Fürth. Incorporated into the organization were the Jewish communities of Ansbach, Nuremberg, Beckersdorf, Wilmersdorf, Sulzbach, Neumarkt, and

---

193 C.A.J.P, NE/48, Altenstadt, "Schreibstücke der Fremden und Armen. Jahresbericht des Verbandes bayrischer Vereine zur Unterstuzüng durchreisender Israeliten für das Jahr 1875".
194 C.A.J.P, ALTENSTADT, "Schreibstücke".

Schwabach, as well as those of smaller villages in the vicinity. In 1874, the organization supported 1,461 *Wanderarmen*, a similar number the following year (1,440). In 1892, the number of supported paupers rose to 2,168, who received, together, a sum of 13,881 Mark. Studying a later report from this fund, dated 1913, it becomes clear that Fürth-Nuremberg was an important center for *Wanderarmen*: The report mentioned 3,600 known welfare recipients, but points out that the actual number was much higher. The report's author estimates that an additional 1,000 welfare recipients did not appear in the fund's records, as a result of which they were not registered by the ZJW. The same report estimates that these unreported welfare recipients, also called "embarrassed poor," constituted about 20% of all welfare recipients, and it is not unlikely that the percentage was similar in other areas. In order to avoid exploitation of the fund's resources, the names of welfare recipients were written on cards. Were they to come back to the same place, they were only entitled to one payment per year. In 1913, the fund's cards included the names of 20,000 individuals, (referred to as *durchreisende Arme*, or passing poor).[195]

The records give details on the applicants' origins: In 1874, most of the welfare recipients (35%) came from Austria, especially Galicia, and 34% from Poland. Fifteen percent of the applicants to the fund were *Wanderarmen* of German origins; one year later, in 1875, they were at 40%. Interestingly, two thirds of all welfare applicants were German speakers, which certainly eased the ordeal of wandering and the absorption process.

Data pertaining to 1875 indicate that the funds in Bavaria had already been organized, and that regional funds had been established

---

195 IFB February 21st, 1913.

Chapter 8: Regional Activity

in several large communities: Ansbach, Augsburg, Bamberg, and Würzburg. (The Fürth fund will be dealt with separately.) In 1875, the regional funds of Bavaria supported 5,393 *Wanderarmen*; according to the reports, 81 communities financed the support.

Payments were not made one a one-time basis. The movement of *Wanderarmen* continued year after year, and turned into a common sight for the residents of Jewish communities in which the funds were located. In Augsburg alone, 6,602 Jews were supported between 1875 and 1880 (figures for 1876 are not available). Many adjacent communities referred the welfare seekers to the regional fund, which they helped finance.[196]

In the neighboring city of Ansbach, a similar organization was established in the 1890s, after the problem there worsened:

> In recent years, the problem has significantly worsened. The increased presence of beggars leads to not infrequent confrontations between the paupers and the police, bringing hardship to the members of our community. In order to overcome this, it was decided to establish the organization, and the police was informed about it as well.[197]

During its first years, the fund's activities were smaller in scope than were those of the Fürth-Nuremberg fund: It supported 554 *Wanderarmen*. Local organizations, such as the ones in Ansbach, Augsburg, or Fürth, were the first step towards the unification of regional organizations under larger frameworks. In December 1899, it was decided to establish a central organization for the state of Bavaria. Its [written] principles teach us that the fund based itself on

---

196 The regional fund in Augsburg was financed by the following Jewish communities: Hainstart, Osterberg. Dillingen, Kriegsfaber, Harburg, Buttenwiesen, Binswangen, Altenstadt, Felheim, Hürben, Nördlingen and Ausgburg itself.

197 C.A.J.P, Gemeinde Ansbach, "Armenkasse zur Unterstützung".

existing organizations, and that it included all the Jewish communities of Bavaria. The renewal of joint activities was carried out with the cooperation of regional organizations supporting *Wanderarmen* and foreign Jews. Essentially, these were large welfare organizations that took control over the welfare system for paupers from many communities. The central welfare organization committed itself to caring for every pauper living in its jurisdiction, and to do its utmost in providing the applicants with work and support. Direct support was to be granted only to "embarrassed poor" and to those who were permanently supported by the communities (the "chronically poor"). Those responsible for the fund had to thoroughly check every welfare applicant. If a community was not able to support an applicant for charity, it was required to announce this to the closest larger community. The applicants had to renew their claim for support every year, thus enabling the funds to better supervise a recipient's financial situation. The instructions further determined that support was to be given from a fund in the territory in which the pauper lived permanently or in which he planned to stay. In fact, this was an extension of the principle of "welfare based on dwelling place," only that now the applicant was no longer required to live in a specific city in order to receive welfare, but, rather, was able to live anywhere within the borders of a whole geographic region (the region of the fund's jurisdiction). This enabled more freedom of movement and a faster transition from location to location, as the *Wanderarmen* knew that they could turn to a number of places for help. It was also a novelty in the Bavarian welfare system: As mentioned earlier, the non-Jewish welfare system in Bavaria was still based on the principle of welfare according to dwelling place (which enabled the applicant to receive welfare only in the place in which he was registered as a resident). In contrast, the Jewish fund in Bavaria granted support if this was not the case, as long as the applicant fulfilled the obligations for welfare. For example, support was also granted to someone in need who was not from Bavaria. Thereby, all geographic restrictions on regional funds were lifted, as well as on the main organization.[198]

It was decided that the non-local poor (Germans and foreign Jews) would be entitled to support from the central Bavarian fund once a year, and only if they turned directly to it. In reality, however, the money came from the regional funds. The system made arrangements ahead of time to prevent exploitation by professional beggars, swindlers and *Schnorrer*, and idlers. Support was given either in cash or by providing employment. The funds were required to report all those who acted dishonestly, with the aim of defrauding the funds, to the central branch in Berlin.

The communities of South Germany organized themselves in a similar manner. In Frankfurt am Main, the welfare activities were centered on the Jewish community board, which supervised the activities of 22 charity organizations there. Ten thousand Mark were spent on welfare in 1890.[199] Established in 1882, the *Verein zur Wanderbettelnsbekämpfung* (Society for the Fight against *Wanderarme* begging) was responsible for the support of the poor. However, the organization was not recognized by all community members, as these were divided into two groups: the Orthodox and the "regular."[200] The example of Frankfurt teaches us that the system was not always clearly defined and that it often depended on a local community's structure, which differed according to place. Frankfurt

---

198 C.A.J.P, Gemeinde Ansbach, "Armenkasse zur Unterstützung".
199 AZJ, Nr. 33, 1890.
200 312 community members supported the *Verein*. It gave welfare mainly to German Jews. In 1890, for example, 870 Jews were supported by it, 547 Austrians (mainly from Galicia) and 522 Jews from Russia and Poland. (see: AZJ, No. 48, 1890). In the regulations of the *Verein*, see: C.A.J.P, Frankfurt am M., "Verein zur Bekämpfung des Wanderbettelns".

was known for its wealthy Jewish community, and Jews who passed through the city often took advantage of the opportunities there. In 1898, 871 Jews received charity in Frankfurt; twenty two years later, that number stood at 2,631 (annually) – and two years after that, it stood at 4,000.[201]

There were many differences among the regional funds, and one of the main reasons for this was the distance of each fund from the border. Applicants to funds that were located deep inside the Reich were more dependent on charity than were those who applied to funds near the border, for the former faced a longer journey back to their places of origin and, as a result, larger travel expenses. On the other hand, funds located close to the border (or on the border) suffered from a large influx of welfare seekers, which made the application process difficult there, too. One reason behind the influx of applications was the fact that many *Wanderarmen* arrived at the border in the hopes of finding someone or something – a person or an institution – who would support them. The risks involved in doing so were great, but the records indicate that they were usually worthwhile. In Königsberg, which was located on the border and which served as an important border station for *Wanderarmen*, the charity institutions were crowded with applicants. The welfare services there included education and a shelter for Jewish *Wanderarmen*, the latter of which had 100 beds and, since 1891, accommodated only those Jews who were fleeing Russia.[202] Königsberg was also home to an organization called *Hachnassat Orchim* (Hebrew for hospitality); among its services was a soup kitchen, established in 1899. And it was in Königsberg, too, that a *Bikur Holim* was founded, where needy Jews received medical treatment

---

201 Wilhelm Neumann, *Reform des jüdischen*, 1910, p. 2–3.
202 *Ha–Maggid*, issue 13, 1892.

Chapter 8: Regional Activity   187

from specialists. Regional funds of a different sort were established near the border, from which *Wanderarmen* either left Germany (to a neighboring country, to their home country, or overseas). There, the objective was to prevent overcrowdedness, which would have emphasized the Jewish presence among Gentiles. Funds located at junctions close to port cities were a preferred destination for *Wanderarmen*. The Hannover fund, for example, which was located on the "salt route" (the salt trade passed through its port), led to port cities to which many migrants travelled. In addition, Hannover was located on a central crossroads, between the capital (Berlin) and the industrial cities of the Röhr region. And so, the Hannover fund not only coped with local poor, but also with *Wanderarmen* and with the so-called "returning *Wanderarmen*," i.e., those who asked to return to their countries of origin after wandering through Germany. It was decided that the latter were to receive support only once a year, and that it was preferable to provide welfare seekers with employment rather than with cash. For the purpose of dealing with the wandering poor, the smaller funds in the Hannover region were required to transfer 80% of their local budget to the central fund in Hannover, with the remaining 20% left to the smaller funds' discretion. In 1890, the *Verein zur Wanderbettelnsbekämpfung* spent 5,054 Mark on welfare.

Although the number of welfare organizations operating within Jewish communities rose during the 1890s, they were not able to cope with the demand for welfare. Annual income reports testify to the fact that the communities' resources were not sufficient to meet the increasing needs of the *Wanderarmen* population. Despite the growing demand for charity, the number of individual donors to welfare causes was small (when compared to the number of organizations). The decentralization led to inefficiency; often, organizations only existed in order to glorify the names of their chairmen. As a result, Jewish communities – like the one in Hannover, for example – preferred to change the support system and to remove *Wanderarmen* from their cities. The burden, however, did not diminish. In Hanover, 20% (5,000 Mark) of the funds spent on charity in 1901 were spent on *Wanderarmen*. All activities connected to the support of *Wanderarmen* were carried out in coordination with local police and the city's train stations. At the city's main train station, the organization placed signs on which directions to the fund were printed. According to one source, support was given mainly to young people:

> To our delight, we provided employment for Jewish laborers and merchants who had been in distress before, and who, in the end, reached the reception station in deep economic distress. We took care of them, supervised their steps, and succeeded in providing some of them with safe positions and satisfying income.[203]

---

203 *S.H.,* "Zentralstelle", No. 343–346.

Chapter 9:

The Establishment of Jewish Worker Colonies

The economic boom of the 1860s and early 1870s increased the demand for laborers and triggered the movement of the lower classes from the periphery to the cities and economic centers. In times of economic crisis, members of these classes were the first to suffer. Lacking an effective welfare system, they were forced to move from place to place, looking for sources of income. In 1880, for example, approximately half a million people in Germany were *Wanderarmen*.[204]

In 1842, Germany implemented the "residential principle" as a basis for receiving welfare. This principle determined that an applicant could receive welfare anywhere, but on the condition that he had lived in the place for a specified amount of time (usually, between one and two years). This made it difficult for the needy to receive welfare, as they were not able to turn to a public welfare institution unless they had stayed for an extended period in the town or city in which the institution was located.[205] Worse, *Wanderarmen* moving from place to place without the ability to provide for themselves could expect imprisonment or isolation in poor houses.[206]

Hans Rosenberg, who studied the economic depression of 1873-1879, wrote that during times of crisis, the strength of society can be measured by its ability to operate independent support systems.[207] During the period discussed in this book, 1860-1914, the welfare system in Germany was active without any involvement of the German state. Rather, it was private institutions, churches, and communal institutions that acted as welfare organizations, independently and subject only to their own guidelines. Jewish

---

204 Jürgen Kuczynski, Geschichte der Lage der Arbeiter in Deutschland von 1800 bis in die Gegenwart, volume III, Berlin 1947, p. 265.
205 This principle was turned into law in December of 1842, a law called *Unterstützungswohnsitzgesetzgebung* [support residence legislation]. The minimal stay for a person to be eligible for welfare was determined by this law.
206 *S.H.*, „Anweisung für die Provinzial–bzw. Landeskasse". Paragraph 5.
207 Hans Rosenberg, *Große Depression und Bismarckzeit*, Berlin, 1968, p. 65.

Chapter 9: The Establishment of Jewish Worker Colonies

institutions played a significant role here.[208] It is, accordingly, interesting to look for differences among various social groups by studying their welfare organizations. In my opinion, the sources of thousands of Jewish welfare organizations in Germany and the extensive archival material on the subject add a new dimension to the study of Jewish-German society.

Generally speaking, the welfare system has always operated within the bounds of limited resources, needing to determine its principles according to the available resources and to define eligibility for welfare. This allocation is based on moral principles as well as the political, economic, and social interests of the society

---

208 The welfare system in Germany has become an important research topic in the last few years and decades. However, the different ways in which welfare organizations were structured requires further research. For example, the status of communal welfare organizations is still not clear: How were they financed? Were the conditions for receiving public welfare implemented by them? Before the end of WWI, a few important works were written on the German welfare system. Here is a partial list:

C.J. Klumker, *Fürsorgewesen, Einführung in das Verständnis der Armut und Armenpflege*, Leipzig, 1918; Emil Münsterberg, *Zentralstelle für Armenpflege und Wohltätigkeit*, Jena, 1897; V. Böhmert, *Das Armenwesen in 77 deutschen Städten*, Dreseden 1886; Emil Münsterberg, *Die Armenpflege*, Berlin 1897. Only in the 1960s did this topic again begin to interest scholars, as it became part of the new discipline of social history. Additional works have been published, but an integral body of research on the German welfare system and its relationship to the development of German economy and industrialization has yet to be published. Here is a partial list of modern research:

F. Tennstedt, Sozialgeschichte der Sozialpolitik in Deutschland, Göttingen, 1981; C. Sachße, F. Tennstedt, Geschichte der Armenfürsorge in Deutschland, Stuttgart, 1980; W. Abel, Massenarmut und Hungerkrisen im vorindustriellen Europa, Hamburg, 1975; C. Jantke, D. Hilger (eds.), Die Eigentumslosen, Freiburg, 1958; C. Jantke, Der Vierte Stand, Freiburg, 1955.

financing the welfare system. In this context, European history has demonstrated that a conflict of interest exists between the reasons for which welfare reforms come into being and the interests of the people financing them. Good examples of this are the English Poor Laws and the social reforms of the 19th century, both in England and in the Germany of Otto von Bismarck.[209]

The sources relating to these welfare reforms also relate to the Jewish communities and to the relationship between welfare givers and welfare recipients. The following discussion – in particular, the comparison of the solutions offered by the Jewish welfare organizations to those of the non-Jewish, German organizations – will demonstrate how the welfare system can aid us in analyzing socio-historical aspects of the period.

The Jewish Worker Colony in Berlin-Weißensee

In 1899, the Organization of Jewish Communities in Germany held a meeting in order to discuss solutions to the *Wanderarmen*

---

[209] Many historians claim, for example, that Bismarck's motives regarding social legislation derived mainly from his fight against the Social Democrats. According to this view, Bismarck tried, through insurance legislation, to turn workers into allowance–recipients from the state, thus weakening their struggle. For an analysis of Bismarck's social policy see here:

Hans–Ulrich Wehler, *Bismarck und der Imperialismus*, Köln & Berlin, 1969, p. 459–464; Hans Rothfels, *Bismarck – Vorträge und Abhandlungen*, Stuttgart, 1970, p. 166–181; Hans Rothfels, *Bismarck, der Osten und das Reich*, Darmstadt, 1960, p. 165–181; Hans Rothfels, "Bismarck's Social Policy and the Problem of State Socialism in Germany, in: *Socio*, 1938, pp. 81–94. 288–302; Karl–Erich Born, *Staat und Sozialpolitik seit Bismarcks Sturz, 1890–1914*, Wiesbaden, 1957, p. 20–32; Hans Rosenberg, *Große Depression und Bismarckzeit*, p. 210–227.

problem. They decided to establish a Jewish worker colony in Weißensee, a neighborhood of Berlin.[210]

A Jewish donor named Meier donated a plot of land for this purpose. The expenses were covered by the Association of Pittsburgh Jews (an American organization). In September of 1902, a colony was established under the name *Jüdische Arbeiterkolonie Weißensee* (Jewish worker colony of Weißensee). Its regulations stated as its objective the reduction of the *Wanderarmen* phenomenon and the improvement of Jewish morals and economic standing. It was further determined that unemployed Jews who were fit for work would be accepted to the colony, and that the colony would also provide temporary shelter to Jews who were not German citizens, the latter of whom passed through, rather than stayed, in Germany.[211]

The establishment of the colony was a novelty in many ways: Until then, welfare solutions had been divided into "closed welfare," which was given to people through organizational frameworks (like shelters for the needy and orphanages), and "open welfare," whereby the welfare recipient returned home after receiving support (as was the case with community poverty committees, welfare organizations, and funds). It should be mentioned here that the Jewish communities of Germany usually adopted the "open welfare" system, and that their reforms preceded those of non-Jewish Germany.

The "residential principle" as implemented by the UWG (*Unterstützungswohnsitzgesetzgebung*, i.e., support residence legislation) is a good example here: According to it one was entitled to charity only after living in the town or city in which the respective

---

210 Jakob Segall, „Arbeiter–Kolonie, Brockensammlung, Arbeitsnachweis, Darlehensvereine", in: *ZDSJ*, 1914, Heft 2, p. 61.
211 Ibid., p. 61.

welfare fund was located. Jewish communities acted differently from non-Jewish communities in that they saw themselves responsible for all Jews dwelling in their midst, notwithstanding how long they had been living there. Therefore, the "residential principle" was never implemented in the Jewish communities of Germany.[212]

The first innovation of the Weißensee worker colony was to bring Jews who were fit for work to a "closed" institution that had previously housed only chronic welfare cases and people who were unfit for work. Another novelty was the educational idea to change the life habits of *Wanderarmen*. Weißensee also trained its inhabitants in manufacturing professions, provided employment, and helped "graduates" find work after the completion of training. The colony was the first institution to temporarily remove problematic individuals from the Jewish communities and to send them to a place in which they would be supervised by local Jews. As a result, the communities' burden of caring for the *Wanderarmen*, which they had shouldered despite their obligations towards the local poor (permanent community members), was alleviated significantly.

Providing professional training for the needy marked a turning point in the local Jewish attitude towards *Wanderarmen*. This turning point occurred in the 1890s, when it was recognized that the *Wanderarmen* problem stemmed not from political reasons, but from economic crisis and unemployment. In his suggested reform in the way in which communities dealt with *Wanderarmen*, Wilhelm Neumann expressed this change in attitude: "The reason behind the existence of *Wanderarmen* and beggars is not political persecution

---

[212] For a detailed analysis of the Jewish welfare system and its relation to the overall German welfare system see: A. Bornstein, *Mi–Kabtzanim le–Dorshei Avodah* (from beggars to employment seekers), published in Hebrew only. p. 180–231.

Chapter 9: The Establishment of Jewish Worker Colonies 195

but, rather, economic."[213] Later on, welfare organizations and the people connected to them considered both the economic and the political realities of Jews fleeing from Eastern Europe: The economic hardship we are experiencing in trade and economy is forcing thousands to migrate from Russia, Galicia, and from the countries of the Balkans. These countries are not particularly friendly to us Jews. Hundreds of families return to us also from England, France, and America, after they have been left destitute. In these cases, it is impossible to castigate these 'air people' who just 'walk the earth' [sic.]. Talk of this kind and the shrugging of shoulders will not solve their problems. Nobody hastily leaves the city of his birth to find his luck in a different country.[214]

Different reasons motivated the Jewish communities of Germany to establish welfare institutions for *Wanderarmen*, some of which are connected to the Jewish welfare tradition as it had developed in Germany throughout the 19th century and before, and some of which stem from the unique nature of Germany's Jewish welfare system. Not infrequently, action taken on behalf of the beggars was rooted in the self-interest of the communities, which, as mentioned earlier, were often frightened by the arrival of foreign Jews. The solutions provided by the communities were guided by two main approaches: One was the integration of Jewish *Wanderarmen* into Germany, whether into the Jewish community they had turned to or into another, in which case the *Wanderarmen* received temporary aid with the purpose of easing the absorption into new surroundings; the second approach aimed to remove the *Wanderarmen* from the

---

213 Wilhelm Neumann, *Reform des jüdischen*, p. 3 (Wilhelm Neumann was one of the leaders in the Central Organization for the Support of Jewish *Wanderarme* in Germany, founded in October, 1910).
214 "Herberge für jüdische Durchreisende", *A.J.Z.*, January 23rd, 1914.

Jewish communities, resulting in stricter standards for giving welfare and the establishment of institutions whose objective it was to help *Wanderarmen* leave Germany. In some cases, both approaches were taken simultaneously, and the motive for giving welfare is not clear: Many local poverty funds, for example, provided temporary support for *Wanderarmen*, and it is difficult to determine if the motivation was to ease the applicants' absorption or to quickly remove them from the communities in which the funds were located.

The homeless shelter in Hamburg, named after Daniel Worms, expressed the same ambiguity regarding absorption and rejection, as did the workers' colonies: The Weißensee colony's yearly report for 1903 tells us that 324 people arrived at the colony during its first year of existence. The colony housed 60 people at the beginning of the year, and 128 by year's end. Since its establishment, 512 Jews had stayed there, 441 of whom were released in order to live independent lives. According to the report, those released had since been absorbed into society:

> [...] some because they returned to their families and others because they found employment through our efforts. Some of those released managed to find work without our help, and yet others were employed by entrepreneurs and contractors connected to the colony.[215]

The annual report for 1904 describes the process of joining the colony:

> When we leave our office, we witness a scene that repeats itself on a daily basis: Two young men applying to be accepted to the colony. One of them, like 80% of the residents of this colony, was

---

[215] *C.A.J.P*, TD–394, "Berlin–Weißensee–Jüdische Arbeiterkolonie und Asyl bei Berlin, über das Geschäftsjahr 1904–1005", p. 7–9.

Chapter 9: The Establishment of Jewish Worker Colonies 197

sent by the poverty committee of the Jewish community. Others arrive with a recommendation, issued by previous residents. The new candidates exhibit the traits of wandering and homelessness. They are scantily clad, and their faces express desperation, worry, and distress. Their bodies, too, show the signs of a life of poverty. Had they not been in possession of a certificate from the local doctor, which testified to their health, we would have assumed that these men were ill. The doctor's reports confirm that the young men are in good health and that their frail appearance is due only to their [economic] hardship. After only a few days, the young men show almost miraculous signs [of recovery]. After the applicants' documents are examined and shown to be impeccable, and after the applicants sign a commitment to behave according to the rules of the place, they are informed of the good news that they have been accepted. A ray of happiness lights up in their eyes. This will be the first day the *Wanderarmen* will have a roof above their heads after a long period of wandering.[216]

The new members of the colony and their belongings were then thoroughly disinfected, so as to keep the hygiene of the colony. The report described this procedure as follows:

> Before [the new residents were accepted to the place], they must enjoy an additional pleasure: a bath. The new residents are brought to the basement, where the shower room and bath are located. While the body is thoroughly cleaned [after one bath], in most cases the clothing needs additional disinfection after the first cleaning. The undergarments, in particular, often need to be thrown away and replaced with new ones.[217]

---

216 Berlin–Weißensee (1903–1904), p. 8.
217 Ibid., p. 9.

This abrupt transition, from wandering to a clearly defined framework with strict rules, was difficult and raised problems of adjustment. In order to introduce the residents to the new framework, the colony emphasized discipline and a uniform code of conduct. A report from 1905 mentions the changes noticed among the residents:

> It is difficult for them [the new residents] to manage to stay clean and to behave according to certain rules. And yet, as they have meanwhile recognized the importance of the rules and their advantages, they [the residents] change beyond recognition. At the workshop they are diligent. Especially during days of rest, it is impossible to recognize them: They dress in nice clothes and look decent and neat. The metamorphosis of their appearance has then been completed, so much so that visitors to the place express their amazement at the fact that these men were once known to them as corrupt beggars.[218]

Out of fear of the cholera epidemic, which had been a serious public health problem since the 1820s, the German authorities implemented a number of measures: Monitoring centers were established, and it was even common, at the beginning of the 20th century, to stop trains coming into Germany from abroad and to check whether any of the passengers were infected. Such a center was established at the Berlin-Ruheleben train station, and foreign Jews who did not possess medical documents proving their health were not allowed to enter Germany. The fear of cholera was also prevalent among the management of the Weißensee colony, as a result of which newcomers and their belongings were thoroughly disinfected. The annual report for 1903 describes this as follows:

---

218 For the 1905 annual report of the worker colony at Berlin–Weißensee, see: *Mitteilungen des D.I.G.B.*, October 1905.

Chapter 9: The Establishment of Jewish Worker Colonies

In the same way that a house shall be clean and aired out, so shall its inhabitants. For many of the people [here] it is not easy to sit in a bathtub and to thoroughly scrub themselves for the first time. Many are still afraid of the water and are not able to appreciate the importance of a hot bath and shower. Once a week, a bath is organized for all the residents, in which neither water nor soap is spared. Every resident regularly receives undergarments, clean bedclothes, and towels. [We] insist that every person treats his clothes as he treats his body.[219]

Among the important functions of this institution was to provide its residents with medical services and a high standard of sanitation and cleanliness. An on-site doctor examined the applicants prior to their being accepted to the colony, and he was also responsible for supervising their health. Furthermore, a strict system of rules and regulations enforced the residents' cleanliness. According to records for 1904/05, the colony continued to supervise the cleanliness of its residents:

The residents' hygiene was checked, and their clothes were regularly disinfected. The health situation was good. The disinfection of clothes, the medical check-ups, the insistence on hygiene standards and on regular showering and bathing led to positive results.[220]

The main objective of the medical check-ups was to detect infectious diseases among the applicants, especially sexually transmitted diseases, which were during this period difficult to heal. The routine was described as follows by a doctor:

Once a month, I conducted a medical check-up, in order to find infectious diseases and in order to check general health. The

---
219 Berlin–Weißensee, (1904–1905), p. 18.
220 Berlin–Weißensee, (1904–1905), p. 15.

residents are cooperative regarding the check-up, as it enables them to complain about their medical problems. It is possible to clearly state that the residents, who had arrived here starved and miserable, are improving quickly. Already after a few weeks they look healthy and fresh.[221]

Regarding infectious diseases, the doctor added the following:

Infectious diseases were rare last year. The last influenza [outbreak], which turned into an epidemic, only affected a few residents. After a few days of rest in bed, the situation of most of the sick improved. We also did not experience diseases affecting the intestines and the digestive system, despite the intense heat.[222]

In the framework of its regular activities, the colony also provided medical services:

We saw to it that a sick room was installed on the second floor of the worker colony. There, we concentrated sick people who needed to be quarantined. In this room we also isolated those suffering from respiratory infections. More serious cases were transferred to a Jewish hospital. When we detected diseases like tuberculosis, serious heart conditions, and especially skin and sexual diseases, we tried to prevent the admission [of those diagnosed with them] to the colony. In such cases, applicants were only admitted after meticulous medical examinations.[223]

The 68 cases dealt with by the colony's doctor included a variety of medical conditions, but a few of the patients only pretended to be sick. The doctor wrote the following comments in his medical file: "I would like to point out that many (perhaps out of fear of work)

---

221 *Berlin–Weißensee*, (1904–1905), p. 19.
222 *Berlin–Weißensee*, (1904–1905), p. 15.
223 *Berlin–Weißensee*, (1904–1905), p. 16.

Chapter 9: The Establishment of Jewish Worker Colonies 201

complained about illnesses they did not have. Each complaint, however, was checked thoroughly."[224]

Serious efforts were invested in providing nutritious foods and in educating the residents in table manners: The food was tasty and various, leaving the residents satiated after every meal. One has to observe the faces of the people eating their lunches: It is possible to discern how satisfied they are with the food, and how they finish their plates with satisfaction and serenity, and how quiet the place becomes. The gentleness with which people bring the spoons to their mouths is noticeable. Every person knows that the moment the first pot of food is emptied, he will receive a second serving, until he is completely sated.[225]

The following account describes the menu at the Berlin-Weißensee colony:

> Lunch consists of a large serving of vegetables, served with meat and potatoes. Every serving of meat weighs 125 grams. The vegetables are lettuce, cabbage, green beans, and peas. Then there are fruits such as plums, plum compote, and sometimes-even peaches. There are also grits and rice. Meat is served once a day for lunch, and

---

[224] In 1904, the check–ups continued. 220 cases of illness were diagnosed, out of which the following were released from the colony: three people suffering from syphilis, one suffering from gonorrhea, one suffering from nerve weakness, one suffering from a serious eye disease, and three suffering from an illness of the digestive system. The statistics from 1903, regarding common diseases at the worker colony, mentioned the following: 16 injuries, fractures and muscle ailments, eight suffering from stomach and intestinal illnesses, three suffering from rheumatism, eight from respiratory ailments, one from heart disease, four from tuberculosis, five from the flu, one from arthritis, six from eye illnesses, six from throat and nerve pains, and two from blood circulation issues and weakness. See: *Berlin–Weißensee*, (1904–1905), p. 19.

[225] *Berlin–Weißensee*, (1904–1905), p. 15.

on Fridays for supper. On other days, supper consists of cheese or sausage, herring and tea, or hot potato soup, with a side dish of fish and whole grain bread.[226]

In order to improve the health of the residents, it was decided that the worker colony would join the *Bar Kochba* sports club. In June 1903, the colony registered its residents there, giving them the opportunity to practice athletics and ball games. The following was said about the sports activities: Excepting complaints about unnecessary conversations during practice, the discipline was, considering the fact that many of these people had never before participated in physical activity, good.[227]

Training took place every Sunday from 10 to 12 a.m. at the facilities of *Bar Kochba*: "Training starts with exercise drills. Then there are group games in which the groups are switched so as to keep the activities interesting for the participants."[228]

Number of Residents at the Jewish Worker Colony in Berlin-Weißensee

From 1902 until 1913, 6,689 people stayed at the Jewish worker colony in Berlin-Weißensee. The number of new members grew constantly, reaching its peak in 1913, when 914 people were accepted to the colony, i.e., 208 more than in the previous year. This is not surprising when one considers that 1913 was a year of deep economic crisis and, as a result, rising unemployment and widespread internal migration. In general, however, the number of residents did not fluctuate much, and stayed at approximately 80 residents per year. In 1909, the colony was able to accommodate 96 residents (the same number as in 1911 and in 1913). As the number

---

226 *Berlin–Weißensee*, (1904–1905), p. 15–16.
227 *Berlin–Weißensee*, (1904–1905), p. 20.
228 *Berlin–Weißensee*, (1903–1904), p. 20.

Chapter 9: The Establishment of Jewish Worker Colonies

of applicants rose, so did the total number of work days put in by the residents. The available data enable us to calculate a resident's average stay at the colony, which dropped by one third between 1902 (when the colony first opened its doors) and 1913. While the average stay in 1902 was 79 days, in 1913 it was 29.

Table 7: Number of Residents at the Worker Colony in Berlin-Weißensee[229]

Year	Number on January 1st	Accepted during the year	Left during the year	Peak number	Total	Average Stay
1902	0	188	138	60	10,224	79.87
1903	60	328	313	82	10,003	79.87
1904	71	419	400	90	26,450	66.10
1905	90	453	459	90	28,129	66.28
1906	84	535	529	92	29,614	55.97
1907	90	594	596	91	26,112	43.81
1908	88	635	633	93	30,678	48.45
1909	90	727	727	96	30,801	42.36
1910	90	635	635	94	29,640	46.67
1911	90	659	661	96	27,014	40.86
1912	88	696	706	81	25,368	35.92
1913	78	914	902	96	25,634	29.41

The reduced duration of stay suggests that the colony's resources were limited, as was its ability to host paupers for extended periods.

---

[229] The peak number indicates the largest numbers of residents in the colony during a year's period. The last column of the table expresses the numbers of days a *Wanderarme* stayed at the colony, from his entrance day to the day he left.

A long stay at the colony was an advantage, for it enabled residents to save money (earned from salaries) for the future, when they would leave the colony and fend for themselves; another advantage was the extensive professional training they received at the colony, which made it easier to find employment. It is possible that the average duration of stay dropped as a result of improved economic conditions and the growth in the German economy between the start of the 20th century and the outbreak of WWI. New sources of employment enabled the colony's residents to shorten their stay, and because the sources do not indicate that the declining average stay was the result of policy instituted by the colony's leadership, we can assume that the process was initiated by the residents, and that it was the result of the period's changing economic circumstances.

Age Demographics at the Colony

The age structure of the colony's residents was almost identical throughout the years: Half of them were between 16 and 23 years old, one third were between 24 and 30 years old, and the remaining 20% were between 30 and 55 years old. On average, they were younger than those registering at the poor funds for *Wanderarmen*. This fact can be explained by the desire of young people to acquire professional skills or to save money. Furthermore, unlike the people applying to *Wanderarmen* funds, the members of the colony were physically fit and able to work.

Most of the colony's residents came from countries outside Germany. The number of German-born Jews was 20%. In Weißensee, the largest group came from the countries of the Austro-Hungarian Empire, notably Galicia; the second largest group came from Russia, as emigration from that country was particularly intense between

1904 and 1907, when Jews were relentlessly persecuted there and the next largest group came from Romania.

The distribution of countries of origin, especially the large percentage of Jews who came from Austria-Hungary, is puzzling, but considering the fact that Galician Jews constituted a large percentage of the *Wanderarmen*, their considerable representation among the colony's residents makes sense. Another explanation for the ethnic division is the fact that *Wanderarmen* of the same background often moved from place to place together.

Table 8: Distribution of the Weißensee Colony Residents According to Country of Origin[230]

Year	Germany	Austria	Galicia	Hungary	Russia	Romania	Other
1902	12 (10.2%)	12 (10.2%)	20 (16.9%)	9 (7.7%)	4 (3.3%)	1 (0.9%)	60 (50.8%)
1903	12 (8.5%)	14 (10.0%)	15 (10.6%)	17 (12.0%)	10 (7.1%)	2 (1.4%)	71 (50.4%)
1904	61 (7.7%)	75 (9,5%)	91 (11.6%)	41 (5.2%)	118 (14.9%)	5 (0.6%)	400 (50.5%)
1905	93 (10.3%)	59 (6.5%)	114 (12.8%)	71 (7.9%)	101 (11.2%)	5 (0.5%)	459 (50.8%)
1906	102 (8.4%)	109 (8.9%)	197 (16.1%)	71 (5.7%)	119 (9.7%)	8 (0.6%)	619 (50.6%)
1907	124 (9.1%)	91 (6.7%)	270 (20.1%)	92 (6.8%)	83 (6.1%)	10 (0.7%)	684 (50.5%)

---

230 The people marked as "others" were either of unknown origins, or from relatively small places. See: Jakob Segall, "Arbeiter–Kolonie", p. 3.

Year	Germany	Austria	Galicia	Hungary	Russia	Romania	Other
1908	163 (11.3%)	108 (7.5%)	274 (19.1%)	63 (4.4%)	75 (5.2%)	22 (1.6%)	732 (50.9%)
1909	145 (10.2%)	113 (7.9%)	288 (20.2%)	79 (5.5%)	56 (3.9%)	18 (1.3%)	727 (50.0%)
1911	133 (10.4%)	78 (6.2%)	252 (19.7%)	68 (5.3%)	65 (5.1%)	19 (1.5%)	661 (51.8%)
1912	170 (12.2%)	121 (8.7%)	227 (16.3%)	89 (6.4%)	63 (4.5%)	17 (1.2%)	706 (50.6%)

Unlike the *Wanderarmen* support funds, the worker colony consisted mainly of laborers and craftsman; members of these two groups constituted, on average, 35% of all residents. As a result of the fact that those who joined the colony were interested in earning a living, and not just in learning a new profession, craftsmen became the most dominant group. The second largest group was that of merchants and of those working in trade as salaried employees. Among the craftsmen, the tailors were the largest subgroup, followed by blacksmiths, carpenters, bakers, painters, slaughterers, fur producers, and plumbers.

Funding of the Colony

Although the worker colony was managed like a commercial enterprise, its core principle was the desire to find a solution to a social issue. Examining the colony's balance sheet, we discover that the colony suffered financial losses over the years, losses that undoubtedly led to its eventual shutting down.

Chapter 9: The Establishment of Jewish Worker Colonies

Between 1903 and 1913, the annual income of the colony was, on average, approximately 7,000 Mark, while the expenses totaled approximately 14,000 Mark. The resulting deficit was covered by one-time donations of individuals who regarded the colony as a philanthropic institution, and who donated in order to benefit those staying there, as well as by donations from organizations that participated in the colony's financing efforts.

The residents of the worker colony received a salary for their labor, which was raised gradually and reached a combined sum of 10,000 Mark per year. The colony also generated income by selling its products and services, thus enabling it to pay its workers for their labor.

Table 9: Income and Expenses of the Weißensee colony[231]

Year	Income	Expenses	Deficit	Workers' Salaries
1903	23,330	23,474	144	816
1904	25,531	26,182	551	1,211
1905	22,303	29,676	4,975	8,630
1906	28,379	32,888	4,507	13,780
1907	27,130	32,968	4,937	11,841
1908	34,576	37,192	2,616	12,066
1909	33,149	38,975	5,825	13,000
1910	33,595	36,853	3,538	13,892
1911	29,079	36,192	7,112	12,678
1912	30,025	38,006	7,680	13,172
1913	30,803	37,045	6,242	8,218

---

231 Jakob Segall, "Arbeiter–Kolonie", p. 23.

Towards the Expected Change

The term "productiveness in the making," i.e., preparation of the residents for manufacturing jobs, does not express in full the colony's intentions. Records of the Weißensee colony's activities show that, in addition to providing professional training, the colony also acted as a mechanism that contributed to the socialization of the lower classes, an example of which we find in the following account, written by a visitor to the colony:

We quickly made our way to the first and second floors of the central building, where one finds large and pleasant sleeping rooms, with windows overlooking a delightful view…However, the most important reason for our visit was to see the people work. When we crossed the well-kept courtyard, we turned left for a pavilion-shaped building. As soon as we entered, we understood that we were in a busy factory. As a matter of fact, this is a production facility for umbrellas and walking sticks, operated by "Schmerling Bertha and Co." This is the most important manufacturing branch of the colony. Of the residents, 45 workers are employed here in a wide range of tasks. We carefully observed the people's faces, rather than their hands. These dedicated workers, who work at a fast pace, are not the same beggars we had known so well! We were tempted to believe that this was an illusion.[232]

The colony's leadership and this becomes clear after studying the records of activities treated *Wanderarmen*, in particular those who were not German citizens, in an arrogant manner; this in spite of the fact that the colony's German-born residents constituted only about 25% of the total number of residents. The arrogant attitude is

---

232 *Berlin–Weißensee*, (1903–1904), p. 10.

Chapter 9: The Establishment of Jewish Worker Colonies

reflected in the colony's reports, in which it is stated that the colony's objective is not only to solve the unemployment problem or to alleviate economic hardship, but also to turn the *Wanderarmen* into "cultured beings," which would facilitate the process of assimilating German customs after leaving the colony. Such treatment was conspicuous during the entire period, with local Jewish organizations often treating *Wanderarmen* in a condescending manner. Those in charge of the colony expressed wonder at the noticeable changes in the residents, who became diligent, disciplined, organized, and clean. One of the records expressed wonder at the residents' increasing tendency to use writing paper, noting that the residents use their own pocket money to buy the writing paper and stamps, and that it is customary for them to send one another letters: "This is an important contribution to the residents' spiritual life."[233]

It is possible to find, in each of the colony's annual reports, proof that its leadership stressed the importance of changing the character and habits of the residents. Local German Jewry regarded the *Wanderarmen* with suspicion, fearing that the failure to change the foreigners' negative habits would eventually harm local Jews. The fear that the colony would not be able to change the residents' negative habits is evident in the annual reports. The authors of the 1905 report, for example, pointed out the residents' diligence while at the same time expressing concern that the colony's efforts might have been in vain, as some of the *Wanderarmen* were not educable.

There is a good atmosphere in the worker colony. Each member is in high spirits and fulfills his duties with diligence. With others, indolence rules, due to prior habits. These people, unlike the first group, cannot get used to order and discipline. Finally, there are

---

[233] Annual report of Berlin–Weißensee for the year 1905. See: *Mitteilungen des D.I.G.B.*, October 1905.

those in whom the nature of vagabonding has been deeply engraved, and they are unable to find serenity in their work. These [people] are to be treated with calm and patience. Sometimes it is even possible to attain favorable results.[234]

The social life of young Jewish men in the colony was supervised by the management. Once a week, lectures were delivered on secular subjects. After the meal, the residents gathered in the dining hall for social activities:

> After dinner, calm descends on the place. In one corner, people smoke (too much, unfortunately); others try to learn how to read and write German; and still others play cards. Some are interested in newspapers. Afterwards, all sing patriotic folk songs, loudly and with great musical understanding.[235]

The worker colony at Berlin-Weißensee was a two-story structure, housing residential rooms, a yard, a synagogue, and a number of workshops in which the residents worked, learned a profession, and received a minimum wage. The residents were employed in a few manufacturing branches located within the colony, in special halls used as workshops. Visitors described the manufacturing activities of the colony as follows:

> One group sits in the divided hall, behind gas burners with which they bend walking sticks and umbrellas. Another group whets the sticks, and yet another group deals with finish, decoration, and with gluing the parts together. At a different department, people work next to drills. Each is given the opportunity to familiarize himself with all the departments and different manufacturing activities. The fast learners earn a living as subcontractors. As the

---

234 *Berlin–Weißensee*, (1904–1905), pp. 16–18.
235 *Berlin–Weißensee*, (1904–1905), pp. 15–16.

Chapter 9: The Establishment of Jewish Worker Colonies 211

manufacturing hall is not large enough for the 45 workers, some of the manufacturing work was moved to the adjacent rooms, where three additional industrial activities of the colony take place: basket weaving (15 men were employed there, manufacturing shopping baskets and bucket handles), the manufacturing of pants hangers, and the sewing and selecting of clothing items made of fur or sheer fabric, or children's clothes (10 people). These jobs will give the people a chance to become integrated as independent workers in worthwhile professions.[236]

As a Jewish institution, the colony insisted on keeping a traditional Jewish character and on following the rules of Jewish religious law in matters pertaining to food and prayer. The report elaborates on this:

> It is already 7 p.m., and the diligent workers have finished their work and are now preparing for *Arvit* [the evening prayer]. We accompany them to the modest but respectable rooms of the synagogue, located in the area of the main building. Here, 70-80 people are present; among them those who have recently been admitted to the colony and are already looking like new people. Never was there a shortage of Jews for prayer services [i.e. for a Jewish prayer forum of 10 men]. On Shabbat and Jewish holidays, Mr. Goldman, otherwise employed at the Jewish cemetery, delivers thought-provoking sermons to the audience. The [daily] morning and evening prayers also provide a structure for the work life, enabling us to work and to observe the Jewish holidays.[237]

Together with its efforts to maintain a traditional Jewish identity, the colony also tried to enhance the German identity of the residents

---

236 *Berlin–Weißensee*, (1904–1905), p. 10.
237 *Berlin–Weißensee*, (1904–1905), p. 12.

and to introduce them to German habits. It is difficult to determine how this was received by the residents, and whether their stay there met their expectations. It is, however, clear that the socialization process had its difficulties. These difficulties were hinted at, not without irony, by a visitor to the colony in 1905. After the visiting group had completed the tour, it was delayed at the dining room:

> Also in the dining room, decorated with pictures of the emperor and his wife, German habits rule. In order to emphasize this, the supervisor asks the colony's residents to sing German folk songs for the guests after dinner. The song 'I Want to Return to My Homeland' was sung loudly at the top of 80 lungs.[238]

The Weißensee colony had a number of objectives, and it is difficult to determine if it succeeded in achieving all of them, just as it is difficult to determine its role in providing solutions to the *Wanderarmen* problem. Some of the residents learned a profession, saved money, were referred to jobs, and went on to live independent lives. The report states the following about former residents of the colony:

> We completed our visit to the Jewish worker colony with the feeling that this place is bustling with activity, of residents and of management. There is hope that people will return to normal lives, and that they will take with them not just the skills acquired here, but also the good spirits they absorbed in this oasis. As for the worker colony we hope that it will continue to flourish and develop.[239]

Another statement has this to say about the graduates of the colony:

---

238 *Berlin–Weißensee*, (1904–1905), p. 12.
239 *Berlin–Weißensee*, (1904–1905), p. 14.

We are proud that many of the graduates are professionals who will be able to make an independent income. Not everyone, however, can fight the urge to return to a life of begging and bad deeds. We were told that those released were given work in Germany, and that those who had left its borders were given work abroad. Sometimes, we receive requests for manpower, and we try to supply it. Of the 263 [residents] of the worker colony [for that year], 190 left it after a short stay. We release the people, give them our blessing, and even try to find out what happened to them and whether or not they returned to their old ways [i.e., turned to poor funds to receive welfare]. Therefore, we ask the different institutions to report to us, through the blacklists, on graduates of the colony who applied for support afterwards.[240]

Others criticized the colony, arguing that it lacked efficiency and failed to achieve its objectives.[241] One of the declared aims of the colony was to serve as a professional career center, directing its graduates to work places. Examining the records, however, we discover that only a minority of those who left the colony did so because they had been referred to a job. Furthermore, the number of jobs offered to the colony's residents dwindled each year: While in 1904 and 1905 the colony was able to refer 42% of those who left to places of work, it was able to do so for only 37% in 1906, 35% in 1907 and 1908, 33% in 1909, 19% in 1911, 17% in 1912, and a mere 13% in 1913. Critics interpreted this drop in demand for workers as an indication of the colony management's failure to achieve its objective. According to Jakob Segall, however, the lowered demand for workers was the result of the economic crisis.[242]

---

240 Annual report of Berlin–Weißensee for the year 1905. See: *Mitteilungen des D.I.G.B.*, October 1905.
241 Jakob Segall, "Arbeiter–Kolonie", p. 21.
242 Jakob Segall, "Arbeiter–Kolonie", p. 22.

Segall is mistaken here, for the period between 1902 and 1914 (with the exception of 1907-1908) were years of economic growth. Therefore, a more plausible explanation is that the attraction of the worker colony fell during this time, and that it did not make any special efforts, during this period of economic growth, to refer its graduates to places of work, assuming that they would be able to get by on their own.

An additional objective of the worker colony was education. Here, one can point to a certain success, for many of the colony's former residents were integrated into the workforce. According to the annual reports, the number of people banished from the colony due to disciplinary offenses diminished throughout the years.[243] This is an indication of the colony's success in instilling educational values (like order and discipline) or, perhaps, an indication of the colony's growing ability to select proper candidates. The economic situation of *Wanderarmen* staying on at the colony after leaving the program usually improved, as workers of the colony received, in addition to a daily wage of between 105 and 119 Pfennig, an additional wage through the colony's subcontracting system. Combined, the two incomes constituted a "respectable income" according to the standards of the period.[244] The remaining sum (that which the residents still had after leaving the colony) enabled them to start an independent economic existence. Additional worker colonies were established in other cities. In Cologne, the Jewish community established a worker colony that consolidated all activities in the Rhein-Birkenfeld region; at the colony, a woodwork workshop was opened. One hundred and thirty-three Jews lived in

---

243 Jakob Segall, "Arbeiter–Kolonie", p. 22.
244 Jakob Segall, "Arbeiter–Kolonie", p. 22.

the colony in 1902, 523 in 1911, and 600 (the peak figure) in 1914. A Jewish colony was also established in Bochum; in 1909-1910, this colony supported 858 *Wanderarmen* between the ages of 20 and 29. "The number is large," wrote a representative of the Bochum Jewish community in his report, sent to the DIGB, on the colony's activities.[245]

The idea of establishing worker colonies did not originate in the Jewish communities. Similar institutions had, in fact, existed in Germany prior to the establishment of the Jewish colonies. The following section, in which we will study the non-Jewish colonies, will reveal the uniqueness of those established by Jews.

Non-Jewish Worker Colonies

The non-Jewish worker colonies in Germany were established at the initiative of Protestant groups associated with *Innere Mission*, members of which began to take an interest in the economic distress of *Wanderarmen*. Two differing positions regarding *Wanderarmen* characterized this group: One regarded the wanderers as a fringe group that must be suppressed (proponents of this attitude refereed to the problem as *Die Bettelplage*, the "beggar plague"); the other stressed the material and physical suffering of Jewish *Wanderarmen*, who, homeless and unemployed (referred to at the time as *Vagabundennoth*, or vagabonds in distress), were eligible for extended support, mainly out of moral and religious considerations.[246]

---

245 *I.F.B.* September 22nd, 1901.
246 Jakob Segall, "Arbeiter–Kolonie", p. 25.

The economic crisis that accompanied the establishment of the German Reich (1871) worsened the wanderers' employment and housing problems, which were particularly severe at the end of the 1870s. The "residential principle," according to which one was entitled to charity only after living in the town or city in which the fund was located for a specified period, greatly exacerbated the distress of the needy, for they could only turn to the public charity institutions after two years of residence. Following the economic boom of the 1860s and early 1870s, workers who had flooded the large cities became a pressing problem. The absence of effective welfare mechanisms, coupled with the lack of a safety net from family or friends, often forced people to migrate to the cities. Of these "urban migrants," many were forced to constantly move from place to place in order to find employment. This was reminiscent of the apprentice lifestyle, in which people who had just completed their training at a guild were forced to move from place to place in order to apply it.

This new *Wanderarmen* existence constantly moving from place to place in search of work of the late 19th century was not congruent with German law, according to which *Wanderarmen* could be put on trial or extradited to regional police who sentenced the migrants to forced labor in so-called *Arbeitshäuser* (labor houses). It was in this way that *Wanderarmen* were categorized as criminals and outlaws, and from the moment they embarked on their wanderings, they were dragged into a vicious circle. Pursued by the police and the municipal authorities, and constantly fearing arrest, the *Wanderarmen* were forced to continue moving from place to place. In order to prevent confrontations between *Wanderarmen* and the law, and in order to prevent *Wanderarmen* from turning to crime, a number of private welfare organizations worked towards the establishment of colonies.

Chapter 9: The Establishment of Jewish Worker Colonies

The idea to establish worker colonies in agricultural areas belonged to Bodelschwingh, a priest who had previously managed a mental institution in Bethal. Bodelschwingh's motives were, naturally, religious. He opposed solving the problem through poor houses (as was the case in England) and also suggested that the authorities stop treating *Wanderarmen* as criminals. At the first institutions established by Bodelschwingh, residents were employed in agricultural work.

Germany's first workers' colony, established in Bielefeld (in Northern Germany) in 1882, accommodated 350 residents; there, the aim was to rehabilitate the mentally ill and those with criminal pasts by instilling a work ethic. Bodelschwingh opposed the practice of beggars and *Wanderarmen* receiving aid from private individuals and from the *Verein gegen Bettelei* (The League against Begging), and it was he who coined the phrase *Arbeit statt Almosen* (work instead of alms). Based on Christian morals and ethics, the institutions he established not only offered material help, but also tried to instill these values into the minds of the residents. Bodelschwingh's target audience included the "irreparably unemployed" or those who chose to work in the colony in order to avoid deteriorating into a life of even greater poverty and suffering. The priest was mainly interested in *Wanderarmen* who had been unemployed for a long time: These would be able to look for employment during their stay at the colony, and would be referred to places of work upon their release. In addition, the residents also included released prisoners, alcoholics, homeless, the disabled, and the mentally ill. The main difference between the poor houses and Bodelschwingh's institutions stemmed from the latter's religious character, the absence of a limit on the number of people permitted to join, and the values (work and discipline) instilled there. In 1883, the *Centralvorstand Deutscher*

Arbeiterkolonien (Central Board of Directors for German Worker Colonies) was founded, after which a new branch was added to the field of social work. Subsequently, a network of over 30 worker colonies, *Wanderarbeitsstätten* (*Wanderarmen* workshops) and *Verpflegunsgstation* (nourishing stations) were established, all with the objective of serving *Wanderarmen*.

By the beginning of the 20th century, however, it had become evident that the hope invested in the colonies had been in vain: On average, only 15% of *Wanderarmen* who completed the training were actually fit to work. Furthermore, the work places offered by the colonies did not attract significant numbers of the unemployed residents.[247] Finally, the religious coercion, the enforced moral indoctrination, and, above all else, the fact that one lost his political voting rights when he joined the colony, deterred many from joining.[248]

In 1893, the colonies, workshops and *Wanderarmen* hostels (called *Herbergen zur Heimat*, i.e., homeland hostels) formed a

---

[247] In the 25 years since the establishment of worker colonies, 200,000 unemployed stayed there. See: Jürgen Scheffler, "Die Gründungsjahre 1883–1913", in: Jahrhundert Arbeiterkolonien, "Arbeit statt Almosen", Hilfe für obdachlose Wanderarme 1884, 1984, Freiburg 1984, p. 28.

[248] The loss of voting rights was based on paragraph 33 of the *UWG* constitutional amendment from May 1869. The law stated that welfare recipients of three years would lose their political rights. An amendment to this from 1909 modified the definition of welfare recipients to "publicly supported." According to the new definition, welfare recipients did not lose their political rights when receiving welfare due to an illness, for educational purposes, for professional training, when the welfare was temporary, and when the recipient was receiving money in accordance to insurance laws. See: Ernst Grässner, Erich Simm, *Das Armenrecht*, p. 413. R. Kluge, *Handbuch für Armenpflege, Ratgeber für die in der öffentlichen oder privaten Armenpflege tätigen Personen*, Hamburg, 1913, p. 47.

Chapter 9: The Establishment of Jewish Worker Colonies

joint organization called *Deutscher Herbergenverein* (German hostel organization). By 1885, 13 colonies had been established in Germany; by 1890, 22; and in 1914, the country was home to 36 colonies, housing 5,000 residents. In the 25 years since the establishment of the first worker colony, more than 200,000 unemployed found refuge in the colonies.[249]

The average stay at a German colony was 4 ½ months, after which the resident was referred to a place of employment. In 1905, Hoffnungstal (a town close to Berlin) established a worker colony that, unlike other colonies, allowed its residents to continue living there after finding work, and even to return to the colony in the event that the absorption process (the absorption into the new job) did not succeed.

Although the Christian worker colonies were active in most of the Reich, they focused their efforts on agricultural areas in Prussia. The colonies were financed by church sources, local government budgets, and private donors; an additional source of income came from work performed by the residents.

Excepting their work on behalf of chronic welfare seekers, for whom institutions of this kind were the only solution, the impact of the Christian colonies was marginal. A similar solution was offered by the workshops for *Wanderarmen* (the *Wanderarbeitsstätten*), which offered *Wanderarmen* temporary employment in order to prevent them from returning to their old ways. These workshops, some of which offered sleeping arrangements, employed between 10 and 20 workers, who worked in carpentry or housekeeping. According to Brauner, a priest from Berlin who presided over several colonies and *Wanderarmen* workshops during the Weimar

---

249 Jürgen Scheffler, "Die Gründungsjahre 1883–1913", p. 28.

Republic, the objective of the workshops was "to fight *Wanderarmen* by finding them and removing them from the streets, in a way that would regulate the stream of *Wanderarmen*."[250]

Workshops differed from worker colonies in that the residents of the former lived there for extended periods. German workshops were planned in such a way that the distance between them never exceeded 25 kilometers: "The organized *Wanderarme* is someone who works in the morning, after which he moves on to the next workshop," states a proposal to reform the *Wanderarmen* support system.[251]

The legal agreement on the *Wanderarmen* issue in Prussia (from 1907) also determined the framework of *Wanderarmen* workshops, which was implemented in Prussia, Hannover, Westphalia, Saxony, Hessen-Nassau, and Württemberg (where poor houses were established according to the English model, housing *Wanderarmen* who were arrested for the offenses of *Landstreicherei*, or vagrancy, and wandering). The workshops provided a solution to the threat posed by migrants wandering the main roads. As with the worker colonies, the workshops' residents received wages for their work. The workshop system was, however, too limited in scope to provide a solution to the problem of unemployment, and its main objective was to reduce the number of *Wanderarmen* on the roads, thus calming public unrest.[252]

Due to their limited funds, non-Jewish organizations dealing with *Wanderarmen* were not able to cope with unemployed

---

250 Shalom Adler–Rudel, "Voraussetzung und Notwendigkeit einer jüdischen Arbeiterkolonie", in: *Jüdische Arbeits– und Wanderfürsorge* (J.A.W.), 1927/1928, p. 150.

251 Shalom Adler–Rudel, "Voraussetzung", p. 151.

252 Shalom Adler–Rudel, "Voraussetzung", p. 151.

Chapter 9: The Establishment of Jewish Worker Colonies

Wanderarmen through worker colonies and workshops. Established by churches (no other organization was willing to do so) on a regional scale (rather than on a city or town scale), the German worker colonies were unable to become an effective mechanism against unemployment and begging.

Although the Jewish worker colonies were established on similar principles, they differed from the Christian colonies in significant ways, the main difference being that the Jewish colonies were set up in urban, rather than rural, areas. The main advantage of the urban setting was the proximity to the labor market, which enabled the residents to find employment soon after leaving the colony. Comparing Jewish worker colonies with those of their Christian counterparts, we discover that the former were more successful. In contrast to the Christian worker colonies, the Jewish colonies never developed into a closed welfare system for the support of those who were unable to fit into society. The worker colony at Weißensee, for example, supported able-bodied Jews who were able to enter the job market after leaving the colony. The Weißensee worker colony, which was relatively small, is a good example of the way in which worker colonies continued to enact the principles laid down by Jewish welfare organizations: The goal was to try to enable the charity recipient to return, as quickly as possible, to a regular, independent life free of any dependence on welfare organizations.

The establishment of the worker colony in Weißensee expressed German Jewry's approach to welfare, according to which it was necessary to find all-encompassing solutions to poverty by establishing large organizations and thus reducing the number of *Wanderarmen* seeking absorption in Germany. The residents of these institutions would benefit from them no less than their founders. The colonies' insistence on "German character" was an expression of the founders' desires to ease the absorption of *Wanderarmen* into new surroundings. The Jewish welfare organizations did not distinguish between German and foreign Jews, and this proves that the main distinction at the time was not between German and foreign (mainly Eastern European) Jews, but, rather, between permanently settled Jews and *Wanderarmen*. Thus, regional Jewish community institutions in Germany were divided into organizations dealing with local paupers on the one hand, and those dealing with foreign paupers on the other hand. Although it is often difficult to determine just how successful these organizations were, we can point to one innovation for which they were responsible: The worker colony at Weißensee was the first concentrated effort to bring indigent Jews nearer to the professional structure and behavioral patterns of non-Jewish society.

The Weißensee colony exemplified the prevalent attitude among German Jews: that socialization was a key factor in the integration of *Wanderarmen* into society. German Jews regarded the colony as a path to secular German society, in which the residents would learn a manufacturing profession and the customs and traditions of the country, and in which they would, perhaps, earn enough money to facilitate their integration into society. At the same time, the colony also exemplified the condescending (and, sometimes, worse) attitude of local Jews towards the *Wanderarmen*. The reciprocal relations were even more complex than portrayed above. This issue requires further research.

CHAPTER 10:

HOSTELS FOR HOMELESS JEWS

As shown in the preceding chapter, the worker colonies stemmed from a specific approach to the problem of *Wanderarmen*, one in which they were housed in a closed institution where they learned a trade and the customs of the new country. Another popular approach, albeit a very different one, was to remove *Wanderarmen* from communities, even if that meant supporting them temporarily; proponents of this approach argued that the money and resources thus spent would enable the *Wanderarmen* to quickly leave the community.

There are early accounts of Jewish communities in Germany establishing hostels for passing paupers. As early as the medieval period, in fact, synagogues reserved a special room (inside the synagogue or next to it) for this purpose. Every medium-sized Jewish community had a "poorhouse" for the sick and the indigent. In his *Sefer Hassidim* ("Book of the Pious," written in the 12th century), Rabbi Yehuda ha-Hassid emphasized the importance of the poorhouse: "a community that has neither synagogue nor poorhouse shall build a poorhouse first." According to records from the period, such poorhouses already existed in Regensburg, Cologne, and Koblenz in, respectively, 1210, 1240, and 1365. Among the donations mentioned in the memorial book of the Jewish community of Nuremberg for the years 1280-1364 we also find donations for the community's poorhouse. And in Frankfurt, where, according to the records, only 12 taxpaying Jewish families lived in 1473, the community managed to maintain a poorhouse in which 23 paupers and sick people lived.[253]

The most noticeable difference between these two periods (medieval and modern] was the size of the stream of applications: During the latter period, especially after the onset of the 20th century, the number of people living in poverty skyrocketed, as a result of which it became necessary for the institutions to adapt to the new circumstances and care for large numbers of applicants, as opposed to the isolated cases of the past.

The network of Jewish welfare funds being established in Germany proves that the *Wanderarmen* phenomenon had spread to every region of the German Reich. The large cities, which

---

[253] On Medieval poorhouses, see: Bergman, Yehuda, *ha–Zedaka be–Israel, Toldoteya u–Mosdoteya* [Hebrew: Charity in Israel, history and institutions], Jerusalem 1943, p. 56.

were particularly attractive to *Wanderarmen*, turned into a kind of bottleneck: In Berlin, the capital, the pressure of migrating paupers was felt for the first time, demanding that the community's different institutions cooperate with one another. As a result, a hostel for the poor was established in the city at the beginning of the 19th century.

The new dimensions of migration forced the community to implement new organizational methods for the purpose of solving the problem posed by *Wanderarmen*, those who wandered from community to community and those who migrated from abroad. Two options for the housing of *Wanderarmen* were available: the private framework, in which a Jewish family offered to host a Jew or a Jewish family, and the institutional framework, an example of which is the aforementioned hostel. Information regarding the former is scarce, for individual acts of charity were rarely documented. The few extant accounts of individual charity are usually memoirs written by members of the host families, and the information they contain does not shed light on the general phenomenon. We do know, however, that thousands of *Wanderarmen* flocked to the cities every year, and that they found some sort of shelter there. The dearth of documentation on hostels for the homeless indicates that the community's institutions did not, for the large part, concern themselves with providing the *Wanderarmen* with organized sleeping arrangements, and that the hosting of *Wanderarmen* was conducted within the private framework. It can therefore be said that (according to existing documentation) private individuals provided the majority of homeless shelters.

In Bavaria, more than 1,000 *Wanderarmen* (and their families) passed through the large metropolitan centers (mainly Würzburg, Fürth, and Augsburg). The funds' records mention financial support for *Wanderarmen*, including food and travel expenses. They do not, however, mention sleeping arrangements (with a few exceptions). We can therefore assume that the paupers stayed with Jewish families, rather than in places provided by the communities' institutions. As a result of the increase in the number of *Wanderarmen*, the relationship between welfare recipients and welfare donors suffered; paupers often did not stay with families providing welfare, but, rather, with other families, mostly related to the welfare donors.

The concentration of groups of the same ethnic background within the Jewish communities, e.g., Galician Jews in Berlin's *Scheunenviertel* quarter or Russian Jews in certain areas in Munich, made it easier for *Wanderarmen* of the same background to move between Jewish communities. Although testimonies from the period often mention the hospitality provided by affluent Jews, the scope of their involvement with *Wanderarmen* should not be exaggerated, in particular during periods when the communities were working to eliminate door-to-door begging and direct charity.

Direct contact between *Wanderarmen* and the local population had several positive consequences: quicker absorption into new surroundings and into the welfare system, mutual aid, and an unmediated relationship between German Jews and the "new immigrants." The official sources do not, however, mention these beneficiary outcomes.

An article that appeared in the *Jüdische Allgemeine Zeitung* in 1915 described the rise of the hostel in Berlin since the 18th century:

> In the last years, almost every community had a hostel for passing Jewish paupers. In 1807, the Jewish community in Berlin maintained such a hostel at *Rosenthal-Tor*. This we learn from a drawing of the period. In the large cities and communities, where so much has happened recently, we find such hostels especially in

the East and in Hamburg. The absence of such a dwelling place in the Jewish community in Berlin resulted in public disturbances by paupers. Jewish paupers, especially those expelled from Russia and Galicia, arrived with their wives and children at the halls of the train station. Many of them wandered around the area of the train station and adjacent streets. It was particularly sad to watch how these starved and exhausted individuals waited at the train station late at night: One should have seen how they were 'housed' in all sorts of alcoves. They lived in the pimp quarter, where often their last belongings were stolen. Young men and women, not even of age, deteriorated into prostitution.[254]

It was in this context that the Jewish community in Berlin decided to establish, in 1909, a hostel for Jewish *Wanderarmen*:

> Thanks to the help and generosity of our brothers and sisters of faith, we were able to arrange a large number of beds on the first floor of [the building at] *August* Street, no. 25. The paupers can stay there, under the supervision of a couple of inspectors, and receive welfare. In the last year, 20,000 meals were handed out and 8,000 sleeping arrangements were provided [there]. In 1912, the number of days spent there by *Wanderarmen* increased to 12,000 per anno and more than 30,000 meals were handed out. The organizations *Ezra*, *Allianz*, and *B'nai B'rith* provided aid that enabled the continuation of support. However, despite the large amount of aid, we still had to reject a few people, as the place became too crowded.[255]

It is possible to divide the Jews who arrived in the large cities into two groups: those who lived in Germany permanently, and those who stayed there for a transitional period before continuing to other

---

254 "Herberge für jüdische Durchreisende", in AZJ, January 23, 1914.
255 AJZ, January 23, 1914.

countries. The latter moved between German-Jewish communities until reaching a port, and their concentration was particularly large in cities close to Germany's borders, large border checkpoints (like Königsberg) and, in particular, port cities. A detailed description of the homeless hostel in Hamburg follows.

The David Wormser Homeless Hostel in Hamburg

Unlike Berlin, which, as an industrial and commercial center, attracted many Jews, Hamburg mainly served as a transit point for migrants departing to North and South America or to England. Many Jews arrived at Hamburg's ports, and it was thus necessary to find a fast and efficient solution to the problem of housing the *Wanderarmen* during their brief stay in the city. In the 1880s, Daniel Wormser, a Jewish resident of the city, decided to act on their behalf. He raised funds from private sources and also received support from the Hamburg police, the latter of which provided a heated hall for homeless Jews to sleep in. "He gathered many of those crowded next to the Hamburg community's offices and accommodated them in migrant housing. Daniel Wormser invested his efforts in preventing Jewish disgrace."[256] A Jewish welfare guide, published by the Jewish Center of Statistics and Demography, mentions 1900 as the year during which the hostel for Jewish homeless was established in Hamburg. According to a different report, however (issued by the same organization), the homeless hostel was founded in 1884.[257]

---

256 Bericht und Abrechnung des Israelitischen Unterstüzungsvereins für Obdachlose", in *Bibliothek und Archiv der jüdischen Gemeinde Berlin–West*. 1909, p. 4.

257 Between 1901 and 1905, reports of the organization's activities were published annually.

Chapter 10: Hostels for Homeless Jews 229

The inconsistent dates indicate possible inaccuracy in other sources, as well. The fact that years of activity were not reported to the central Jewish institutions or brought to their attention reflects a reality in which organizations were established on a regional, local, or otherwise limited basis, on the initiative of single individuals or communities. Records pertaining to these organizations' activities are also meager, making it difficult for the researcher to measure their scope on the local level. The welfare guide mentions two additional *Wanderarmen* hostels: One in Cologne (established in 1913) and one in Frankfurt (established in 1922).[258]

Hundreds of thousands of migrants passed through Hamburg beginning in the early 20th century, and a solution to the ensuing housing problem had to be found quickly. To this end, special halls (called "migration halls") were established on the dockside of the port. These halls accommodated Jewish paupers, as did, beginning in 1884, the Daniel Wormser Homeless Hostel. The latter was initially called *Unterstützungsverein für obdachlose israelitische Handwerksburschen und arme durchreisende Israeliten* (Welfare organization for homeless young Jewish craftsmen and for poor wandering Israelites).[259] Although it is possible that the pogroms of 1881 triggered the establishment of the hostel, the report states a different reason:

The number of *Durchwanderer* [wanderers], i.e., young people from Germany, Austria, Hungary, etc., has increased significantly.

---

258 J. Segall, Führer durch die jüdische Wohlfahrtspfelge in Deutschland, (published by) Z.W.J., 1928, p. 22.
259 In England, a similar organization was established in 1885 called "Temporary Almshouse for poor Jews." The initiative came from a private individual named Simcha Cohen, known by his contemporaries as "Cohen the Baker". See: Aryeh Gertner (ed.): *Yehudei Angliya ba–'Et ha–hadasha* [England's Jews in Contemporary Times, Hebrew]. Jerusalem. 1981, p. 132.

Since 1871, Germany has become an industrialized country, developing at a rapid pace. And so, Jewish craftsmen, laborers, and young merchants moved from place to place looking for work."[260]

As the communities' available funds and resources were not sufficient to meet the needs of these *Wanderarmen*, they turned to other organizations for help. The report mentions that inexperienced *Wanderarmen* often fell into the hands of missionaries who seduced them with alluring offers of support. The stated objective of the organization was to enable Jewish paupers to stay in Hamburg for a short time (during which they were provided with sleeping arrangements and clothing) and to prevent the deterioration of the homelessness problem, thus enabling the paupers to leave Germany. Although the report from 1909 (dedicated to the hostel's 25th anniversary) clearly states that the *Wanderarmen* had arrived in Hamburg because of economic hardship, previous annual reports emphasized the direct relationship between the pogroms in Russia and the stream of charity applicants:

> Migration from Russia increased in the years 1892, 1900, and 1905. The Russo-Japanese War and the Russian Revolution forced masses to flee. Many organizations referred us as the proper system and institution through which to deal with whomever wants to migrate. Large migration halls were built here, as well as a kosher kitchen in which the preparation of food was supervised. A special synagogue was acquired by Daniel Wormser (now owned by the "Hamburg-Amerika-Line") provided religious services.[261]

Regarding the admission process, the report states the following:

> After examining the applicants, we provided them with housing and supported them for several days. Sometimes this was done in

---

260 Jüdische Obdachlose Hamburg (Bericht 1909), p. 5.
261 Jüdische Obdachlose Hamburg (Bericht 1909), p. 6.

Chapter 10: Hostels for Homeless Jews 231

collaboration with the organization for the welfare of foreigners, established through the DIGB. Women's groups and other organizations helped us in finding clothes and handing them out to the people in the migration halls, so that they [the homeless] would look dignified.

The organization was also active in alleviating the ordeal of the sea voyage, establishing kosher kitchens on ships bound for America.

Migrants traveling to New York and to South America will find kosher food [on the ships]. Separate kosher kitchens were installed in the ships. This alone required an investment of 3,000 Mark per year, despite the fact that the kitchenware, the food, and the staff's wages were paid for by the shipping company. This kosher kitchen [established on the Hamburg-Amerika-Line] was supervised by the Hamburg Rabbinate.[262]

It is difficult to determine if the residents of the Wormser hostel did indeed intend to leave Germany, or if some of them actually intended to stay in Hamburg, to which purpose they took advantage of the services provided by the hostel. During the initial phase of the *Wanderarmen* phenomenon in Hamburg, most of the arrivals tried to earn a living. Later, as the stream of migrants intensified, *Wanderarmen* were forbidden from moving within the country freely; they were brought directly to the ports, from which, after a brief stay, they departed overseas.[263]

It is not apparent from the sources whether most residents of the hostel really intended to leave Germany. It can be assumed that some stayed in the hostel planning to settle in either Hamburg or in a

---

262 Jüdische Obdachlose Hamburg (Bericht 1909), p. 7.
263 See: Paul Lasker, *Über Aus– und Rückwanderung*, Lecture held on Wednesday, September 17th, 1902, Hamburg.

different city in Germany. The annual report of the Daniel Wormser Hostel for 1912 states the following:

> This year, we dealt with a large number of individuals and families who, despite the fact that they had tickets for the sea voyage, stayed in the 'migration halls' and were supported by us. There were also migrants whose family members stayed with us until they could unite with their families. [This was the case when one family member immigrated first, after which his relatives joined him.]Taking care of the sick also fell on our shoulders. Only someone who knew the place from before 1909 can appreciate the work being done here. The sum allocated for these people is so high that every member participates in raising donations. The statistics in front of us show that the meals served at the Daniel Wormser Home exceeded by far the number of people sleeping there. This resulted from the fact that the hostel provided meals to Jews who, although they had already found employment [in Hamburg], would receive their wages only at the end of the week.[264]

> The editor of the special report from 1909 argued that the pogroms in Russia and Poland (in 1881) were the main reason for the hostel's establishment. "It was then that anti-Semitic acts against the Jewish population occurred in Russia," the report stated. "Many Jews escaped from there after terrible bloodbaths took place in a number of cities, among them Odessa, Kiev, Elisabethsgrad, etc. The leadership of the *Alliance* in Paris decided to establish different committees that would help send [Jewish] paupers to America and Canada. Their distress was intense until Daniel Wormser came along and founded his organization."[265]

---

[264] Jüdische Obdachlose Hamburg (Report for 1912).
[265] Jüdische Obdachlose Hamburg (Report for 1909), p. 1–2.

Chapter 10: Hostels for Homeless Jews

Although the Jewish *Wanderarmen* population was partly made up of refugees from the pogroms in Russia, there was also a considerable number of *Wanderarmen* who came to Germany for purely economic reasons. Homeless hostels (including Daniel Wormser's), however, did not bother to check the motives of the shelter seekers. The Wormser hostel was active for 30 years, and it can be assumed that it did not limit itself to sheltering persecuted Jews from Russia and Poland.

The Jewish paupers slept in the community center on Alba Street. With the help of a donation made by Herman Pinkus (15,000 Mark) and money from the Daniel Wormser foundation (9,000 Mark), another hostel was established on Westerstraße, which was inaugurated on July 4, 1904. According to the heads of the institution, "Nothing could have been more fitting than this to celebrate the 25th anniversary of the organization."[266]

The new hostel contained the following:

> ... three floors of large and ventilated rooms with enough space for 35 people. Each room has shower facilities and running water. In addition, each floor has a hot water faucet and a bathroom. The ground floor has a kitchen, a dining room, a room for recreational activities, and an office. In the basement there are shower rooms and wardrobes. The basement also houses disinfection facilities, where the clothes of the arrivals are cleaned. Beneath the roof are storage rooms and drying rooms for laundry. The hostel is named after Daniel Wormser. Sixty thousand Mark were necessary to build the hostel and to adapt it to its current purposes. Only someone who witnessed our distress of previous years can understand how lucky we are now, after the establishment of this hostel.[267]

---

266 Jüdische Obdachlose Hamburg (Report for 1909), p. 8.
267 Jüdische Obdachlose Hamburg (Report for 1909), p. 8.

In order to understand the continuous activities of the hostel, it is necessary to make use of the annual reports, which were published beginning in 1901. The report from 1901 also described the activities of previous years:

> The organization's activities in 1900 were extraordinary, considering the increased volume of migration from Germany. This should not come as a surprise, as the reasons behind our brethren's decision to leave Eastern Europe [i.e., pogroms] are constantly growing. While many organizations only deal with people looking for a new home [i.e. migrants who became so of their own free will], almost no one deals with those who were forced to leave in distress [i.e. refugees]. We are filling this void.[268]

On the identity of the hostel's residents, the following was stated: "Regarding nationality, the vast majority of those arriving are from Galicia. Others came from Russia, Romania, Hungary, and Germany. And there are those whose origins lie in America and Southern Europe." On the services provided by the hostel: "Until now, we have provided sleeping arrangements, meals and, if necessary, travel expenses. We established a 'clothing department' in 1900, and are now able to provide additional clothing. The migrants from Russia are housed in the halls on board the 'Hamburg-Amerika-Line' and eat from the kosher kitchen there. Others are staying in different hostels in town."

The hostel also took care of the sick, mainly by referring them to one of the hospitals in town. The cost for medical treatment was, on average, 1,420 Mark per patient. In 1900, the cost of maintaining the hostel totaled 20,039 Mark, the bulk of which was spent on food (11,985). A year later, the hostel's expenses increased, totaling 23,345 Mark:

---

268 Jüdische Obdachlose Hamburg (Report for 1901).

Chapter 10: Hostels for Homeless Jews

This number was inevitable, for – and the statistics show this – migration increased. While Russia was then experiencing a peaceful period, the situation of Jews from Galicia, Hungary, and, again, Romania deteriorated. Thus, a large group of people, members of which were physically fit and willing to work, had a hard time finding employment because of their Jewish origins! These people had no choice but to look for work elsewhere, as did those who immigrated to America or England and succeeded there. However, many [of the Jews from Galicia, Hungary, etc.] are not advancing, for they continue to live in their countries and starve. Many of those living in hostels are *Rückkehrarme* [returning *Wanderarmen*, i.e., paupers who have decided to return to their countries of origin], and their numbers are rising, as are the number of regular *Wanderarmen*. Due to a lack of resources, these *Rückkehrarme* are deteriorating into wandering and beggary, and their only way to prevent this is to return quickly to their native countries. Therefore, it is our obligation to care for them and to establish organizations for *Rückkehrarme*.[269]

The activities of the Hamburg hostel were noticed in other cities as well. The annual reports show that the institution established relationships with the communities of Berlin, Breslau, and Posen, as well as with Jewish organizations that dealt with migration. The hostel's funding sources were not independent from one another, and it was funded by additional Jewish communities: Dresden, Munich, Stuttgart, Bielefeld, Würzburg, Strasbourg, Augsburg, and Chemnitz; in addition, the hostel received donations from private donors and from larger Jewish organizations. The joint financing efforts prove that Jewish communities all over Germany had a stake in ensuring that *Wanderarmen* reached a port city from which they

---

269 Jüdische Obdachlose Hamburg (Report for 1901).

would be able to leave Germany, and it was for this reason that the communities agreed to finance a remote hostel. While donations might have been given for purely philanthropic reasons, the hostel's activities and methods point to something else: these donations served certain interests (such as reducing the burden on Jewish communities).

The Daniel Wormser Hostel was soon unable to accommodate all those asking to stay there, as a result of which the institution enlarged its scope. The hostel was also responsible for providing sleeping arrangements for Jews in the area of the port. In 1901, 11,988 people stayed at the docks; the hostel supported them, as well. The annual reports detail the material help given to those who stayed in the hostel; in 1901, for example, 8,273 Jews passed through Hamburg, and the report tells us that they received, in total, 32,382 meals, 7,193 coffee mugs, and 3,292 lunches. Of these, 2,603 individuals received money for travel expenses, which they used to either immigrate abroad or to return to their native countries; 1,996 received money for new clothes; and 736 received money for hospitalization expenses.

Companies whose ships traveled to America also maintained halls on Hamburg's docks (called *Auswanderungshallen*, or emigration halls). The people staying there received aid from the Daniel Wormser Hostel (mostly food and clothes). The report from 1903 asks the following: "How can Jewish residents of our city still remain aloof after the organization has proven, for 20 years, what it is within our power to achieve, supporting thousands of our people every year and guaranteeing them a better future." The authors of the report were annoyed with the indifference of many Jews who did not participate in financing the hostel at a time when its financial

Chapter 10: Hostels for Homeless Jews 237

status worsened and its deficit stood at 4,800 Mark. The burden on the hostel's resources intensified in 1903, for it was during that year that many Jews who had previously immigrated to America returned to their countries of origin as a result of the economic crisis in America, which left many without a source of income. These returning immigrants arrived in Hamburg and stayed there briefly before continuing their journey.[270] The number of people who sought aid increased in 1905, and this in spite of the fact that fewer Russian Jews – they had formerly constituted the majority of applications – applied for aid that year. And yet, the report from 1905 states the following:

> The organization is still committed to helping every destitute *Wanderarme* arriving in Hamburg, so that he can achieve his aims in the best way possible. We must also help those wanting to immigrate during their stay in Hamburg.[271]

At the port, a large clothing warehouse was established, handing out clothes to needy applicants. The author of the annual report from 1905 complained that, "we [often] receive things that are not suitable to our aims. People are sending torn packages and tattered articles of clothing that cannot be worn. These are not even worth the cost of shipping. We give the people we support respectable clothes fit for wearing while looking for work."[272]

In 1905, the hostel covered the travel expenses of 1,467 people moving within Germany. During the following years, too, the organization continued its activities on a scale similar to that of previous years. In 1912, its activities significantly increased:

---

270 Jüdische Obdachlose Hamburg (Report for 1903).
271 Jüdische Obdachlose Hamburg (Report for 1905).
272 Jüdische Obdachlose Hamburg (Report for 1905).

1912 and 1913 were busy years, demanding great effort on the part of the organization. The number of migrants from abroad, and of those who arrived for a short time in order to look for employment, was significantly higher than that which was recorded during the previous year. The traffic at the Daniel Wormser Hostel resulted in large amounts of money being spent on meals and travel expenses of *Rückkehrarme*. Due to the war in the Balkans, the migration halls were crowded. In 1913, 100,000 lunches were provided by the kosher kitchen. We also made an effort to provide the Jewish migrants with proper clothes, for these clothes enabled immigrants to receive entry permits to America. Most of the people staying at the migration halls intended to move overseas: Argentina was also a popular destination, but the stream of immigrants headed for that country decreased as a result of the fact that the economy there was not as strong as it had been during the previous war. On the ships headed for America there is always a kosher kitchen. The lines headed for North and South America accommodate us on this matter. At the kosher facilities, between 20 and 25 diligent and trustworthy Jews are permanently employed as cooks.[273]

Data pertaining to the support of homeless Jews in Hamburg, both by the hostel and by the migration halls, show that their number was very high. Between 1900 and 1913, a total of 400,000 sleeping arrangements were provided in Hamburg.

---

[273] In 1912, the migration halls supported 20,972 Jews who received 90,297 meals from the kosher kitchen. In 1913, the halls supported 38,997 Jews who received 157,167 lunches. At the Wormser House alone, 2,097 Jews received lunches in 1912 and 2,304 in 1913. In 1912 and 1913, the number of sleeping arrangements provided was 4,780 and 5,929 respectively. The number of breakfasts served was 5,223 in 1912 and 7,150 in 1913. In addition, the Wormser Hostel also served lunch and dinner (24,397 meals in 1912 and 19,755 meals in 1913). See: Jüdische Obdachlose Hamburg (Report for 1913).

Chapter 10: Hostels for Homeless Jews

Table 10: Number of Jews supported by the Daniel Wormser Hostel and the migration hall in Hamburg

Year	Sleeping Arrangements at the Wormser Hostel	Sleeping Arrangements at the Migration Hall	Total Expenditure in Marks
1900	8,828	19,409	20,542
1901	8,273	11,988	23,345
1902	7,646	19,501	23,770
1903	5,491	20,381	22,204
1904	4,424	36,020	25,884
1905	3,699	28,931	24,425
1906	2,939	45,445	28,278
1907	1,948	29,007	23,598
1908	1,649	12,177	25,360
1909	1,759	21,572	22,046

The statistical data refer only to *Wanderarmen* who were supported by organizations associated with the Jewish community. *Wanderarmen* who did not stay in these institutions spent the night at other places, about which we have little systematic information. As for the Hamburg Hostel, it dealt with more people than the *Weißensee* worker colony, albeit with people who stayed in Hamburg for fewer days at a time: Usually, migrants would stay in the city for between a few days and a month, after which they would move on. Both institutions were considered "closed welfare" institutions.

In contrast to the previously established *Wanderarmen* support networks, which had been founded in the 1870s, the *Weißensee* and the Hamburg Hostel commenced their welfare activities in 1900. The fact that these two institutions were established relatively late indicates that German Jewry changed its approach towards *Wanderarmen*: The first turning point was in the 1880s, when the principle of direct, individual charity was abandoned. The DIGB's struggle against the phenomenon of door-to-door begging was accompanied by its effort to replace the traditional manner of giving charity (directly) with a widespread organizational charity framework. By doing so, the DIGB was also able to develop methods of supervising the movement of *Wanderarmen* within Germany. Another major change, occurring on or about 1900, was the clear distinction between community welfare institutions and special institutions that only dealt with the *Wanderarmen* group. Until the new century, most Jewish communities in Germany dealt with foreign paupers through the community institutions, i.e., through community welfare funds. As the number of *Wanderarmen* began to grow, however, local Jews faced enormous difficulties in dealing with the burden through the existing framework. Therefore, in addition to the local Jewish community welfare system, a nationwide welfare network was established in order to deal with Jewish beggars. It should be noted here that the main distinction was not between local (German) and foreign Jews, but, rather, between settled Jews and *Wanderarmen*. Accordingly, there is little mention of the countries of origin of the people receiving support, neither in the records of the *Weißensee* worker colony nor at the Daniel Wormser Hostel.

Chapter 10: Hostels for Homeless Jews 241

The two institutions that were discussed in this chapter represent two opposing approaches to the *Wanderarmen* problem: one promoting their integration into German society, the other their expulsion. Reality proved both approaches unsuccessful. This becomes apparent when comparing Jewish and non-Jewish *Wanderarmen*, and the organizations dealing with both. The main difference between the Jewish and non-Jewish institutions boils down to operational principles. Jewish welfare institutions had been an integral part of the community well before the *Wanderarmen* issue had become a nationwide problem. Mechanisms for dealing with foreigners, charity principles (e.g., working for the economic independence of the charity seeker, individual help) – these had been an integral part of the Jewish welfare system in Germany, and all that the Jewish communities had to do in order to meet the growing demand for charity was to broaden the scope of existing systems. Accordingly, the two new welfare mechanisms (one helping local Jews, the other *Wanderarmen*) adopted the Jewish communities' existing welfare customs. The Christian welfare system, on the other hand, had to build its own welfare infrastructure *ex nihilo*, for it could not rely on the insufficient example set by church communities.

Although, as mentioned earlier, the Jewish welfare system distinguished between welfare for local Jews and *Wanderarmen*, it was on behalf of the latter group that the system usually operated. The various solutions to the problem – e.g., local welfare funds, border funds, regional organizations, worker colonies, and homeless hostels – were groundbreaking in terms of their organizational capacity and their ability to care for large numbers of charity seekers over extended periods. An example of this sophistication was the work of Albert Ballin (1857-1918), whose father had earned his living by helping poor Jewish migrants: Ballin served as director of the renowned *Hamburg-America Line*, whose ships transported many migrants to and from America.[274] In non-Jewish society, however, a similarly sophisticated system for dealing with *Wanderarmen* did not exist, even though the phenomenon there was similar in scope.

Both approaches, then, existed simultaneously: one in which the goal was to help *Wanderarmen* leave Germany as soon as possible (exemplified by, among other institutions, the Wormser Hostel and local funds), the other in which the goal was integration (exemplified by the worker colony at *Weißensee* and similar organizations). Although both approaches ultimately improved the lives of the migrants and paupers, they also contributed to the deterioration of relations between German Jews and *Wanderarmen*. Differences in language, appearance, and demographics further exacerbated the alienation between the two groups. However, what really perpetuated the distinction was the different treatment these two groups received from the welfare organizations.

---

[274] Cecil Lamar, Albert Ballin, Business and Politics in Imperial Germany, 1888–1918, Princeton 1967.

CHAPTER 11:

THE WEIMAR REPUBLIC AND THE END OF THE JEWISH BEGGAR

The end of WWI also marked the end of the ZJW (Central Organization for *Wanderarmen*, see previous chapters): In the weeks and months following the cessation of hostilities, the regional *Wanderarmen* funds were swamped with Jewish paupers asking for one-time financial support that would enable them to return to their countries of origin. Many of these applicants were foreigners who had lived in Germany for a while. Then, in 1915, the ZJW ceased to function – not because it lacked the resources necessary to deal with paupers, but, rather, because the war put an immediate end to the Jewish *Wanderarme*n phenomenon. The demand for workers dwindled significantly during this period, as did the number of people who sought employment. A survey conducted among Jewish communities in Germany revealed that they were not interested in renewing the ZJW's activities. Even in Berlin, where the defunct organization's headquarters had been located, the community showed no interest in continuing joint welfare efforts. The war had created new problems that could not be solved with the old methods and tools.[275]

The circumstances surrounding and following the end of WWI were not the only factor in the demise of the ZJW. Although the organization had (during the four years that separated its founding and the outbreak of WWI) been responsible for all local Jewish organizations in the territory of the Reich, it nevertheless failed to establish a permanent line of action and to impose its authority on local organizations. At a meeting of the central branch in Berlin that took place months before the outbreak of WWI, the chairman stated that the registration system was not working properly: "Of the 43 branches of the organization active all over Germany this year, the central branch has yet to receive information regarding 17,000 Jewish *Wanderarmen*. Even the Berlin branch has not passed on information about several thousand *Wanderarmen*."[276] The chairman further complained about a lack of discipline, examples of which he found in the fact that funds were neither fulfilling their obligation to transfer 20% of their income to the central fund in

---

275 Shalom Adler–Rudel, "Die jüdische Wanderfürsorge in Deutschland im letzten Jahrzehnt", in: *ZDSJ*, 1924, p. 109–110.
276 IFB, May 14th, 1914.

Chapter 11: The Weimar Republic and the End of the Jewish Beggar

Berlin nor disclosing the number of people they supported. He reported that many funds were acting in opposition to the central organization's instructions (that is, independently).

Further exacerbating matters was the absence of any noticeable improvement in the relationship between the central organization and several regional organizations that had refused to join it; the organizations of Baden, Württemberg, and Alsace-Lorraine continued their policy of not collaborating with the ZJW. During the meeting mentioned above, the member organizations of the ZJW requested that the organization approach the local organizations and ask them to join the ZJW. The decisions taken at the meeting reveal the organization's many shortcomings, e.g., its demand that the funds not hand out money and charity without first distinguishing between different categories of applicants, its complaint that the funds were not doing enough to protect the communities in their area from *Wanderarmen* who were not willing to work. The committee called on its members to make every possible effort to establish direct contact with *Wanderarmen* making their way to Germany from neighboring countries, especially Russia, and to warn them that "support from local Jewish organizations is not limitless."[277]

With the end of WWI, the distinction that had previously been made between *Wanderarmen* and local unemployed Jews became blurred. From then on, both groups were treated as one. And as the Jewish *Wanderarmen* problem became more and more marginalized, Jewish beggars were increasingly dealt with by the employment agencies and welfare organizations for Jewish laborers. In 1921, the employment offices were an inseparable part of the system dealing with *Wanderarmen*, especially on the local level. The demographic

---

277 IFB, May 14th, 1914.

characteristics of those who applied to the employment offices were, however, different than those of the *Wanderarmen*.

In the first years of the Weimar Republic, the collaboration between Jewish and official German community welfare organizations increased. In addition, those who operated the Jewish community welfare system, which controlled a wide variety of welfare institutions, became a national source of skilled professionals. The sources mention that many officials from the Jewish welfare system later applied to the German system and held key positions there. The cooperation between the two welfare systems began as a solution to significant problems, a solution which was to benefit both sides. In 1919, contacts between Jewish leaders and the Prussian government were established on the issue of dealing with Jewish migrants from the East and with *Wanderarmen*. In the framework of these contacts, the Prussian Ministry of the Interior agreed to recognize the *Arbeiterfürsorgeamt* and to deal with the legal aspects of foreign Jews staying in Germany, as well as those pertaining to Jewish migrants coming there.[278]

After WWI, questions related to migration became central to Jewish welfare organizations. Germany's defeat in WWI and the ensuing economic crisis diminished the country's former appeal as a place in which foreign Jews could find economic opportunities and prosper. Accordingly, many *Wanderarmen* and Jewish migrants changed their preference from Germany to America.

Jewish organizations in Germany feared that the *Wanderarmen* would move to the Jewish communities of the larger urban areas in considerable numbers. These organizations worked to scatter groups of *Wanderarmen* who had gathered in the cities, arguing

---

[278] Shalom Adler–Rudel, "Die jüdische Wanderfürsorge", p. 107.

that there presence there would lead to a housing shortage. The real reason, however, appears to be the Jewish leadership's desire to avoid creating crowded quarters of Jewish paupers, which would have highlighted the economic distress of the paupers and triggered unfavorable reactions from the Germans. In Berlin, for example, where poor Jews concentrated in the so-called *Scheunenviertel*, it became necessary to provide them with shelter and food. For this purpose, the Jewish community in Berlin purchased a house at *Wiesenstraße*. Jewish paupers staying there were also referred to places of work, and when, in 1920, the need for agricultural workers increased, Jewish employment offices provided suitable manpower.[279] Between the years 1920 and 1922, Jewish workers were also referred to heavy industry in the *Ruhrgebiet* (North Germany). At the same time, Jewish *Wanderarmen* of German origin continued to receive support.

Germany's economy began to seriously wobble in 1914, but it was after the defeat, and the ensuing reparation payments, that the rate of inflation reached crippling levels, resulting in the hyperinflation of the early 1920s. The economic depression exacerbated the plight of the Jewish *Wanderarmen*. From then on, Jewish organizations focused their efforts on helping Jews leave Germany (especially for England and America); however, they also helped paupers who could not migrate to find work.[280]

The efforts of the past – of training *Wanderarmen* in workshops and in Jewish worker colonies – were reduced. It became clear that the reason for the economic distress of the *Wanderarmen* and the paupers from Eastern Europe was not their lack of "productivity,"

---

279 Max Kreuzberger, "Jüdische Wanderfürsorge", in *Soziale Praxis und Archiv für Soziale Volkswohlfahrt*, No. 36,1925, p. 795.
280 Wilhelm Neumann, *Die deutsche Zentralstelle*, 1914/15.

but, rather, the economy's inability to absorb additional workers. And so, the hopes invested in the idea that professional training would succeed on a large scale were disappointed. In reality, no institution was able to provide a general solution to the *Wanderarmen* issue.[281]

After WWI, the majority of *Wanderarmen* were German-born Jewish paupers, as opposed to foreigners, and they increasingly turned to the welfare finds for aid. Between 1917 and 1924, welfare activity focused on the ravages caused by the war. It was only later that the ZJW returned to its original welfare activities. The year 1924 marked a turning point in the manner in which Jewish organizations dealt with migration: That year, the *Hauptstelle der deutschen Juden* (Central Bureau of German Jews) was established, unifying under one framework all previous organizations dealing with Jewish migration. The new organization kept the previous objectives, e.g., the supervision of the migrants' comings and goings, the insistence on registration. The *Hauptstelle* was headquartered in Berlin, with additional branches in Bremen, Hamburg, Hannover, Cologne, Duisburg, Bochum, Frankfurt a. Main, Kassel, Würzburg, Nuremberg, and Leipzig. The idea of establishing workers' colonies and workshops (like *Weißensee*) was mentioned at a meeting of the *Hauptstelle*.[282]

In 1925, centralization efforts were further advanced with the establishment of *Jüdische Arbeitsgemeinschaft für Wanderfürsorge* (Jewish Association for *Wanderarme* Welfare), which was, according to a contemporary of the period, a sign of "a new era in the history of Jewish support organizations in Germany."[283]

---

281 Max Kreuzberger, "Jüdische Wanderfürsorge", p. 795.
282 Max Kreuzberger, "Jüdische Wanderfürsorge", p. 796–797.
283 Shalom Adler–Rudel, "Die jüdische Wanderfürsorge", p. 114.

Chapter 11: The Weimar Republic and the End of the Jewish Beggar

On the eve of the Nazis' rise to power, in 1933, the Jewish *Wanderarmen* problem had still not been solved. It was also dealt with differently than it had been previously: Migrants seeking to leave Germany received support, but only from migration organizations. From October 1928 until March 1929, 1,701 Jews received migration visas, 96% of whom were entitled to unemployment insurance.[284]

A report released by the central organization for migrants in 1930 indicated an increase of 25% in the number of migrants; the percentage of *Wanderarmen* of German background rose similarly. Efforts to solve the problem through the establishment of a worker colony continued that year, and the report states that the preparations for its establishment were "at their height," and that "it will probably be established in the next winter." This was, according to the source, "possible because of the support received from the Prussian government." These efforts, however, were only remnants of those previously made, and were ultimately unsuccessful.[285]

The waning days of the Weimar Republic also marked the end of the *Wanderarmen* phenomenon, of paupers moving from one Jewish community to the next in search of support and income. By then, the *Wanderarmen* issue had become part of the general issue of migration. Upon coming to power, the Nazis destroyed any attempts made by the Jewish communities to independently deal with welfare. The Nazis did, however, adopt the organizational framework of Jewish welfare when establishing their own welfare system, called *Winterhilfe* (Winter Help). The aim of this organization was to bring together the different welfare activities – including those of Jews

---

[284] *J.A.W.* 1928/1929, p. 85.
[285] "Hauptstelle für jüdische Wanderfürsorge in Berlin", in: *J.W.S.*, 1930, p. 480.

and other minorities – under one national framework. *Winterhilfe* was short-lived, silenced completely by the outbreak of WWII.

In manufacturing their anti-Jewish propaganda, the Nazis made use of stereotypes pertaining to the Jewish lower class, in particular to those of the *Wanderarmen* and beggars. Accordingly, the last echo of the *Wanderarmen* phenomenon, heard not long before Nazi Germany destroyed European Jewry, was the sinister image of the parasitic Jew.

BIBLIOGRAPHY

1) Archival Sources

a. *The Central Archives for the History of the Jewish People, Jerusalem (C.A.J.P)*

NE/48 Altenstadt, *Schriftstücke der Fremden-und Armenvereine-Unterstützung. Jahresbericht des Verbandes bayrischer Vereine zur Unterstützung durchreisender Israeliten für das Jahr 1875.*

NI/98 Ansbach, *Armenkasse, Entwurf von Satzungen für den Verband jüdischer Hilfsvereine in Bayern , 1896-1904.*

NI/98 Ansbach, *Armenkasse, Verein zur Unterstützung armer jüdischer Durchreisender, 1896-1914.*

NI/98 Ansbach, *Armenkasse, Verein zur Unterstützung armer jüdischer Durchreisender, 1896-1914.*

NI/96 Ansbach, *Kollektion, 1851-1905.*

NI/99 Ansbach, *Armenkasse, Landesverein zur Unterstützung notleidender jüdischer Kultusgemeinden, 1894-1902.*

NI/97 Ansbach, *Unterstützung mehrerer Vereine, 1892-1902.*

Wr/339 Bad Kissingen, *Protokoll des israelitischen Wohltätigkeitsvereins, 1877-1916.*

Wr/98 Bad Kissingen, *Protokoll des israelitischen Wohltätigkeitsvereins für Frauen, 1878-1923.*

B XII 4 Bamberg, *Armenwesen, 1881-1893.*

B II 4a Bamberg, *Aufrufe zur Unterstützung, 1852-1933.*

B II 5 Bamberg, *Kollekten, 1877-1894, 1903-1905.*

B XII 48 Bamberg, *Vereinigte Wohltätigkeitsstiftungen, 1883-1913.*

B II 16 Bamberg, *Waisenverein (auch Wanderunterstützungsverein), 1895-1929.*

B XII 49 Bamberg, *Wanderunterstützungsverein, 1993-1913.*

TD 394 Berlin-Weißensee, *Jüdische Arbeiterkolonie, 1903-1904 Jüdische Arbeiterkolonie und Asyl in Weißensee bei Berlin.*

TD 394 Berlin-Weißensee, *Jüdische Arbeiterkolonie und Asyl bei Berlin, über das Geschäftsjahr 1904-1905.*

Ns/31 Burghaslach, *Armensachen, 1895.*

K Ge 131 Damstadt, *Verein zur Beschränkung des Wanderbettelns und Hilfsverein, Protokollbuch, 1911-1921.*

K Ge 130 Darmstadt, *Verein zur Unterstützung israelitischer Hilfsbedürftiger, Rechnungen und Belege, 1899-1903.*

Wrs/Ess. Esslingen Württemberg, *Unterstützungsliste für durchreisende arme Israeliten, 1871-1880.*

TD-1133 Frankfurt, *Verein zur Bekämpfung des Wanderbettelns, 1907.*

N11 317-80 Genzenhausen, *Armenkassenrechnungen, 1845-1906.*

N 11/8 Gunzenhausen, *Unterstützung durchreisender polnischer Juden (Verschiedene Anträge)*.

Wr/461 Heidinsfeld, *Protokolle der israelitischen Armenpflege 1895-1907*.

Wr/459 Heidinsfeld, *Protokolle des Romann-Bacurim Wohltätigkeitsverein, 1840-1892, 1883-1922*.

Wr/339-40 Kissingen, *Protokolle des israelitischen Wohltätigkeitsverein, 1860-187, 1877-1935*.

Wr/346-357 Kissingen, *Jahresrechnungen und Belege des israelitischen Wohltätigkeitsverein, 1877-1879, 1881-1906*.

Wr/363-364 Kissingen, *Kassen Kontobuch des israelitischen Wohltätigkeitsverein, 1888-1910, 1919-1923*.

Wr/363-364 Kissingen, *Kassenbuch des israelitischen Wohltätigkeitsverein für Frauen, 1878-1923*.

Wr/341-2 Kissingen, *Sammelakte des israelitischen Wohltätigkeitsvereins (auch Heimatschein), 1886-1913, 1877-1928*.

Wr/379 Kissingen, *Verzeichnis der duch die Unterstützungskasse unterstützten Armen, 1873-1874*.

Wr/365 Kissingen, *Wochenbuch des israelitischen Wohltätigkeitsvereins für Männer, 1904-1932*.

Abt. II, H5 Königsberg, *Bittgesuche, 1880-1885*.

H 12 16 Königsberg, *Bittgesuche, 1886-1900, 1901-1910*.

Abt. II, H11 Königsberg, *Centralarmenkommission, 1901-1907*.

Abt. II, H6 Königsberg, *Notstand in Ostpreußen, 1868*. F 10 Kronach, *Armenwesen, 1877-1903*.

RI 79 Neuwied, *Akte des Wohltätigkeitsvereins, 1882-1906, 1907-1910*.

RI 98 Neuwied, *Kassenbuch der Unterstützungskass, 1853-1927.*

RI 84-84 Neuwied, *Rechnungen und Belege des Wohltätigkeitsvereins 1893-1901, 1903-1905, 1905-1918.*

Neuwied, *Statuten und Protokolle des israelitischen Frauenvereins für Wohltätigkeit, 1855-1871.*

RI 94 Neuwied, *Unterstützung und Armenwesen, 1893-1895.*

RI 95 Neuwied, *Wohltätigkeit, 1902-1904.*

RI 270 Regensburg, *Anträge von Unterstützung, 1892-1900.*

RI 286 Regensburg, *Armenpflege, 1864-1865.*

RI 279 Regensburg, *Kassentagebuch des Unterstützungsfonds für arme israelitische Durchreisende, 1893-1896.*

RI 280 Regensburg, *Spenden für arme durchreisende Juden.*

RI 267 Regensburg, *Unterstützungen 1842-1903.*

RI 278 Regensburg, *Unterstützung armer und durchreisender Israeliten, 1879-1887.*

RI 269 Regensburg, *Unterstützungen und Zuschüsse 1869, 1882-1889.*

RI 271-2 Regensburg, *Unterstützungswesen, 1893-1896.*

Pf/36 Speyer, *Satzungen des vereinigten israelitischen Wohltigkeitsverein in Speyer, 1910.*

TD-123 Stuttgart, *Vereinigung zur Unterstützung durchreisender israelitischer Armen, 1908-1909.*

PL/TD, 9 Thorn, *Verein gegen die Hausbettelei, 1882.*

Rh/W XXII Worms, *Israelitischer Unterstützungsverein e.V. zu Worms, 1905.*

Wr/1020 Würzburg, *Einzelunterstützungen der israelitischen Kultusgemeinde, 1871-1898.* Wr/1024-5 Würzburg, *Rechnung des israelitischen Wohltätigkeitsfonds mit Belegen, 1888-*

1890. Wr/1017 Würzburg, *Sammelakt betreffend israelitischen Armenwesen, 1830-1879.*

Wr/1019 Würzburg, *Satzung des Vereins Osre Dalim, 1869-1879.*

Wr/993-1003 Würzburg, *Tagebuch der israelitischen Wanderunterstützungskasse 1863-1869, 1865-1868, 1868-1870, 1869-1874, 1874-1879, 1888-1894, (13 Akten mit Register).*

Wr/1018 Würzburg, *Unterstützung für auswärtige Juden 1830-1879.*

Wr/1022 Würzburg, *Verhandlungen der israelitischen Kultusgemeinde mit dem städtischen Armenrat, Unterstützungsgesuche, 1910-1917.*

b. Staatsarchiv Fürth

30/62 *David und Karoline Sondheimer-Stiftung für arme Bräute, 1901.*

c. Staatsarchiv Nürnberg

8348-8350 *Verhältnisse der Israeliten im Bezirksamt Beingries bzw. Hebsbruck, 1863-1878.*

d. Niedersächsisches Staatsarchiv, Hannover

HANN 478 *Das Armenwesen der Juden betreffend, 1842-1865*

HANN 1462 *Der Aufenthalt russischer Juden in Deutschland, 1906-1921.*

HANN 7430 *Der jüdische Armenverband, 1872-1893.*

HANN 4625 *Die Unterhaltung der Armen in der Synagogengemeinde Gifhorn, 1819-1872.*

HANN 80 *Die Aufsicht über das Vermögen der jüdischen Synagogen, Armenanstalten und Stiftungen, 1843-1920.*

H 33/881 Grünstadt, *Wohlätigkeitsverein der Israelitischen Gemeinde Grünstadt, 1830-1868.*

HANN I N7 Hildesheim, *Armenwesen, 1842-1860.*

HANN 65 Hildesheim, *Das jüdische Armenwesen 1849-1860.*

HANN 801 CD Hildesheim, *Die Kammeragenten Meyer Michel David. Testamentarische Stiftung zu einem Institut und Einrichtung für arme Juden, 1790-1868.*

HANN 137 Hildesheim, *Die beantragte Vereinigung des christlichen und jüdischen Armenwesens.*

HANN 74 Hildesheim, *Die Bildung eines Vorstandes zur Verwaltung des Landesrabbinats und allgemeine jüdische Armenkasse zur Besorgung der jüdischen Angelegenheiten der größeren Armenverbände, 1863-1875.*

HANN 80 Bf 64 *Im Amte Diepholz soll keine Herberge für Betteljuden geduldet werden, Verpflegung der armen einheimischen Juden, 1814.*

H 31/457 Ingenheim, *Armenwesen der Gemeinde Ingenheim, 1850-1881.*

HANN 74/175 *Jüdische Synagogen, Schul-und Armenwesen, 1859-1892.*

HANN 31 *Landesrabbinat-Verwendung der Mittel, insbesondere Beihilfe an den Provinzial-Fonds für Armenunterstützung und Dienstalterzulagen... 1868-1877.*

HANN 80/37 Lüneburg, *Angelegenheiten der jüdischen Gemeinde, 1802.*

HANN 80/569 Lüneburg, *Der jüdische Armenvorstand, 1843-1874.*

HANN 131/20 *Reparation sowie die Verwaltung des Armenverbandes, 1846-1875.*

N 74 Solingen, *Aufhebung der jüdischen Armenverbände, 1871-1932.*

HANN 465 *Übersicht der von den Israeliten zu tragende Synagogen, Schul-und Armenwesen usw. 1862-1865.*

HANN 74/95 *Vagabunden, Betteljuden und dergleichen 1795.*

HANN 174 Zellerfeld, *Das jüdische Synagogen, Schul-und Armenwesen 1814-1937.*

e. Staatsarchiv Hamburg

9225/330 "Anweisung an die Grenzbüros", in: *Zentralstelle für jüdische Wanderarmenfürsorge.*

9225 *Anweisung für die Provinzial-bzw. Landeskasse, ausgedruckt von der deutschen Zentralratstelle für jüdische Wanderarme, Steglitzerstraße 85, Berlin.*

9225/60 *Bericht über die weitere Entwicklung der Gesamtorganisation seit dem 27. November 1910.*

9225/315 *Erster Bericht der Provinzialkasse Sachsen-Anhalt und Thüringen für Wanderarmenfürsorge, 1.10.1910-31.12.1911.*

9225/84 Joachim Hermann, *Das Wohlfahrtswesen des Deutschen-Israelitischen Gemeindebundes und seine Organisationen.*

SA 1505 *Politische Polizei, Zentralkommission für die Gesamtorganisation der Wanderfürsorge.*

9225/330 *Satzung der Deutschen Zentralstelle für jüdische Wanderarmenfürsorge.*

9225/665 *Satzung für die Provinzialkasse Hannover-Braunschweig für jüdische Wanderarmenfürsorge.*

9225 *Statistik über die Grenzbüros.*

9225/454 *Stenographischer Bericht über die Delegierten-Versammlung zur Beratung, Berlin, 20. Und 21. Oktober 1891, israelitischen Wanderarmenunterstützungsvereins, 1925-1938.*

9225 *Zentralstelle für jüdische Wanderarmenfürsorge, 1910-1914.*

f. Generallandesarchiv Karlsruhe

236/6058 *Das Armenwesen der Israeliten, 1811-1870.*

357/2547 *Die Schenkung des Abraham Epstein von Karlsruhe an den Israelitischen Wohltätigkeitsverrein Chebro Gemilut Chasadim, 1862.*

357/2557 *Judensachen, Die Armenunterstützung der Israeliten betreffend, 1861.*

357/2471 *Stiftungswesen, 1866.*

g. Speyer Landesarchiv

H34/76 *Inventar der Quellen zur Geschichte der jüdischen Bevölkerung, 1815-1945, in Rheinland-Pfalz und im Saarland von 1880.*

H33/795 Bezirk Frankenthal, *1847.*

H3/610 Bezirk der Pfalz, *1848-1849.*

h. Hauptstaatsarchiv Württemberg

E146 BU 118 *Juden-Armensachen, Spezilia nach Oberämtern, 1813-1871.*

E146 BU 803 *Belästigung der israelitischen Bevölkerung durch polnische und ostpreußische Juden, 1874.*
Archiv des Diakonischen Werkes, Berlin-Dahlem. ZI II *Wanderarmenfürsorge, 1925-1928.*
C 1c *Zentralwohlfahrtsstelle der deutschen Juden, 1925.*
CA/6 100/4 *Zentralwohlfahrtsstelle der deutschen Juden.*

2) Newspapers and Magazines

Allgemeine Zeitung des Judentums. Berlin/Leipzig, 1868-1914.

Allgemeine Israelitische Wochenzeitschrift.

Concord, Zeitschrift der Zentralstelle der Volkswohlfahrt.

Dokumentation zur Geschichte der jüdischen Bevölkerung. Die Juden in ihrem gemeinschaftlichen und öffentlichen Leben. Bd. III. (Publ.) Landesarchivverwaltung Rheinland-Pfalz. 1972.

Ha-Magid, 1892-1868.

Im Deutschen Reich. Berlin, 1895-1914.

Israelitisches Familienblatt, Hamburg. *Jahrbuch für Caritaswissenschaft.*

Jüdische Arbeits-und Wanderfürsorge. Berlin, 1927-1930.

Jüdische Wohlfahrtspflege und Sozialpolitik. 1930.

Menora, Jüdisches Familienblatt für Wissenschaft, Kunst und Literatur. Wien/Frankfurt, 1926.

Mitteilungen des Deutsch-Israelitischen Gemeindebundes. Berlin, 1873-1914. *Schriften des Deutschen Vereins für Armenpflege und Wohltätigkeit, Heft 28, Verhandlungen.* Leipzig, 1869.

Sozialpraxis und Archiv für Sozialvolkswohlfahrt. 1925.

Zedakah, Mitteilungen der Zentralwohlfahrtsstelle der deutschen Juden. (Publ.) Eugen Caspary, Jakob Segall, Paul Frank, 1921-1928.

Zeitschrift für Demographie und Statistik der Juden. Berlin, 1905-1930.

Zeitschrift für jüdische Wohlfahrtspflege in Deutschland. 1928.

3) Books and Protocols of the period

Albrecht, H.: *Handbuch der sozialen Wohlfahrtspflege in Deutschland.* Berlin, 1902.

Archiv für Wohlfahrtspflege (Publ.): *Die Wohlfahrtseinrichtung in der Stadtgemeinde Berlin. Eine Auskunft und Handbuch.* Berlin, 1927.

Arnold, Friedrich: *Die Freizügikeit und der Unterstützungswohnsitz.* Berlin, 1872.

Ave-Lallement, Friedrich Chr. Benedict: *Das deutsche Gaunertum in seiner sozialpolitischen, literarischen und linguistischen Ausbildung zu seinem heutigen Bestande 1852-1862.* Bearbeitete und gekürzte Ausgabe. Wiesbaden, 1914. (Reprint).

Baeck, Leo: "Jüdische Wohlfahrtspflege und jüdische Lehre," in: *JWS*, 1930. Baneth, Noami: *Soziale Hilfsarbeit der modernen Jüdin.* Berlin, 1907.

Bergman, Eugen von: *Zur Geschichte der Entwicklung deutscher, polnischer und jüdischer Bevölkerung in der Provinz Posen seit 1824.* Tübingen, 1883.

Bericht der Großloge für Deutschland u.o.B.B. 1882-1907, Festausgabe: Berlin, 1907.

Bericht der Großloge für Deutschland u.o.B.B. Berlin. Berlin, 1907.

Bericht und Abrechnung des Israelitischen Unterstützungsvereins für Obdachlose für das Jahr 1903 (bis 1913). Hamburg.

Bing, Anton: *Statistische Untersuchungen über private Wohltätigkeitspflege.* Frankfurt/Main, 1904.

Böhmert, V.: *Die Armenpflege.* Gotha, 1890.

Böhmert, V.: *Das Armenwesen in 77 deutschen Städten.* Dresden, 1886. Böhmert, V.: *Der Branntwein in Fabriken.* Leipzig, 1889.

Böhmert, V.: *Der Kampf gegen die Unsittlichkeit,* Leipzig, 1888.

Boss, S.: "Die Beseitigung der Wanderbettelei. Eine schwierige Aufgabe der heutigen Judenheit," in: *AZJ* July 31st, 1872.

Bosse, Friedrich: *Die Verbreitung der Juden im Deutschen Reich, auf Grundlage der Volkszählung vom 1. Dezember 1880.* Berlin, 1885.

Brandenburgischer Herbergs-Verband (Publ.), *Wanderarbeitsstätten in der Provinz Brandenburg.* Brandenburgischer Herbergs-Verband, Berlin. 1908.

Brandt, Siegfried: *Die Wohlfahrtseinrichtungen der jüdischen Gemeinde Berlin.* Dissertation, University of Cologne. 1923.

Brauner, Paul: "Die christliche Wanderfürsorge," in: *JAW,* 1928.

Breslauer, Bernhard: "Die jüdische Wohltätigkeit und Wohlfahrtspflege in Deutschland," in: *Archiv für Volkswohlfahrt,* 1908.

Breslauer, Bernhard: *Die Organisation der Privatwohltätigkeit in Berlin.* Berlin, 1891. Brinkmann, Zimmermann: *Ehrenamtliche und berufsamtliche Thätigkeit in der städtischen Armenpflege.* Leipzig, 1894.

Brückner, N.: *Die öffentliche und private Fürsorge*. Frankfurt/ Main, 1892.

Central-Ausschuss für die Innere Mission der deutschen evangelischen Kirche (Publ.): *Statistik der Inneren Mission der evangelischen Kirche*. Berlin, 1899.

"Die jüdische Wohltätigkeit und Wohlfahrtspflege in Deutschland," in: *ZDSJ* 1909. D.I.G.B. and Z.W.D.J. (Publ.): *Handbuch der jüdischen Gemeindeverwaltung und Wohlfahrtspflege 1924/25*.

Deutsche Zentralstelle für jüdische Wanderarmenfürsorge (Publ.): *Erster Rechenschaftsbericht der Deutschen Zentralstelle für jüdische Wanderarmenfürsorge*. Berlin, January 28th, 912.

Dyk, S.: *Über die Möglichkeit der Beschäftigung von circa 50 jüdischen Wanderarbeitern in Deutschland*. Berlin, 1927.

Eminhausen, A.: *Das Armenwesen und die Armengesetzgebung in europäischen Staaten*. Berlin, 1927.

Feilchenfeld, Wilhelm: *Jüdische Wohlfahrtspflege in Berlin. Beilage zum Bericht der Großloge in Deutschland*. Berlin, 1909.

Festschrift anlässlich der Feier des 25-jährigen Bestehens des Hilfsvereins der deutschen Juden, gegründet am 28.5.1901. Berlin, 1926.

Festschrift zum 25-jährigen Jubiläums der Berthold Auerbach-Loge 1883-1908. Berlin, 1908. Fischer, Alfons: *Grundriss der sozialen Hygiene*. Berlin, 1913.

Fischer, H.R.: *Unter den Armen und Elenden Berlins, Streifzüge durch die Tiefen einer Weltstadt*. Berlin, 1887.

Francke, Paul: *Zur Geschichte des öffentlichen Arbeitsnachweises in Deutschland*. Dissertation. Halle-Wittenberg, 1913.

Freund, Ismar: *Die Emanzipation der Juden in Preußen.* Berlin, 1912.

Freund, Richard: *Armenpflege und Arbeiterversicherung, Prüfung der Frage, in welcher Weise die neue soziale Gesetzgebung und Armenpflege einwirkt.* Leipzig, 1989.

Fritz, Georg: *Die Ostjudenfrage.* München, 1915.

Gedenkblätter zur Erinnerung an das 175-jährige Jubiläum des Wohltätigkeitsvereins im ehemaligen Amt Starkenburg (Sitz Horsch), 1739-1914.

Göhre, Paul: *Die evangelisch-soziale Bewegung, ihre Geschichte und ihre Ziele.* Leipzig, 1896. Goldschmidt, S.: *Die soziale Fürsorge in der jüdischen Religion.* Kattowitz, 1913.

Goodman, Paul: *Die Liebestätigkeit im Judentum.* Frankfurt/Main, 1913. Hampe, Th.: *Fahrende Leute in der deutschen Vergangenheit.* Leipzig, 1902.

Hanauer, W.: "Die jüdische Wohlfahrtspflege in Deutschland, ihre geschichtliche Entwicklung und ihre gegenwärtigen Leistungen. In: *Zeitschrift für die gesamte Staatswissenschaft.* Frankfurt/Main, 1913, p. 724-726.

Harkner, Heinrich: *Die Arbeiterfrage.* Vol. 2. Berlin, 1916.

Haupstelle für jüdische Wanderfürsorge (Publ.), *Bericht über die Tätigkeit für die Zeit vom 1. April 1925 bis 31. Dezember 1926.* Berlin, 1927. In: *JWS*, 1930.

Hilfsverein der deutschen Juden (Publ.): *Festschrift anlässlich der Feier des 25-jährigen Bestehens des Hilfsvereins.* Berlin, 1926. Hamburg, 1909. Horwitz, Jakob: "Zedakah und Wohlfahrtspflege." In: *JAW*, 1927.

Jacobson, B: *Der D.I.G.B. nach Ablauf des ersten Decenniums seit seiner Begründung.* Leipzig, 1879.

Jösten, Dr.: *Zur Geschichte der Hexen und Juden in Bonn.* Bonn, 1900.

JWS (Publ.): "Zentralwohlfahrtsstelle der deutschen Juden. *JWS*, 1932, p. 243.

JWS (Publ.): "Zur Geschichte der jüdischen Fürsorgetätigkeit in Bremen." In: *JWS*, 1931. p. 432.

Kahn, Bernhard: "Die jüdische Auswanderung." In: *Ost und West*, 1905.

Kaleko, S.: "Das Wohnungselend im Berliner jüdischen Wohnviertel." In: *JWS*, 1930. Kaplan-Kogen, Wlad: *Die jüdischen Wanderbewegungen in der neuesten Zeit (1880-1914)*. Bonn, 1919.

Kirsch, Markus: *Betteln und Hausieren ist hier verboten. Eine Studie der sozialen Frage.* Frankfurt, 1890.

Kluge, R.: *Handbuch für Armenpfleger. Ratgeber für in der öffentlichen und privatenArmenpflege tätige Personen.* Hamburg, 1913.

Klumker, C.J.: "Armenwesen." In: *HWB der Staatswissenschaften*, Vol. 1, Jena, 1935. Klumker, C.J.: *Fürsorgewesen. Einführung in das Verständnis der Armut und Armenpflege.* Leipzig, 1910.

Klumker, C.J. *Wohlfahrtsämter.* Stuttgart, 1920. Klumker, C.J. *Zur Theorie der Armut.* Leipzig, 1910. Lamm, Fritz: *Aus der Geschichte der Armenverwaltung.* Berlin, 1913.

Lamm, Fritz: "Die jüdische Darlehnskasse." In: *JAW*, 1927.

Lasker, Paul: *Über Aus-und Rückwanderung.* (Lecture held on Wednesday, September 17th, 1902), Hamburg, 1902.

Lazarus, Arnold: *Die Armenpflege für Ortsangesessene.* Frankfurt am Main, 1916.

Liebestätigkeit und Wohlfahrtspflege. Berlin, 1930.

Lemmermann, Karl Johannes:*Womit beschäftigen wir unsere Wanderarmen in unseren Wanderarbeitsstätten?: Zsgest. auf Grund einer Umfrage bei sämtlichen Wanderarbeitsstätten Deutschlands.* Buchdruck des Stephansstift, Hannover. 1910.

Liese, Wilhelm: *Geschichte der Caritas.* Freiburg, 1922. Vol. 2.

Liese, Wilhelm: *Wohlfahrtspflege und Caritas im Deutschen Reich.* Mönchengladbach, 1914. Lisco, Gustav: *Das wohltätige Berlin.* Berlin, 1846.

Mascher, H.U.: *Das Staatsbürger, Niederlassungs-und Aufenthaltsrecht.* Potsdam, 1868.

Menes, A.: "Über die Einkommensverhältnisse der deutschen Juden in Vor-und Nachkriegszeit." In: *JWS.* 1932. p. 87.

Michaelis, Alfred: *Die Rechtsverhältnisse der Juden in Preußen seit dem Beginn des 19. Jahrhunderts. Gesetze, Erlasse, Verordnungen, Entscheidungen.* Berlin, 1910.

Michaelis, Alfred: "Steht den ausländischen Juden in den preußischen Synagogengemeinden ein Wahlrecht zu?" In: *AZJ*, May 31st, 1912.

Mönkmeier, W.: *Die deutsche überseeische Auswanderung.* Jena, 1912.

Münsterberg, Emil: "Armenwesen." In: *Handwörterbuch der Staatswissenschaften.* Jena, 1923. Münsterberg, Emil: *Das Landarmenwesen.* Leipzig, 1890.

Münsterberg, Emil: *Die Armenpflege.* Berlin, 1897.

Münsterberg, Emil: *Die Armenpflege. Einführung in die praktische Pflegetätigkeit.* Berlin, 1897. Münsterberg, Emil: *Die Fürsorge für Obdachlose in den Städten.* Leipzig, 1895.

Münsterberg, Emil: *Zentralstelle für Armenpflege und Wohltätigkeit.* Jena, 1897.

Neumann, S.: *Die Fabel von der jüdischen Massenwanderung. Zweiter Beitrag.* Berlin, 1884. Neumann, S.: *Zur Statistik der Juden in Preußen von 1860-1880.* Berlin, 1880.

Neumann, Wilhelm: *Die deutsche Zentralstelle für jüdische Wanderfürsorge.* Seperatausdruck aus dem Monatsberich. Januar, 1913.

Neumann, Wilhelm: "Entwicklung der jüdischen Wohltätigkeitseinrichtungen. Fürsorge und Selbsthilfe." In: *Mitteilungen des Deutsch-Israelitischen Gemeindebundes.* Mai, 1901. Neumann, Wilhelm: *Reform des jüdischen Wanderunterstützungswesen.* Berlin, 1910.

Ollendorf, Friedrich: "Von Zielen und Wegen jüdischer Wohlfahrtspflege." In: *Vom Wesen der Wohlfahrtspflege.* Berlin, 1918.

Ottenheimer, Hilde: "Die geschichtlichen Grundlagen der jüdischen Wohlfahrtspflege in Deutschland." In: *J.W.S.* 1937/8.

Pedott, Joseph.: *System der Armenpflege und Armenpolitik.* Berlin, 1906.

Ruppin, Arthur: *Die Juden in der Gegenwart. Eine sozialwissenschaftliche Studie.* Leipzig/Köln, 1904 (1911).

Salomon, Alice: "Die Bedeutung der sozialen Berufsarbeit." In: *Concord. Zeitschrift der Zentralstelle für Volkswohlfahrt.* 23. Jahrgang, 1916.

Schäfer, Theodor: *Leitfaden der inneren Mission.* Hamburg, 1914.

Schell, Adolf: *Der wandernde Arbeitslose im Aufgabenkreis der*

Arbeitsvermittlung und Arbeitslosenversicherung. Frankfurt, 1927.

Schmoller, Gustav: *Die soziale Frage.* München/Leipzig, 1918.

Segall, Jacob: *Die Entwicklung der jüdischen Bevölkerung in München, 1875-1905.* Berlin, 1905.

Segall, Jacob: *Die geschlossenen und half offenen Einrichtungen der jüdischen Wohlfahrtspflege in Deutschland.* Berlin, 1920.

Segall, Jacob: "Die Leistunden der Armenkommission der jüdischen Gemeinde zu Berlin." In: *AZJ,* Heft 7, 1914.

Segall, Jacob: "Wanderarmenfürsorge in Deutschland bis zum Jahr 1914." In: *Zeitschrift für Demographie und Statistik der Juden.* Heft 3, 1914.

Sombart, Werner: *Die deutsche Volkswirtschaft im neunzehnten Jahrhundert.* Berlin, 1913. *Soziale Kultur und Volkswohlfahrt während der ersten 25 Regierungsjahre Kaiser Wilhelm II. Ein Gedenkwerk in ausgewählten Einzelabschnitten.* Berlin, 1913.

Statuten des israelischen Unterstützungsvereins für obdachlose Handwerksburschen und arme Durchreisende. Hamburg, 1884.

Stenographischer Berich über die Delegierten-Versammlung zur Beratung der Hilfsaktion für die russischen Juden. Berlin, October 20th and October 21st, 1891.

"Tätigkeit der Haupststelle für jüdische Wanderfürsorge 1.1.1930 – 30.6.1932." In: *J.W.S., 1930, p. 42.*

Theilhaber, Felix: *Der Untergang der deutschen Juden.* Munich, 1911.

Thiele, A.F.: *Die jüdischen Gauner in Deutschland, ihre Taktik, ihre Eigentümlichkeiten und ihre Sprache, nebst aufsführlichen Nachrichten über die in Deutschland und an dessen Grenzen sich aufhaltenden berüchtigsten Gauner.* Vol. 2. Berlin, 1840, 1842.

Uhlborn, Gerhard: *Die christliche Liebestätigkeit in der alten Kirche.* Stuttgart, 1882.

Uhlborn, Gerhard: *Die kirchliche Armenpflege und ihre Bedeutung für die Gegenwart.* Göttingen, 1892.

Vereins jüdischer Arbeiterkolonie Weißensee bei Berlin (Publ.): *Vierzehnter Rechenschaftsbericht des Vereins jüdischer Arbeiterkolonie Weißensee bei Berlin,* Geschäftsjahr (1902-1915). 1915.

"Verhandlungen der D.I.G.B." In: *Berufen konstituierenden Sitzung der deutschen Zentralstelle für jüdische Wanderarmenfürsorge.* Berlin, 1910.

Verwaltungsbericht der Zentralstelle für Wohlfahrtspflege in der Synagogen-Gemeinde. Hamburg, 1921/1928.

von Treitschke, Heinrich: *Ein Wort über unser Judentum. Separatabduck aus dem 44., 45. Und 46. Bande Preußischer Jahrbücher.* Berlin, 1881.

von Tyszka, Carl: "Die jüdische Bevölkerung Münchens nach dem Stande vom 1. Dezember 1905. " In: *Zeitschrift für Demographie und Statistik der Juden,* Heft 6, 1907.

Wassermann, Rudolf: "Die Entwicklung der jüdischen Bevölkerung in der Provinz Posen und das Ostmarkenproblem." In: *Zeitschrift für Demographie und Statistik der Juden.* 1910.

Weber, A.: *Armenwesen und Armenfürsorge*. Leipzig, 1907.

Willner, Max: "Zentralwohlfahrtsstelle der Juden in Deutschland." In: *Jahrbuch für Caritaswissenschaft*. 1866.

Wolf, Albert: *Fahrende Leute bei den Juden*. Leipzig, 1909.

Zionistischer Hilfsfond in London (Publ.): *Die Judenpogrome in Russland*. Köln/Leipzig, 1910. ZWJ (Publ.): *Führer durch die jüdische Wohlfahrtspflege in Deutschland*. Berlin, 1926.

4) Recent Scholarship

Althammer, Beate (Publ.): *Bettler in der europäischen Stadt der Moderne. Zwischen Barmherzigkeit, Repression und Sozialreform*. Frankfurt, 2007.

Aschheim, Steven E.: *Brothers and Strangers: The East European Jew in German and German Jewish Consciousness, 1800-1923*. Wisconsin: University of Wisconsin Press. 1983.

Benad, Matthias and Hans W. Schmuhl: *Bethel-Eckardtsheim: Von der Gründung der ersten deutschen Arbeiterkolonie bis zur Auflösung als Teilanstalt (1882-2001)*, Stuttgart: Kohlhammer, 2005.

Brinkmann, Tobias: "Zivilgesellschaft transnational. Jüdische Hilfsorganisationen und jüdische Massenmigration aus Osteuropa in Deutschland, 1868-1914." In: Rainer Liedtke/ Klaus Weber (Publ.), *Religion und Philanthropie in europäischen Zivilgesellschaften. Entwicklungen im 19. und 20. Jahrhundert*. Paderborn et.al. 2008, p. 138-157.

Bung, Kristen, *Von der Wandererfürsorge mit alleinstehenden Wohnungslosen-die Entwicklung der Nichtseßhaftenhilfe unter besonderer Berücksichtigung sozialpolitischer Aspekte.* (PhD Dissertation). Bochum, 1985.

Dohrn, Verena; Gertrud Pickhan (Publ.): *Transit und Transformation. Osteuropäisch-jüdische Migranten in Berlin 1918-1939.* Göttingen, 2010.

Glanz, R. *Geschichte des niederen juedischen Volks in Deutschland* (1968); Scheiber, in: M. Zohary and A. Tartakower (eds.), *Hagut Ivrit be-Eiropah* (1969), p. 268–75.

Gauding, Daniela: "Die jüdische Arbeiterkolonie in Weissensee." In: Alza Cohen-Mushlin et.al. (Publ.): *Beiträge zur jüdischen Architektur in Berlin.* Berlin, 2009, p. 70-82.

Geremek, Bronislaw, *Geschichte der Armut: Elend und Barmherzigkeit in Europa*, Artemis Verlag, München 1988.

Gestrich, Andreas et al. (Publ.): *Being poor in modern Europe: Historical perspectives 1800-1940.* Oxford, 2006.

Hennings Verena: *Jüdische Wohlfahrtspflege in der Weimarer Republik.* Frankfurt, 2008. Hering, Sabine (Publ.): *Jüdische Wohlfahrt im Spiegel von Biographien.* Frankfurt, 2006. Herzog, Arno: *Jüdische Geschichte in Deutschland. Von den Anfängen bis zur Gegenwart.* München, 2002.

Kaplan, Marion A. *Jewish Daily Life in Germany, 1618-1945.* Oxford: Oxford University Press. 2005.

Kiebel, Hannes (Ed.), *Ein Jahrhundert Arbeiterkolonien: Arbeit statt Almosen-Hilfe für obdachlose Wanderarme 1884-1984;[zur Jubiläumstagung d. Zentralverb. Dt. Arbeiterkolonien am 17. Oktober 1984 in Berlin].* VSH Verlag Soziale Hilfe: Berlin. 1984.

Kipp, Angelika: *Jüdische Arbeits-und Berufsfürsorge in Deutschland 1900-1933.* Berlin, 1999. Liedtke, Rainer:

Jewish Welfare in Hamburg and Manchester, 1850-1914. Oxford, 1998.

Lowenstein, Steven M. et.al.: *Deutsch-jüdische Geschichte der Neuzeit. Bd. 3: Umstrittene Integration 1871-1918.* München, 1997.

Lowenstein, Steven M.: *The Mechanics of Change: Essays in the Social History of German Jewry (Brown Judaic Studies)* Scholar Pr: Toronto, Canada. 1992.

Reinke, Andreas:*Geschichte der Juden in Deutschland 1781-1933.* Darmstadt, 2007.

Rolshoven, Joanna: *Das Figurativ der Vagabondage. Kulturanalysen mobiler Lebensweisen.* Bielefeld: transcript. 2012

Rolshoven, Joanna: *Vagabunden und Vagabondage. Eine Exploration in bewegliche Lebenswelten.* Graz: KFU/ÖH. 2010.

Rolshoven, Joanna: "The temptations of the provisional. Multilocality as a way of life." In: *Ethnologia Europaea. Journal of European Ethnology.* Voll 37:1-2. Copenhagen: Museum Tusculanum Press. 2008.

Sachße, Christoph and Florian Tennstadt, *Geschichte der Armenfürsorge in Deutschland, Bd.1, Vom Spätmittelalter bis zum 1. Weltkrieg.* Kohlhammer: Berlin, 1998.

Toury, Jacob**,** *Soziale und politische Geschichte der Juden in Deutschland, 1847-1871: Zwischen Revolution, Reaktion u. Emanzipation.* Droste: Berlin, 1977.

Uerlings, Herbert (Publ.): *Armut. Perspektiven in Kunst und Gesellschaft. Eine Ausstellung des Sonderforschungsbereichs 600 „Fremdheit und Armut".* Darmstadt, 2011.

Volkow, Shulamith: *Die Juden in Deutschland 1780-1918.*

München, 1994 (Enzyklopädie Deutscher Geschichte, Bd. 16).

Urry, John: *Mobilities*. Cambridge: Polity Press. 2007

5) Works of literature quoted

Agnon, S.Y. Agnon *And the Crooked Shall be Made Straight*. Translated by Michael P. Kramer. New Milton, CT: Toby Press LLC. Forthcoming (2013).

Goldmann, Nachum. *The Autobiography of Nachum Goldmann*, New York: Holt, Rinehart and Winston. 1969.

Kassák, Lajos. *Als Vagabund unterwegs, Erinnerungen*. Berlin: Verlag Volk und Welt. 1978.

www.ingramcontent.com/pod-product-compliance
Lightning Source LLC
LaVergne TN
LVHW020926090426
835512LV00020B/3223